Hegel's Dialectical Political Economy

Hegel's Dialectical Political Economy

A Contemporary Application

Paul Diesing

Westview Press
A Member of the Perseus Books Group

All rights reserved. Printed in the United States of America. No part of this publication may be reproduced or transmitted in any form or by any means, electronic or mechanical, including photocopy, recording, or any information storage and retrieval system, without permission in writing from the publisher.

Copyright © 1999 by Westview Press, A Member of the Perseus Books Group

Published in 1999 in the United States of America by Westview Press, 5500 Central Avenue, Boulder, Colorado 80301–2877, and in the United Kingdom by Westview Press, 12 Hid's Copse Road, Cumnor Hill, Oxford OX2 9JJ

Library of Congress Cataloging-in-Publication Data
Diesing, Paul.
Hegel's dialectical political economy : a contemporary application / Paul Diesing.
    p. cm.
  Includes bibliographical references and index.
  ISBN 0-8133-9131-8
  1. Hegel, Georg Wilhelm Friedrich, 1770–1831—Contributions in social sciences. 2. Hegel, Georg Wilhelm Friedrich, 1770–1831—Contributions in dialectic. 3. Hegel, Georg Wilhelm Friedrich, 1770–1831. *Grundlinien der Philosophie des Rechts.* I. Title.
H59.H44D57 1999
320.1'1—dc21   99-20305
                                                                                                                   CIP

The paper used in this publication meets the requirements of the American National Standard for Permanence of Paper for Printed Library Materials Z39.48–1984.

10   9   8   7   6   5   4   3   2   1

Contents

Acknowledgments   vii
List of Acronyms   ix

1   Introduction   1

2   Background: Metaphysics, History, and Philosophy   9

     Metaphysics, 9
     History, 11
     Philosophy, 16

3   Dialectic   25

4   The *Philosophy of Right*   37

     Preface, 38
     Introduction, 39
     Abstract Right, 42
     Morality, 45
     Ethical Life: Approaching the Concrete, 46
     The Federalist Papers and the United States, 68
     Summary, 70

5   Dialectic of Society   77

     Use and Value, 77
     Family, 82
     Children Grow Up, 86
     Economy, 87
     Law, 94
     Government, 96
     Summary, 98

| 6 | Dialectical Research | 101 |

The Oligopoly–Competition Cycle, 103
The Dialectic, 117
The Context of the Oligopoly–Competition Cycle, 122

| 7 | Rational Political States Today | 129 |

The Search for a Rational Political State, 132
A Trial Run: The U.S. Political State, 133
Corporate States Today, 148

| 8 | The Useful Dialectic | 161 |

Social Problems, 161
And Socialism? 169
Conclusion, 172

Bibliography	175
Subject Index	183
Author Index	187

Acknowledgments

I am extremely grateful to several people who most generously mulled over portions of earlier drafts and made very helpful criticisms and suggestions for improvements: Harry Brod, Keith Fitzgerald, H. S. Harris, James Lawler, Bertell Ollman, and Tony Smith.

Paul Diesing

Acronyms

AARP	American Association of Retired Persons
BASF	Bayerische Anilin und Soda Fabrik
BOF	Basic Oxygen Furnace
CAB	Civil Aeronautics Board
CED	Committee for Economic Development
CFR	Council on Foreign Relations
EC	European Community
EPA	Environmental Protection Agency
EU	European Union
FOB	Freight on Board
FTC	Federal Trade Commission
GATT	General Agreement on Tariffs and Trade
GDP	Gross Domestic Product
GM	General Motors
IMF	International Monetary Fund
MITI	Ministry of International Trade and Industry
NAFTA	North American Free Trade Agreement
NAM	National Association of Manufacturers
NRC	Nuclear Regulatory Commission
OECD	Organization for Economic Cooperation and Development
ÖGB	Österreichischer Gewerkschaftsbund
ÖI	Österreichische Industrieverwaltung
OPEC	Organization of Petroleum Exporting Countries
OPIC	Overseas Private Investment Corporation
OSHA	Occupational Safety and Health Administration
PACs	Political Action Committees
RFC	Reconstruction Finance Corporation
ROI	Return on Investment
UAW	United Auto Workers
VAT	Value-Added Tax
VW	Volkswagen

*Ein grosser Mann verdammt die
Menschen dazu, ihn zu explizieren.*
—**Hegel, aphorism no. 54**

This book arose out of a certain dissatisfaction with existing commentaries on Hegel's work.
—**Plant,** *Hegel*

1

Introduction

Any one writing about Hegel's political theory will have to face the fact that readers will bring with them a huge variety of interpretations and misinterpretations of Hegel, some of them quite absurd. Such as: Hegel was a staunch defender of the autocratic Prussian monarchy. Hegel thought reality was all in our heads (or in God's head); he was an idealist. Hegel was a rabid anti-Semite, a precursor of Nazism (Liebeschütz 1967). Hegel was a philosopher, so he must have been writing for other philosophers about philosophical topics, such as the ontological status of natural law and natural rights, Kant's categorical imperative, or the correct definition of free will or the state. Hegel *could not* have started the *Logic* with the category of Being; he must have meant Substance (Reck 1960, 117ff). Zygmund Pelczynski complains about the "enormous difficulty and obscurity of the dialectical method" (1984, 63) and then ignores it. Hans Georg Gadamer, writing about Hegel's dialectic (1976, 76) dismisses the *Philosophy of Right* as "nothing but a textbook for academic instruction," though it's full of dialectic. He focuses instead on the *Logic*, which is *about* dialectic. As Jacques D'Hondt (1988) observes, the *Logic* changed the dynamic of change into an arid dance of concepts. It "transformed life into the ashes of pure thought."

Most of the misinterpretations and misunderstandings come from commentators' attempts to read their own logic and their own theoretical categories and problems into Hegel. "Invariably interpreters have molded Hegel into their own image" (D'Hondt 1988, vi). If commentators succeed in reading their ideas into Hegel, they present their interpretations as Hegel's own ideas; if they fail, they criticize Hegel for his difficult and obscure writing, or for his errors. We all do that, of course; it's a standard human cognitive process, especially for men. But some interpreters' logic and categories are close to Hegel's, whereas others' are far away; and some interpreters are flexible and open, whereas others are more rigid and closed.

Many commentators begin with an assumed distinction between "is" and "ought," fact and value. Either Hegel is describing some existing state or he is arguing for an ideal state that ought to exist and that we ought to try to establish. And since Hegel is a philosopher, not a social scientist, he must be telling us what ought to be. So how does Hegel describe his ideal state, and what are his supporting arguments? Are these arguments valid, or can I earn some professional points by showing their invalidity? In my opinion, Hegel rejected both of these distinctions. He did not distinguish philosophy and social science but combined them in his work. His argument is both empirically descriptive and normative; he studies the historical development of rights, not a timeless ideal state.

Or sometimes a critic will assume a deductive logic: A philosophical argument must develop basic definitions and distinctions, then deduce conclusions from those definitions. For example, Richard Schacht (1972) asks, What is Hegel's definition of freedom? To answer the question, he first provides the philosophical context: other philosophers' definitions of freedom, including those of Locke and Kant. Then Schacht picks out sentences from the *Philosophy of Right* that are relevant to that context and ignores everything else. The sentences he picks out show the inadequacy of previous philosophers' definitions and, finally, give Hegel's "definition": Freedom is living according to the laws and institutions of a perfectly rational state (1972, 325). The philosophical context controls what Schacht is looking for: some kind of law that will control one's impulses and inclinations. But that's Locke and Kant, not Hegel. Schacht moves from Locke's natural law to Kant's a priori laws to Hegel's social customs and laws. Then Schacht asks, Since few if any existing states are perfectly rational, what if one's own state is not perfectly rational? No freedom? So much for Hegel's "definition." And since the "definition" is inadequate, nothing valid can be deduced from it. Its only use is to provide material for other philosophers like Schacht to argue over in the attempt to construct an adequate definition and theory—and to refute still other philosophers.

In my opinion, Hegel was not constructing a timeless, universal definition of freedom; he was trying to describe and understand the freedom that existed in some actual states that were able to manage their own problems and conflicts more or less.

A standard error made by political scientists is to ask, How does Hegel define the state, and how does he distinguish it from civil society? (See for example, Pelczynski 1971, chap. 1, who goes on to complain that Hegel's definitions and distinctions are not clear.) According to political scientists like Pelczynski, we must distinguish state from society because society is the domain of sociologists and economists, whereas the domain of political science is government. But Hegel did not distinguish sharply government and society; civil society participates in the governmental process, and government participates in the economy. So his work is at once political, economic, and social.

As for substantive interpretations of Hegel's theories, Terry Pinkard (1988, 3) comments that there are almost as many different interpretations of Hegel as there are interpreters, and Hegel did not subscribe to hardly any of the outrageous beliefs ascribed to him. But how do I know that my interpretation is the only correct one? I don't; the others seem wrong insofar as their approach differs from mine. So we are faced with a variety of approaches to Hegel.

It would seem appropriate, then, to state the approach of the present work and to partly distinguish it from other approaches. Hopefully then readers will not read some other approach into the present work and make nonsense of it.

The approach that differs most sharply from mine is that used by many, but not all, professional philosophers and political philosophers. The approach, illustrated above (Schacht, Pelczynski) assumes an ahistorical deductive or deontic logic that requires clear definitions and sharp distinctions, such as the distinction between is and ought, or between government, economy, and society. To understand Hegel, one must clarify his obscure text by working out implicit definitions and deductions, sharpen vague and shifting distinctions, bring out confusions and ambiguous meanings, and thus reconstruct some sort of meaningful argument. This process might be called "Making Sense of Hegel."

This approach also requires that one refute other philosophers' interpretations of Hegel by exposing their misreadings, conflations, non sequiturs, inconsistencies, and so on. Then one compares Hegel's reconstructed argument with those of still other philosophers on the same subject. The other philosophers can be Hegel's predecessors, as in the Schacht example above, or they can be recent or contemporary. The comparison enables one to evaluate Hegel's argument, or some critic's argument. Does the argument accurately describe and refute the other philosophers? Do Hegel's conclusions follow from his premises, and are those premises plausible? What contribution does the argument make to the philosophical debate?

A second rather similar approach to Hegel would be to downplay the logical deductions and definitions and focus simply on the theory, what Hegel "taught." The theory would consist of a series of assertions about the proper structure of government, the functions of each branch, the proper mode of election or appointment or inheritance, and so on. Then Hegel's theory can be compared with other political theories, or with critics of his theory, and evaluated as before: How well does it refute the critics or withstand criticism? How consistent is it? And so on.

For example, a commentator might have a conception of the modern state as a democracy, in which voters elect their representatives in government, and in which the various branches of government check each other. The commentator can find that in Hegel, after a fashion: There's a two-house legislature, an executive, and a judiciary somewhere, and apparently some kind of electoral process. But what's the monarchy doing there? We don't need that; we have voters. And look! The three branches of government don't check each other; they are interconnected! And there's too much bureaucracy there and hardly any real citizen participation; Hegel's state is too hierarchical, too corporate (Hardimon 1994, chap. 6, sec. III; conclusion). Michael Hardimon is reading the U.S. Constitution into fragments of Hegel and criticizing him when the two don't match.

I admit that Hegel did occasionally criticize other philosophers in his incidental remarks and footnotes, so there is some validity in the approaches described above; but I regard such remarks as incidental to the theory itself.

My approach differs from the above two approaches as follows:

1. Hegel's logic is dialectic, a nondeductive, nondefinitional logic of historical process. For a deductive logician, "dialectical logic" is an oxymoron, an absurdity, unless one is thinking of Kantian dialectic. So readers who don't think dialectically can think of dialectic as a heuristic for studying historical processes, not a logic. Readers familiar with Whitehead's process philosophy can apply Whitehead's thinking to Hegel to help them accommodate to Hegel's historicism. (Disciples of Popper should stop screaming at this point.)

2. But if dialectic is a heuristic, it is a means of locating the empirical dynamics of actual current societies. For example, for Hegel the market (as of 1820) is a process of increasing interdependence between demanders and suppliers. As suppliers, people learn to produce and provide what customers are demanding, but they also learn to produce new products; new products beat the competition. As customers, people learn to like and use what is being supplied; then they develop quality standards and demand quality, but they also explore new products. They also learn to want what other people are consuming and to try to equal or surpass others in their discriminating good taste. Thus, the supply side and the demand side, in adapting to each other, each push the market to continually expand the range of products offered and the levels of quality supplied and demanded. The market continually gets more complex; it never approaches any sort of equilibrium.

Perhaps, then, one could call Hegel a political economist, not a philosopher. Similarly, Marx has been called a sociologist by some, an economist by others, and a philosopher by still others. But Hegel rejected these distinctions, in my opinion. As a philosopher, he was looking for the reason

Introduction 5

in actual societies, the dialectical structure that made them work while also gradually transforming them. But, like a social scientist, he was studying the social structures and processes of his own time, not a timeless ideal state.

3. Hegel's dialectic also requires the present approach to be holistic. Hegel's theory is an interconnected structure that must be understood as a whole; but the society he describes is also treated as an interconnected whole, in which all institutions are interdependent and internally related. There is no separate and distinct government, legal system, economy, masculine personality, and so on. Each institution participates in and shapes the others. Henning Ottman (1977, 392) makes the same point: He observes that Hegel was an all-around thinker, combining economic, political, historic, artistic, theological, and philosophical thought. Consequently any attempt to focus only on Hegel's logic, or legal theory, or economics, or theology, or political theory as a separate topic is certain to miss important aspects of that theory. Disciplinary specialists will have to be flexible, tolerant, and open minded in reading the present work.

A holistic interpretation of Hegel's political theory requires some familiarity with its context: Hegel's other writings. *The Philosophy of Right*, as a mature work, builds on and develops ideas that appear in earlier political and nonpolitical writings. Some familiarity with those writings would help one understand the *Philosophy of Right*. Ottman, who like me takes Hegel's holism seriously, draws a disturbing implication in his section on "the dialectic of whole and part" (1977, 11). To really understand Hegel, he says, one cannot just quote a sentence out of context, such as "The true is the whole" (mistranslated as "The truth is the whole"). Nor can one take a single publication out of the context of all of Hegel's publications—and unpublished manuscripts, class lectures, and correspondence. So a full understanding of, say, his treatment of the legislature requires a study of everything he wrote and said. But this is impossible, Ottman admits. Besides, even to attempt it would be to prevent one from undertaking the necessary detailed study of a single publication. The whole and the parts depend on each other, but they also exclude each other. That's dialectic.

In addition, Hegel was thinking about his own time; it helps to put him in his own time, his historical context, in order to understand him; that is, it would help to relate his writings to contemporary political events such as the French Revolution and the Prussian reform movement. Hegel's context also would include the cities he lived in, the people he knew there, and any political activities he committed. For instance, an interpreter might ask, Why did Hegel get into a boat and row around beneath the windows of the Berlin prison? Who was jailed there? Why did he write privately delivered letters in support of some dissident, hoping to get him a job, or why did he visit a political prisoner in a Berlin jail? Knowing Hegel's political convictions should help us interpret some ambiguous published remark that managed to get past the Prussian censor.

Thus, David MacGregor (1992, chap. 2) asserts that Hegel disguised parts of his argument to evade the Prussian censorship that was set up in 1819. He was not always successful; the censor forbade publications of part of Hegel's comments on the 1830 English Reform Bill. One type of evasion was to criticize crude, uncivilized aspects of Roman society, hoping that the astute reader would realize that the practices criticized were quite common in 1820 Prussia. Armin Bogdandy (1989, 247) points to *The Philosophy of Right* ¶319, on the importance of a free press, as a vague, murky, disguised criticism of the Prussian censorship that, if taken seriously, "throws his whole theory of law overboard." We shall pass quickly over ¶319 in our detailed study.

Hegel's occasional references to English society, based on his reading of English newspapers, journals, and political pamphlets, points to another context: empirical information about English society as of 1800–1830. Since Hegel apparently developed his later political ideas in part by mulling over English society and politics, we might understand those ideas better by getting familiar with his empirical sources. By extension, some familiarity with Prussian politics and society might also help.

Also, Hegel was thinking and writing in ordinary German, and translation always tends to lose subtle meanings, such as implicit connotations of *Geist* or *wirklich* or *Begriff*. The result, for people who do not know German, is a stilted, wooden caricature of Hegel. Raymond Plant (1973, 205) makes the same point.

By now we have an impossible task; the context has gotten too large. The solution is to depend on other writers for the larger context of the *Philosophy of Right*. Commentators such as MacGregor have provided a detailed account of Hegel's times as they affected his thinking. Other commentators have discussed Hegel's other writings; political writings such as the Jena manuscripts and the article on the English Reform Bill are especially relevant. For example: "It is difficult to avoid seeing in Hegel's remarks here a form of self-criticism of his own youthful enthusiasm for the revolutionary spirit" (Brod 1992, 47). Also, "We have seen how Hegel's political writings present a consistent and progressively unfolding panorama of the way in which his political theory evolved through constant confrontation with historical reality" (Avineri 1972, 81). Plant (in Maker 1987, chap. 3) provides a fine account of the development of Hegel's political thought that can supplement the present work.

And Hegel's political thought didn't end with Hegel; it continued to develop in his successors. Marx acknowledged that his life-long revolutionary critique of political economy was a painstakingly detailed and passionate elaboration of what Hegel summed up in two terse pages (par. 243–248) of PR (Weiss 1974, 254). Also Bernard Bosanquet (1899) brings out some changing meanings of Hegel's concept "corporation," and T. H. Green brings out other possible meanings. According to Robert MacIver (1947, 483) "the most plausible interpretation of Hegel is that of Bernard Bosanquet, particularly in his *Philosophical Theory of the State* (1899). John Dewey develops other Hegelian concepts.

Familiarity with such Hegelians would be helpful; and familiarity with Hegel's contemporaries, whose ideas Hegel used or negated, such as Kant and Adam Smith, also would help.

So my approach will be dialectical, empirical, and somewhat holistic. It agrees completely with the approach of Ottman and Bogdandy (1989, 257), who emphasize Hegel's dialectic and holism as contributions that are still valid and important today. We will treat Hegel's work on political economy, the *Philosophy of Right* (hereafter PR), as a study of a whole western European society, including its government, as of 1800–1820 or so.

Consequently, this work will be most useful, and comprehensible, to political economists and philosophers who think in terms of dynamic social processes—tensions, conflicts, pressures, path dependence—rather than static abstract models. For example Loukas Tsoukalis (1997, 69), discussing European trade and markets, points to "the ever-widening gap between traditional theory and the real issues at stake. . . . The emphasis is now clearly on the so-called dynamic effects" of the economic and political integration and the single currency. In other words, the European economy is changing rapidly. By "traditional theory" he presumably means the static mathematical ceteris paribus models of neoclassical and supply-side economics.

Process-oriented researchers use terms like "cumulative causation," "circular causation," "backwash," "virtuous circle," and "spread." Researchers who think that way can use Hegel's method and concepts in their studies of current economic developments. In particular, institutionalists and some post-Keynesians will recognize some dynamics that they have already studied, and some familiar concepts, as will Marxists. Indeed, I have used institutionalist, Keynesian, and Marxist concepts in explicating Hegel's ideas and dialectic.

Marxists may find Hegel useful in dealing with their current intellectual and research problems. Current Marxist theory is in considerable disarray and is moving in a wide variety of directions, such as "market socialism" (Ollman 1998) and a merger with international-relations realism (Linklater 1990). Some Marxists are collaborating with their neighbors, the institutionalists; others write about reinterpreting or reinventing Marxism, and there is even a journal on the topic. One encounters "post-Marxists" and reads thoughtful books like *After Marxism* (Aronson 1995).

The problem for Marxists has not been the collapse of the Soviet Union, which for most Western Marxists always has been a caricature of Marxist theory. It has rather been that times have changed since 1867, and theories have to adapt to these changes. Labor today is not the factory labor of 1848; women are different; the economy is global; technology, corporate structure, and finance have changed enormously. One cannot treat Marx's writings as a Bible containing timeless truths to be interpreted and clarified endlessly. He was interpreting his own time, and we must do that as well. Moreover, his interpretations were based on detailed empirical research, and we must do that too.

The main point of this book is to show how Hegel's dialectic can be used in empirical research today. Then the results can be used to revise Marxist theory, expand institutionalist theory, or do other social research.

Chapters 2 and 3 are preparatory chapters that present my interpretation of Hegel. Chapter 2 provides a minimal context, a brief sketch of Hegel's whole philosophy. Chapter 3 presents my understanding of Hegel's dialectic. Chapter 4, the central chapter, will be a detailed study of Hegel's mature political treatise, the PR. We will go through the text a "logical" step at a time to locate the dialectic and put the argument together. As we follow the movement of the dialectic, we will see the interdependence of 1820 social institutions being laid out step by step. This will also give the reader practice in dialectical thinking, to prepare for the last four chapters. Dialectic is a way of thinking, among other things, so it cannot just be described; it must be practiced.

Chapters 5–8 apply Hegel's dialectic and his political and economic concepts to current society. Chapter 5 takes the various dialectical dynamics that Hegel describes in PR and traces their development into the present. Chapter 6 shows how one can do dialectical research in economics (and other fields). Chapter 7 shows how we can use Hegel's analysis of his own state as a guide for locating the structure of some current political state, its economic and social context, and the problems that exist or loom ahead. Finally Chapter 8 shows how one can use dialectical thinking to interpret some personal or social or political problem and devise a possible solution.

2

Background: Metaphysics, History, and Philosophy

Metaphysics

We begin with the problem of translation. Hegel's central metaphysical term is *Geist*, a word with multiple meanings and connotations in ordinary German. One possible translation is "ghost"; *Heilige Geist* means "Holy Ghost" or "Holy Spirit." *Geistliche Lieder* means "religious songs." *Geisteswissenschaften* used to be translated "social sciences," but more recently has become "cultural sciences." So direct translation does not work. Translating *Geist* as "Spirit," capitalized even (in German all nouns are capitalized, even Dirt), is inevitably misleading; it suggests some supernatural power causing everything to happen.

It is more helpful to see how Hegel uses the term. He begins his *Phenomenology of Geist* with the simplest kind of *Geist*, the sensation of light or darkness: "It's dark." What have we here? Well, sense-perception, consciousness, mind. That is one kind of *Geist*, subjective *Geist*. We might as well call it mind, consciousness, or experience, as a start. Of course, "mind" gets more complicated as the *Phenomenology* moves along (Stillman 1987).

Mind does not just perceive; it always goes outside itself actively, for instance by asserting that it's dark. Now suppose we meet someone and say "Hello, how are you?" or paint the wall of our house, or construct a patio for sitting outside, or design and plant a garden. These are intentional actions; we pick out the color, design the patio, select the flowers and their location. The plans and intentions are subjective: I plan; I intend, but the result is objective. However, the garden or the sentence has our mind, our intention, in it; I did it. That is objective *Geist*. As objectified, our designs and skills and maintenance are clearly visible to other people.

Where did we get the idea of saying "Hello" or having a patio to sit on, or a house to live in? We learned it from other people, who learned it from other people. That is culture, which gets transmitted from generation to generation. Culture, then, is objective *Geist*, as in *Geisteswissenschaften*, cultural sciences. "Objective spirit means the spirit which has issued forth from its inwardness and embodied itself in an external and outward world. . . . It is in general, the world of *institutions* . . . law, society, state, customs, manners" (Stace 1924, 374).

Mind is a product of culture and carries culture in it as its content. We learn to speak a particular language, say hello, eat with a fork, and so on. But conversely, mind is always changing culture, remaking it; we do not just pass it on. Language is slowly changing; we invent new kinds of gardens and new sentences and new house designs. So mind makes culture, and culture makes mind. Such an idea is commonplace enough in the social sciences, taking slightly different shapes in different writers: structure and agency (Bhaskar), history and subjectivity (Gottlieb 1987), substance and subject (Hegel [1807] 1967, 80), structuration (Giddens 1984), praxis: "By acting on the external world and changing it, man changes his own nature" (Ball and Farr 1984, 248).[1]

Anthropologists have long distinguished material and ideal culture. Ideal culture is what we carry in our mind and personality, such as language, rules of politeness, skills, goals, self-concepts. Material culture is composed of the material products of our activity: machinery, tools, buildings, roads, nature preserves, polluted air, impoverished soils, and so on. Material culture, which we have made, is the setting of our life. Urban geographers call it the "built environment."

One can also distinguish particular cultures in ordinary German, as anthropologists also do: *Zeitgeist* is the culture of the time, current culture; *Volksgeist* is national or popular culture, literally, "folk culture"; *Weltgeist* is world culture, for instance, the international economy or international political institutions.

Finally, there is a third kind of *Geist*. This kind occurs when we think about our culture and try to understand it. This is subjective *Geist* (mind), which studies objective *Geist* (culture), studies itself and communicates its findings. The result is self-knowledge or self-experience, self-consciousness. Hegel calls this "absolute *Geist*." As H. S. Harris observes, the Absolute is with us from the start; science is self-comprehension (1995, chap. 9). In the *Phenomenology*, "the final object of our knowledge is not 'God,' but ourselves as *knowers*" (Harris 1995, 14). In self-knowledge as in ordinary consciousness, our presuppositions and ways of thinking come out of the culture we are trying to study, but we can use these freely to construct a variety of representations or expressions of the culture.

Hegel distinguishes three kinds of absolute *Geist*, namely, art, religion, and philosophy (1956, 53). Art expresses its own culture in "feeling"; theology expresses it in devotional terms that describe a Deity or deities patterned on the given culture. As Hegel observes in his early theological writings, "The God of a people is nothing else but a 'mirror' of the people, the picture of their time" (Scheit 1973, 51). Philosophy expresses itself in thought. What happened to social science, *Geisteswissenschaft*? I believe Hegel included it in philosophy; like philosophy, social science expresses in concepts the experiences and perspectives of a particular location in society and uses these concepts to interpret aspects of a society. Elsewhere, I have shown, following Karl Mannheim's argument ([1929] 1936), how various schools of social science express the perspective of a particular class or some other social location and interpret social processes from that perspective (Diesing 1982). Thus, a combination of two or three perspectives would give a better picture than any single perspective.

Notice the difference between the three kinds of self-consciousness. Philosophy and social science produce concepts and theories, perhaps knowledge, that enable us to think about ourselves and our society and perhaps to work out ways to change ourselves. Art and religious ceremonies express portions of our life experiences more vividly and thus produce shared consciousness. Such experiences—for example, a church service or a requiem—constitute a shared feeling of our togetherness and help unify small communities or congregations (Plant 1980, 81).

All three kinds of *Geist* make history. Culture provides the setting for human action: practices, values, conflicts, equipment, problems, opportunities; reflections on culture improve one's self-knowledge, perhaps, and so help shape planning and policymaking. Action, finally, makes history.

History

In the *Philosophy of History*, Hegel begins by distinguishing four stages in the history of culture, but things rapidly get more complex. There are substages and variations in different areas, overlappings, and even a repetition of earlier epochs (Hegel 1956, 345). Since our main interest is in the last substage, modern time (because this is the stage to which PR refers), we shall avoid most of the earlier complexities.

The earliest stage of history available to us through writings is the Oriental world from China to Egypt. In this stage, large areas, like China or the valleys of the Nile and the Euphrates, were ruled by an all-powerful emperor. The emperor was owed the deepest reverence, and he alone was in direct contact with God. The populace barely survived through small farming, hunting, and fishing, and they contributed their labor to imperial projects such as palace construction, warfare, and domestic service. Ordinary people were worthless—"All are alike degraded"—and could be sold, or killed, or in India kill themselves, for instance, if one's husband or child had died.

This sort of culture brings with it a theology that glorifies the one God, all-powerful, all-wise, creator of the whole earth, loving and caring for us all, but watching our every move and punishing persistent evil doing. God has laid down the rules we must follow, but he forgives our minor infractions if we are trying to be good. There were also some secondary deities, at least in China, who kept watch over specific rivers and provinces. As Hegel observed, "The more powerless and passive people feel, the more almighty their God is as compensation" (Scheit 1973, 51).

The most expressive art of this period is architecture: not the tiny clay huts of the populace, but grand imperial palaces, pyramids, and enormous temples in which people worshipped the Deity. The populace experienced this art and theology as devotion to the almighty God or emperor. The worshipper in the enormous temple or cathedral experienced humility: I am nothing; God is almighty. O Almighty, be merciful to me, a sinner.

The second stage of history is the Greek world. Hegel (1956, pages in subsequent paragraphs refer to this work) begins by contrasting Greek geography with that of the Oriental world. The Oriental empires were located in vast river valleys or great plains, which could be controlled easily by the imperial military force. Greece was a series of small territories, separated by mountains, narrow peninsulas like the Isthmus of Corinth (Sparta), or the sea (Crete and other islands). Communication was mostly by boat, so the small communities could defend themselves against large imperial armies. Consequently, Greece consisted of a variety of small, independent farming and fishing communities. People from many different races and cultures emigrated to the various communities, which therefore developed great heterogeneity internally and externally. Yet the small size facilitated the development of community.

This was an age of heroes: sailors who made long, precarious voyages bent on trading, colonization, piracy, or conquest; warriors who organized a defense of their city; inventors of new construction techniques or city governments.

The cities were originally governed by princes, who were regarded as heroes because of their bravery in defending their city, their preeminent insight and wisdom, or their ancestry (229). They built the city walls, to which these "princes of the heroic times generally attached their dwellings." Yet, since the princes' "superiority is only the individually heroic, resting on personal merit, it does not continue long," (230) so government structures kept changing.

The Greek culture of heroes was expressed in a theology of multiple divinities: Athena, Ceres, Apollo, and so on. There was no one almighty

God who ruled the earth from a far-off heaven; Zeus was a god like any other, and he lived nearby on Mount Olympus. Each god had a specific task (228): Ceres taught the first farmers the art of agriculture and continued to watch over the fields; Prometheus brought us fire; Poseidon invented the horse; Apollo kept the sun in orbit; Athena insured the continued wisdom of the Athenians. The gods were "personalities, concrete individuals" (246). "Athene the goddess is Athens itself, the real and concrete spirit of the citizens" (252).

The primary art of this period was sculpture: statues of individual gods, goddesses, or heroes—Venus, Achilles, Odysseus, the discus thrower. Sculpturing enabled the artist to capture the unique characteristics of some deity or hero. In addition, the Greeks cultivated and displayed their bodies through sports, so sculpture could express this sense of individual bodily beauty, which was central to Greek culture (239, 241–243). "This is the subjective beginning of Greek art—in which the human being elaborates his physical being, in free, beautiful movement and agile vigor, to a work of art" (242). Hegel also mentions painting, which enabled the artist to depict the charms of Venus in color, and song and dance.

As for philosophy, the statesmen and philosophers—Pericles, Thucydides, Socrates, Plato, Aristophanes—expressed the political culture of their time to the citizens (260–261).

We skip the third period, the Roman world, because of its complexity. However, a new theological development occurred in this period: Jesus. Jesus was a new sort of god: He was human. He gave us his teachings through his disciples, performed a heroic deed on the cross, then ascended to heaven where he continues his work. Later the saints—Paul, Boniface, Stephen, Joan of Arc, and so on—were also human; they performed very good deeds on earth to help other people, then ascended to heaven where they continue their work. Jesus and the saints showed that God can be present and active in some exceptionally noble human beings; divinity can be here in some of us, rather than off in Olympus or Valhalla or heaven.

Because these divinities are also human, people can experience a deep personal relation to a particular one: Jesus loves me and cares for me; he died for me. See his intense suffering in this picture, one might say. Or one might keep a statue of one's patron saint in one's car for protection against accidents.

We also skip most of the fourth period, western European or Teutonic history. Somehow, this period includes within it the subperiod of Mohammedan civilization. The last subperiod is "the modern time," postfeudalism, which is the historical setting for PR.

The transition from feudalism to the modern world involved the growing importance of towns, which developed the earliest reactions against feudal violence (384). Towns were the location of craftsmen, merchant traders, and bankers. At first towns were protected by the local lord, at a cost; but higher nobles, kings, and the church also levied taxes irregularly according to their needs. So the cities, especially the larger ones like Hamburg and Venice, tried to become independent; they put up walls, and some joined together in self-defense leagues. So the nobles got no more taxes.

But the basic event that sounded the death knell of feudalism was the invention of *gunpowder* (402). The king's heavy artillery could break through the duke's castle walls, leaving him defenseless. Later, when guns were developed, city dwellers became the equal of armored knights on horses, armed with spears and swords. Castles became historic monuments, along with the nobles who inhabited them. So technology brought an end to feudalism.

To be sure, other factors were also involved. The expansion of trade, which Hendrik Spruyt argues was the critical "exogenous variable" (1994, 6, 25) was also centrally important for Hegel. Expanding trade contributed to the growth of cities, which eventually replaced feudalism.

The growing cities facilitated a gradually increasing division of labor in city handicrafts. Several people could be involved in tool making, construction, weaving, or food processing. Improved transport, especially in ships, permitted vastly extended trading and therefore expanded production in the port cities, and this expanded production called for increased productivity and an expanded division of labor.

The Protestant Reformation accompanied this increase in productivity and contributed to it in various ways (Tawney 1926). One contribution was a reversal of the negative Catholic moral ideal of chastity, poverty, and obedience (Hegel 1956, 422–423). Such an ideal enjoins the sinful, insignificant human being to empty himself and prostrate himself before almighty God; this ideal belongs to the Oriental period, not to the modern world. The Lutheran ideal reverses this notion and promotes self-development: Marriage expands life by promoting interdependence; work and industry develops people and enriches them; and following one's own conscience is part of living in a free society.

Another contribution of the Reformation was the elimination of ecclesiastical control over an individual's business and trade dealings, a control priests exercised in the confession box (Tawney 1926, 39ff.). Individuals were directly related to God and so could take responsibility for their own life and business. As Hegel put it, "Since then the individual knows that he is filled with the divine spirit, all the relations of externality are eliminated. There is no longer a distinction between priests and laymen. We no longer find one class in possession of the substance of the truth, as of all the spiritual and temporal treasures of the Church.

... Each man has to accomplish the work of reconciliation in his own soul." (1956, 416). Divinity was now in each individual, not just in the saints and heroes. By extension, the feudal nobility and the saints were no longer owed submission and deference.

The Lutheran theology of this period, Hegel's own era, involved increased emphasis on the Holy Ghost or the "divine spirit," as in the Hegel quotation above. What's "spirit?" The key Bible passage reads, "Whenever two or three are gathered together in my name, there I am in the midst of them" (Matthew 18:20). This does not mean that there is an invisible ghost floating around; it means that these people share a common activity—worship, conversation, work. Activity is what they share. "The very essence of spirit is activity" (Hegel 1956, 73). Of course, the theologian would insist that what they share is worship, and they do; but for Hegel such theology expresses a characteristic experience for city dwellers in this period: equal participation in collective work or activity. John Dewey (1934, 202) develops this concept at length: "Shared experience is the greatest of human goods." Experience for Dewey meant doing, making, so shared experience consists of people making or working together, for instance, playing music.

The most expressive art of this period was music, since in music many people can share the same experience and contribute their own bit to it. Music began to develop as an aspect of early Christian church services, first with priests' chants and then choral chants. The different voice levels—soprano, alto, and so on, singing in octaves and fifths, gradually acquainted people with harmony and dissonance, so the chants could become polyphonic and then contrapuntal. By the sixteenth century, contrapuntal techniques were well developed. In a contrapuntal movement, such as a fugue, three or four voices enter at different times with a theme or countertheme. The voices meet each other in dissonance (conflict), which moves the music toward resolution and more dissonance; that is why it is called a movement. It moves.

Then in the Lutheran church services, unlike Catholic worship, the whole congregation sang together, filling the church with their spirit. They shared a common activity, worship, in music. Those hymns required organ accompaniment, so organ preludes, postludes, and so on developed. Contrapuntal masses, passions, and instrumental sonatas and concertos became more complex, until in Bach's Mass in B Minor or Beethoven's Ninth Symphony many unique contributions, large and small, produced a complex, whole experience that no individual could produce. That is the musical version of the Holy Spirit.

Opera provided an even richer opportunity to express the spirit (culture, *Zeitgeist*) of the time. Consider Mozart's *Marriage of Figaro*, a story of the overcoming of a decadent feudal morality by bourgeois morality. Figaro represents the ambivalence of a loyal courtier; but the women understand the problem, and with careful organization, they get the duke to admit his wrongdoing and beg for forgiveness. Napoleon is said to have called the *Figaro* libretto "the revolution in passion."

Hegel summarizes the three periods selected above by saying that in the first period one is free—the emperor, almighty God; in the second period some are free—the heroes, the nobles, the gods and goddesses; in the third period all are free, through the spirit, the experience we share.

Just to complicate matters, we can note that in the nineteenth century after Hegel, much music became more individualistic, with solo piano, technically dexterous violin solos and concertos, and songs expressing deep individual feelings. Also poetry and fiction developed to express the depths of individual consciousness. Bourgeois individualism was intensifying with the development of capitalism, but that goes beyond Hegel's scheme.

Philosophy

Hegel's task in PR was to give a philosophical description of the emerging or emerged political structure of the modern period. This state was growing out of, and replacing, the feudal state in which monarchs ruled by arbitrary decree, serfs owed much unpaid labor to their protecting lord, the lord had the right to the first night with every bride *(Marriage of Figaro),* and city dwellers had no codified laws to protect their commerce from royal interference. In such a state only the nobles were somewhat free; in Hegel's state, the city dwellers and even the serfs would achieve objective freedom.

The historic event that stimulated Hegel's interest in politics was the French Revolution, which occurred when Hegel was nineteen (Ritter 1969, 192ff; Brod 1992, chap. 3: Both accounts are based on Hegel's correspondence and early political writings). The revolution's call for liberty, equality, and fraternity excited Hegel. The new world has been born! "The halo over the heads of the oppressors and gods of the earth disappears" (Ritter 1969, 194). But by 1795 the Terror, the mass killings, gave Hegel cause for serious doubts. The revolution had wiped out the old oppressive order but had not substituted a new order. "Liberty for all" and fraternity remained subjective visions; their objective institutionalization was missing. So Hegel pondered the question of what these institutions were or would be in countries other than France.

In Prussia, Hegel supported the reform party, in government from 1807–1822, which was attempting to institutionalize representative government, a limited monarchy, and bourgeois freedom (Bogdandy 1989, 237–250). Reforms included the freeing of serfs in 1807 and the partial emancipation of the Jews, which Hegel supported (PR, ¶209R).[2] But by 1819, reaction to the reforms was setting in. The Karlsbad decrees imposed press censorship and censorship of university teaching, research, and publications. Earlier, in Württemberg, Hegel had studied proposed constitutional changes in 1798–1803, which the nobles turned down because the changes would reduce their privileges (Ritter, 202). Napoleon's code, which he unsuccessfully urged on Spain (PR, ¶274A) but successfully promoted in France and northern Italy (Plant 1973, 112), was another example of codified laws that protected city dwellers from royal interference.

But the key event that suggested a solution for Hegel was his reading of James Steuart's *Inquiry into the Principles of Political Economy* in the late 1790s (Ritter 1969, 218; Plant 1973, 64). Hegel came to realize that economic development was the main precondition for a political order in which all are free. Christianity and the Lutheran reformation established the idea of individual responsibility and independence, but this idea remained a subjective belief that required a material basis for its realization. The developing urban manufacturing and trading economy was that basis. Any individual could work, learn skills, buy and sell, satisfy his needs, and become what he wanted to become. That was freedom. In countries where trade, manufacturing, and the division of labor were well developed, such as England and parts of Germany, the needed political changes would occur somehow; in less developed countries like Spain, the new constitution would not take hold; the culture was not ready for it.

Consequently, the French Revolution by itself, with its demand for liberty, equality, and fraternity, was not sufficient. The new order would have to be there objectively already, in urban economic development. Nor was the success or failure of specific attempts at constitutional revision in various countries critical. The issue was rather how pervasive had the new urban economy become in a country, and how influential politically was the business class as a result. An influential business class would reshape the political process so it could deal with the new economy efficiently, even without a revolution.

This realization led Hegel to read the other English economists—Smith, Say, and Ricardo—and immerse himself in economic studies, especially of the English economy (Ritter 1969, 217–220). As Joachim Ritter observes, the economy occupies a central place in PR.

However, Hegel did not adopt the English economists' way of thinking entirely. He used them to learn about empirical matters: human needs, work, the division of labor, capital, taxes, and so on. But their approach was static, whereas his was dynamic and historical. They modeled a static, complete capitalist society, unrelated to the medieval past, just as the French revolutionaries had a vision of a completely new society; but Hegel wanted to understand a capitalist society that was in process of developing out of a surviving feudal past and that would continue to develop. Hegel named the economists' way of thinking the Understanding, and his own way, Reason.

The Understanding is represented by English philosophers: Hobbes, Locke, and Hume, as well as the English economists. This way of thinking expresses the new and growing individualism of traders and producers in the cities. It begins with the fully developed individual with wants, skills, and property, which he or she uses to produce and exchange so as to satisfy his or her wants. Individuals are selfish, with limited benevolence (Hume); the Hamburg merchant who sells manufactured goods to Polish customers via Danzig traders knows or cares nothing about his customers, nor they about him.

Accordingly, this philosophy or economics makes sharp distinctions. One is between past and present: The present economy and polity are based on eternal natural law and have nothing to do with the medieval, feudal past. Today's government is an exchange governed by the social contract; obedience is exchanged for protection and law enforcement. Another distinction is between universal and particular. Particular exchanges in the market are governed by universal laws of supply and demand, unknown to the traders; and conversely the laws have nothing to say about how particular merchants will fare in the marketplace. That is their business. The task of philosophers, then, is to deduce and express the laws of nature that control government and economy.[3]

As part of the Understanding, the domain of philosophy includes logic. This is a deductive, true–false logic descended from Descartes and Leibniz. One begins with undeniable, true axioms, or at least plausible assumptions, and then deduces laws of nature. The deduction requires exact, clear definitions of each term and clear distinctions between all concepts.

Hegel's own philosophy, called "Reason," attempted to go beyond these sharp, static distinctions to locate underlying connections, ambivalences, and dynamics. The abstract models of the economists were a good first approximation, a simplified clarification; but they left out context and underlying dynamics.

First, present society grows out of the past and carries its past with it. "The stages of history that a culture seems to have superseded it still carries with it in the depths of its present." The society Hegel studied carried its past with it; it was an antagonistic mixture of a declining feudalism and a growing capitalism, as in the *Marriage of Figaro*. It also had figurehead emperors or monarchs and cathedrals from a more distant past. Limited market exchanges occurred in a context of traditional production, farming, family practices, loyalties, dominance and submission relations, power, and so on.

Next, for a dialectical thinker, universal "laws" of supply and demand are abstractions from a more complex picture. They describe tendencies, but there are opposing tendencies and other factors involved. Thus, the labor market does not simply follow the law of supply and demand (Branchflower and Oswald 1994; Card and Krueger 1995). The lowering of wages does not automatically lead to a rise in employment, and a minimum wage can promote rather than reduce employment. Obviously, other factors, such as the increasing value of a loyal, trained workforce, are operative. Market power is another complicating factor; oligopoly and monopoly, with their concentrated market power, are pervasive tendencies in the dynamics of competition, not just "interferences."

As for "laws unknown to the traders," this was probably correct in 1800 and earlier; but corporations have come to understand the laws and control them; for example, an oligopolistic price leadership and managed government subsides and tariffs. These topics will return in Chapter 6.

Instead of an abstract deduction of universal natural laws, Hegel's philosophy tries to locate the "essence" or deep structure behind surface appearances. What's "essence?" To get at this concept, we turn to the Kantian doctrine that Hegel regularly negated. According to Kant, when we observe society, no matter how carefully, what we get are appearances: How it looks to us, not how it is in itself. To get the "essence" in itself, we must turn away from observation, which is always *our* observation, and use impartial reason to construct the essence. Hegel denies these distinctions. The essence must appear if it is an essence, he asserts; it appears in the continually varying surface phenomena, at least for the discriminating observer. The task of the philosopher is to collect many empirical phenomena and then construct the underlying essence, using logical thought. Note that this task combines careful empirical work with reasoning (two things that Kant separated); it combines social science and philosophy. Hegel's concept is similar to Bhaskar's "critical realism" (Lawson 1997).

An example might clarify the concept of essence or structure. In the early 1950s, Robert Bales researched the process by which a small group develops its own culture *(Geist)* or structure. In other words, he wanted to study structuration (Bales 1953; Parsons and Bales 1955, chap. 5). Bales set up an interaction process laboratory consisting of several chairs arranged in a circle, with a microphone up above. The room had glass walls; these were one-way mirrors behind which researchers sat watching and taking detailed quantitative notes. A group of six people was led into the room and given a small administrative problem to study. They were supposed to come up with a recommended solution in forty minutes. The microphone recorded the whole conversation for later study, and the hidden researchers coded and tabulated each statement by a group member as it occurred. After the session, each member filled out a questionnaire, and some members were interviewed informally in the hall as they left the meeting. Each group met for one hour once a week for four weeks.

The result was a mass of data, the appearance. Each statement by one member was coded in one of twelve categories, and the twelve in turn were divided into reactive and proactive sets. A reactive statement responded to another person's statement; a proactive statement, by the same person who had just reacted, said something new.

The total set of statements, plus the questionnaire and interviews, provided six roles into which the group members placed each other; the biggest talker, the receiver of the most statements by others, the one with the best ideas, the one who guided the discussion toward a solution, the best-liked member, and the worst-liked member or "scapegoat." Each person could occupy more than one role.

The groups varied greatly in their degree of agreement on who occupied each role. But in all the groups the best-liked member was least likely to have a second role. Conversely, the best ideas and task guidance roles were most likely (.82) to be occupied by the same person. The talking and receiving roles were also highly correlated with best ideas in the high-agreement groups, but not in the low-agreement groups. Obviously the low-agreement groups had a lot of disagreement during discussion, as well; they did not get along. "Things go from bad to worse, with a last meeting that breaks records for disagreement, antagonism, tension" (Bales, 1953, p. 148).

Then Bales looked at the type of contributions made by the best-idea person and the best-liked person. The idea specialist ranked high on giving opinions and giving suggestions. The liked specialist ranked high on showing solidarity, agreement, tension release; on asking other people for opinions and suggestions; and also on expressing tension increase, antagonism, and disagreement. Obviously the idea specialist talked about the administrative problem to be solved. The liked specialist talked mainly about the problem as well; but he also focused on people's feelings and relations more than other people did (Bales 1955, 279–280).

The data interpretations, plus several I have omitted, seem to converge on two opposite roles as essential to a small problem-solving group, according to Bales. One role, combining ideas and guidance, focuses on the problem to be solved, the task. The other role focuses also on the people and their feelings. In the high-consensus groups the two specialists communicated with each other often and positively (usually). Bales calls this pair the "inner circle" (1953, 298) and connects it to the two opposite problems the small groups had to face:

1. Get the assigned task done in forty minutes.
2. Maintain friendly, positive interpersonal relations.

These two problems correspond to Talcott Parsons's instrumental–expressive dichotomy. We can call this "inner circle" the *essence* of the small group structure. The two specialists are interdependent; if friendly relations are not maintained, the group will not get much done, as with the low-consensus groups; and if the task is not done, the members will feel frustrated and have low self-esteem and probably hostility.

As it happens, the essence of the most effective groups is similar to the family structure that Hegel describes in PR. Parsons and Bales (1955) also argue that the same structure appears in American families and in many other cultures.

The dual role structure that appears in the data obviously is not a universal law like the presumed laws of the market; it is one tendency among several, such as continuing disagreement and a breakup into factions or a tendency to separate best-idea and guidance roles. Which tendency comes to dominate depends on the interaction between a variety of personality factors and values and specific decisions (agency) in each group, as Bales observed. However, insofar as the dual role structure or something close to it comes to dominate the other tendencies the group is effective in its problem-solving task. It works, it is actual. In that sense the structure is the *essence* of the problem-solving group. Similarly, the social structure Hegel describes in PR is more fully apparent in some countries than others, but even in England, the country to which he refers most frequently for illustrations, the structure is not fully present (MacGregor 1992, chap. 2). In Germany it is scarcely present at all (Friedrich 1953, 527–539).[4]

Note that Bales's inner-circle structure is not an ought-to-be; it gradually develops, more in some groups and less in others. Similarly, Hegel's state gradually developed, more or less in different countries. It would make no sense to instruct the groups at their first meeting, "You should begin by electing a best-liked member and a task leader." In each case, the group gradually developed its own structure out of the available materials. Similarly, each western European state developed out of the historic, cultural, geographic, economic, and religious materials available. Some states became close to Hegel's essence, others, like Prussia, were farther away; but pronouncing an "ought" would not have helped. Nor would it have helped to impose a constitution on some country, as Napoleon tried to do in Spain.

The kind of logic that is needed to bring out the essence or structure that appears in the data is dialectic. Dialectic works to disclose the underlying structure through the many internally related factors in a complex social process, like group or family interaction. This topic will be discussed in the next chapter.

In summary, Georg Lukacs (1923, 13, 21–23) asserted that (Hegelian) Marxism was not a theory, not a rehash of what Marx taught, but a method of studying a concrete social totality of internally related factors; the method was dialectic. In Hegel's words: "The true is the whole. But the whole is only the essence which completes itself through its own development" (Hegel [1807] 1967, 81; Kaufmann 1965b, 32). In the terminology of cognitive psychology, Hegel's "Reason" requires a divergent cognitive style, that is a tendency to seek out the big picture, in its still bigger context, rather than to limit oneself to a specific area of intensive research. Each totality combines objective and subjective *Geist*, that is, culture and consciousness or substance and subject or structure and agency.

So PR is an example of absolute mind: Hegel got his way of thinking from his own culture, and he used his thinking to study the culture in which he grew up. Mozart expressed his own culture in music; Hegel studied and analyzed and expressed it systematically in concepts.

But remember, present society and culture grows out of the past and carries its past with it; Hegel's culture grew out of the whole history of Western philosophy, as Steven Smith emphasizes (1989, 217–223). Smith shows in detail how Hegel built on and against his predecessors. Similarly, Mozart learned much from Bach, who followed Buxtehude's techniques, and so on.

Notes

1. I believe Barber (1988) distinguishes the two opposites too sharply and thus loses the dialectical relation. According to Barber there are two parallel strands in Hegel's dialectical method: one fixed, the other moving, the one set in stone and the other fluid as water. The moving strand is spirit—the yeast of human consciousness, which, by resisting unity, rebelling against orderliness, and insisting on the productivity of negation, reveals itself as a revolutionary principle of radical action. The fixed strand is history, not history underway, but history cut and dried, completed.

Barber's distinction is much too sharp. For Hegel, each of these produces the other. "Spirit," consciousness, is a product of its own time, of history underway. History is never completed; it is always underway. Rebelliousness is a part of the continuing transition from dependence to independence in children. And people do make history, but not as they please; they must make it out of presently available materials transmitted from the past.

2. A note about my references to the *Philosophy of Right:* An "R" refers to an explanatory note that Hegel added to the text. "A" (addition) indicates student class notes that an editor added. "N" (or Note) is a translator's note.

Metaphysics, History, and Philosophy 23

3. Another distinction that came later, I might add, is between philosophy and social science, and between economics, political science, sociology, social psychology, political sociology, political economy, and so on; here scholars reproduce the division of labor that they express in their concepts.

4. So in at least this respect, Hegel's concern with structure or essence is similar to that of Parsonian functionalists since 1953. Both are concerned with describing the sort of structure that works, is actual. For Hegel, an actual social structure promotes human freedom; for Parsons, it continues to exist, if it is a whole society; or, if it is a subsystem, it contributes its part toward maintaining the whole system. Of course, there are differences as well. Hegel wishes to describe a state that is in continual change due to social dynamics, whereas Parsons focuses more on what a modern society can do to maintain itself by controlling internal strains, conflicts, inefficiencies, anomy, alienation, and so on. Parsons and Bales would have agreed with Bosserman: "Social life . . . is a totality because of the dialectical tensions at play within its interior life holding the various parts together, bringing order out of variety" (Bosserman 1968, 234). For Parsons the tensions would exist among the A-G-I-L subsystems, exemplified by Bales's task specialist and socio-emotional specialist.

3

Dialectic

There have been many different interpretations of Hegel's dialectic, and more keep appearing. One source of the differences is the fact that Hegel treats dialectic somewhat differently in different publications. My interpretation, which I do not claim is the only correct one, is based on Hegel's political philosophy, which deals with objective *Geist:* social institutions. Dialectic takes a somewhat different form in the first part of the *Phenomenology*, which is about the historical development of consciousness and self-consciousness in abstraction from its economic and political context. My interpretation is similar to and derived from Herbert Marcuse (1941), Shlomo Avineri (1972), and more recently, Sean Sayers (1985), Tony Smith (1993), and Bertell Ollman (1993).

The one interpretation that I believe is simply wrong is the one that describes dialectic as a three-step movement: One begins with some concept, the thesis, continues with the opposite concept, the antithesis, and then combines the two, the synthesis. Hegel calls this the Kantian triplicity. This approach treats dialectic as an a priori deductive process, somewhat similar to Thomistic syllogistic and symbolic logic. It is not. "Neither Marx nor Hegel ever used the 'thesis, antithesis, synthesis' formulation. We owe the phrase to Fichte" (Heilbroner 1980, 42).

Another version rather similar to the triplicity has been painstakingly developed by Alexandre Kojève(1969, chap. 7) and is based entirely on the *Phenomenology*. Kojève asserts that Hegel did not himself use dialectical logic at all; he merely described the basic dialectical process in society. This process *always* goes through three stages:

1. Something is there, for instance a field.
2. Someone negates or mediates the field, plows it up and plants beans. Work is *always* the second step of the dialectic (Kojève 1969, 230).

3. The beans grow up and the field overcomes its mediation, moving to a higher level of existence as a farm (208).

I believe this is much too narrow an interpretation, verging on absurdity, though it captures one central kind of dialectical process, the structure–agent interaction.

At the other, better extreme, Kaufmann (1965a), after blasting the Kantian thesis-antithesis-synthesis idea, as Kojève also does (1969, 208), asserts that though Hegel said a lot about how dialectical thinking should proceed, he does not follow his own rules. He just moves around in all sorts of ways in his argument. Dialectic? "There is none" (160). Instead, there is a vision of history moving along through conflict, passion, unintended results, and the irony of sudden reversals. J. N. Findlay (1958, chap. 3) agrees that Hegel moves his argument along in many different ways, but Findlay adds that there are several central themes, one of which is the continuation of conflict, even after mediation or synthesis. For instance, Kojève's farm will experience continuing conflict between the farmer and the immediate tendency of the field to grow weeds, run off in the ditch after a rainstorm, or reseed itself. Another central theme is "self-differentiating unity," for example, the unity of Bales's small groups as they developed a group culture by differentiating several roles (see my discussion in Chapter 2). Pinkard (1988, 19) gives a good, quick summary of dialectic as the "grasping of opposites in their unity, or the positive in the negative," quoting Hegel.

I believe these interpreters have brought out several important aspects of dialectic, including its nonexistence (as rigid systematic logic, that is). Now we begin again, focused on PR.

The abstract deductive logic of the Understanding, based on clear definitions, sharp distinctions, and external relations between causes and effects, is an invention of the modern world, beginning with Descartes and Leibniz. Descartes made drastic changes in the earlier Thomist logic, which in turn was based on Aristotle's syllogisms. Hegel's dialectic also comes out of Greek philosophy, but its source is Socrates, not Aristotle. For Socrates and Plato, dialectic meant dialogue, a discussion by supporters of two opposite views. Dialectic was a process. Similarly, for Hegel dialectic is a process of interaction between two opposites in society, such as the task-oriented leader and the person-oriented leader (see my discussion of Parsons and Bales in Chapter 2). The two opposites tend to "contradict" or negate each other because they are moving in opposite directions; the task-oriented leader wants to get things done, quick, and so tends to be impatient with jokes, praise, side tracks, idle chatter; the person-oriented leader wants to keep people friendly and cooperative, and so tends to be annoyed by the frantic push-push to the next issue, the next disagreement, which leaves bad feelings simmering and cuts off some people who want to speak. The conflict or "contradiction" produces a variety of effects over time: mutual damage or destruction, mutual inclusion of the opposites, learning to get along and even work together, division of tasks, reversal or alternation of control.

None of these various effects are predetermined; there are no "laws" of the dialectic, as Engels supposed, and certainly not exactly three laws. Albert and Hahnel correctly criticize Engels on this point (1978, 50–55). Bales's conflicting group leaders developed different relations in different groups, ranging from mutual respect to strong conflict. Similarly, labor–management relations have varied widely in different countries and time periods.

Findlay summarizes dialectical processes nicely: "By the presence of 'contradictions' in thought or reality, Hegel plainly means the presence of opposed, antithetical *tendencies*, tendencies which work in contrary directions, which each aim at dominating the whole field . . . but which each also require their opponents in order to be what they are" (1958, 74). Sayers (1985, 35–36) calls this the crucial insight of dialectic: Opposites interact and interpenetrate, and through tensions and conflict transform one another over time. I agree. Joel Kovel puts it this way: "The capacity to hold together opposites so that the life immanent within their contradictions can grow" (1997, 20). Yes.

David Gordon uses the term "functional interdependence" to characterize his opposites (1996b, chap. 3). He describes a corporate culture of autocratic management, which feels forced by competition to squeeze ever more productivity out of less labor at minimum wage cost ("lean and mean"). This policy requires its opposite, more managers to supervise workers and lower management, line balancers and other technicians to speed up the process, lawyers to prevent unionization and work slowdowns, and so on. The managers need bonuses and stock options to encourage their push for greater productivity and profits. Managerial costs in turn require more pressure on labor. Rising managerial costs and declining wage costs "foster and reinforce each other, deepening their interdependence" (62). Over time both falling wages and management size have increased.

Of course, the opposites do not just transform each other; they also transform the group, family, institution, society, person in which they interact. That is, dialectic is a "logic" or heuristic of process that deals with how societies and persons develop over time. Dialectic moves from past to future.

The past does not vanish in this process; it continues into the present and future in a changed way. The technical term for such change of the past is *Aufhebung*; past tense, *aufgehoben*. This term means, literally, "lifted up" to a higher level, transformed, but it is usually translated as "sublated." I do not know what "sublated" means, but two examples might clarify the process.

One example: Think of a tiny three-room summer cottage with an outhouse; over time, the owners added a porch to the cottage; then later they put a bathroom in a former bedroom and added a second floor with bedrooms and bath; later still they expanded the kitchen and added a family room with fireplace in back. The old house is still there, as the source and unifying center, but only its original occupants who share its history can still recognize its remaining walls and spaces. It has become absorbed in the new house. The expansions were necessary because of all the visitors who loved the old cottage and returned, and because of the children who grew up, got married, and kept returning with their children. Here the dialectic is between the house and its occupants; it's the kind Kojève studied. That is, the cottage gave its occupants enriching experience, which helped change them; then they changed the cottage to fit their changing family structure, and so on.

A second example: Hegel's intellectual development (as described in detail in Plant 1973, chap. 1–5, and in Scheit 1973, chap. 1–5, two different and supplementary accounts). The youthful Hegel admired the ancient Athenian sense of community and brotherhood and was dismayed at the personal isolation, selfishness, and narrow inwardness of the people around him in Germany. He was enthusiastic about the French Revolution, especially its call for fraternity (Plant 1973, 51), until the Terror disillusioned him. He thought that perhaps a new folk religion would produce social cohesion. Later he wanted a religion that would abandon a remote God in a distant heaven and treat Jesus as a human prophet calling for love, harmony, and reconciliation (Plant 1973, chap. 2). Still later, he shifted to a Lutheran conception of the Holy Ghost who is in all of us and who unites us (Scheit 1973, 68–75). Then Hegel realized that this religious community remained inward, subjective, withdrawn from society; an objective community is needed. Such community is produced by the economic division of labor, which produces a unity of differences (Scheit 1973, 80, 104–107). Then Hegel read Steuart on the historical evolution of society and realized that he himself had been alienated from his own society through his attachment to ancient Greek life. His task then became to understand his own society and economy and explain it to people so they (and he) would appreciate it and become reconciled with it (Plant 1973, chap. 3). To understand his own society and economy, Hegel had to follow Steuart's lead and read the English economists; here he learned how economic development was the primary motor of history, though some political management of the economy was necessary to maintain social cohesion. Then various post-revolutionary reform attempts focused his attention on political processes.

One can recognize these themes in PR and other later works: a longing for a vanished community and a search for some way to reconcile people and bring them back together; some kind of religion as a basis for community; later a focus on how the economic division of labor produces a unity of differences; still later, the need for political maintenance of the economy to help it unify the community. But in PR and other later works these early themes have been transformed, developed, put into a new context: *Aufgehoben.*

The early concern with community is still there, but the conception of community *(Gemeinde)* has shifted from Greek life, to some sort of religious *Gemeinde,* to economy and politics. Greek society has become an earlier stage of history rather than a model for the present, and religions have been relegated to the realm of Absolute *Geist:* reflections of their own society and its past.

Reconciliation is mentioned two or three times in PR; but the favored technique of reconciliation has long since shifted from homogenizing a *Volk* by implanting a religious devotion in their culture (Scheit 1973, 26–32), to a religion of love, to educating people about their own society, to mediating differences of interest derived from the division of labor. The concern has shifted from bringing individuals back into their society to mediating between opposed interest groups so they could work together on their shared problems. Consequently, the earlier tactics of reconciliation have been superseded. As Hardimon observes (1994, chap. 7, sec. III), Hegel's account of the insoluble and intensifying problems of the modern state will not reconcile people to such a state. It could disillusion them instead; but it also could encourage them to manage the problems Hegel mentions and help them to reform their own society. Hegel's focus had shifted from Greek society to current society, and his concern had shifted to political mediation of differences and political maintenance of the economy.

The dialectic in this example is the interplay between Hegel's own thinking and the influence on him of political events and of his reading. Experience and reading changed his old ideas and gave him new ones, which impelled him to search for new ideas in his reading and focus on newer political events, which again changed his previous ideas. This is an internal–external dialectic; that is how people develop and transcend their earlier ideas and concerns.

If dialectic is a continuing process of interaction between two opposites—masculine and feminine, individualism and community, internal and external, worker and employer, universal and particular . . . —we can suspect that there will turn out to be two opposite kinds of dialectic. Of course. The primary kind—for example, the kind Kojève studied—occurs within a culture or society or personality, even if no one is watching. That is how history occurs: It is a product of dialectical processes—conflicts, struggles, mutual learning and reconciliation, unstable balances of power, continuing expansion of some changes and then breakdown and reversal, gradual mutual destruction. Hegel calls this kind of dialectic "the dialectic it has in it," referring to some institution like the market or the legal system. The second kind occurs in philosophers minds when they try to understand their own culture according to Hegelian techniques. One dialectic is objective, the other subjective. However, if the subjective one is any good, it is going to have to catch up with the objective dialectics the philosopher is studying (Brod 1992, 39). "Dialectic is . . . both a movement of the mind, and something mind-independent that imposes itself from the realm of Being. The form and its transformations are *revealed by* enquiry and abstraction, but the form and transformations as revealed *are* the essence of the reality under study" (Meikle 1979, 29). Dialectic *ist mehr als eine Methode: sie ist die Bewegung der Sache selbst* (is more than a method; it is the movement of the thing itself—Scheit 1973, 151). "A two-fold application of the dialectic emerges: . . . first, it shows the types of movement which reality takes; and second, it is the means by which such movements are studied" (Bosserman 1968, 288).

Thus, the subjective dialectic is a method of studying society. Howard Sherman sums it up nicely in his "Dialectics As a Method" (1976): "Briefly, 'dialectics' means an approach to problems that visualizes the world as an interconnected totality undergoing minor and major changes due to internal conflicts of opposing forces." Scott Meikle gives a similar summary: "Marx's dialectic has all to do with grasping a whole in motion, and uncovering the contradiction that constitutes the moving principle of its development" (1979, 14).

The recognition that there are two dialectics helps explain some of the differences between Hegel interpreters. Some of them, such as Kaufmann and Gadamer, focus on the subjective dialectic, and others, such as Sayers and Kojève, focus on the objective dialectic. Some interpreters, such as Findlay and Scheit, recognize both kinds; and others try to "clarify" dialectic as a poor type of deductive process, or ignore both kinds.

The task of the philosopher's subjective dialectic is to locate and describe the essence or "deep structure" of some totality, some social system or personality. The essence is dynamic, with its own internal tensions and conflicts that drive the social system on and produce its history. The dynamic is "the dialectic it has in it," the objective dialectic. The dynamic appears in all the varied empirical data that the social system produces over time. A well-structured system, like the most successful of Bales's small groups, might produce an increasingly regular set of data, cyclical or linear, whereas a more normal conflict-ridden system would produce disorganized data distributions, as with U.S. voting patterns, or sharp breaks like the French Revolution.

Consequently, the philosopher's dialectic also has two opposite, interdependent aspects, an empirical and a rational phase. Empirically, philosophes have to collect mountains of data about the system they are studying: Hegel read a daily English newspaper, journals, many political pamphlets, and books by English economists, and he wrote a long essay on the 1930 Reform Bill. Marx read all the annual reports of Leonard Horner, the English factory inspector (MacGregor 1992, chap. 2, p. 45, chap. 9). In addition, from 1847–1858 he "had his hands full" of daily studies of English, German, French, Irish, and Scotch economic affairs; he wrote economic commentaries for the *New York Tribune;* and he offered to write a book on English economic literature from 1830–1852 (Rosdolsky 1968, 17–22). Bertell Ollman (1993) has studied and organized Marx's empirical investigations of economic processes. But the philosopher's "reason" must then locate the inner dynamics and structure that show through all those varied data or "appearances" and compose the basic long-run developmental tendencies of the system.

How does a researcher locate a dialectical process in society? One is looking for a pair of interdependent opposites, such as supply and demand or policymaking and implementation, and then for the pattern of their interaction over time and its context. Of course one can start with known opposites, such as worker and employer, or Hegel's favorite, universal and particular (example: policymaking and implementation). That is easy, perhaps too easy; one might just squeeze the opposites on to the data. But one can also look for new opposites! That's harder.

To look for a new pair, or to study the interrelations of some known pair, one starts with lots of empirical data, as Hegel did. Since dialectic deals with patterns of change over time, one needs time series data: cycles, steady change, irregular fluctuations, gradually increasing complexity of variations, regular alternation, and so on. Such data constitute the "appearance," the outward expression of the dialectic; the research must then somehow move to the essence, the structural dynamics, that produce those appearances.

If the data show a consistent expansion or increase of some quantity and a decrease of a different one, such as wealth and poverty, one tries to find the interdependence and processes by which each produces the other. If the data show regular alternations or cyclical fluctuations, one obviously examines the peak period to see what sort of factor seems to be active, and then searches near the turning points to see what processes are preparing a reversal. Perhaps the active factor unintentionally activates its opposite, as in the Bales data (see my discussion in Chapter 2), or perhaps it intentionally activates the opposite that it needs for its own completion, as with policymaking and implementation—with unexpected results, of course.

For example, Bales found a fairly consistent alternation in his small groups between concentration on the problem to be solved and relaxation, a joke, laughter, diversion away from the problem. A focus on the problem to be solved tended to build up tensions because of disagreements, status struggles, and so on, until someone entered the process with a joke or other tension-reliever; then he or someone else returned to the problem. "The problem of equilibrium is essentially the problem of establishing arrangements whereby the system goes through a repetitive cycle, within which all of the disturbances created in one phase are reduced in some other" (Bales 1953, 123). "We note joking and laughter so frequently at the end of meetings that they might almost be taken as a signal that the group has completed . . . the task effort. . . . This last minute activity completes a cycle of operations involving a successful solution both of the task problems and socio-emotional problems confronting the group" (143). Thus, the time series data pointed to the two problems the groups had to manage, and those problems in turn pointed to the task specialist and the socio-emotional specialist as the essential roles, the essence or "inner circle" of the group's role structure.

Once one has a plausible pair of opposites, one can try them out by estimating their mutual relation and seeing whether it would fit the data. Polarized opposites like capital and labor or husbands and wives can conflict and damage one another, or one can dominate the other in a hostile or in a friendly, benevolent manner, or the two can develop a mutual respect and division of labor, and so on. Interdependent opposites such as social and psychological processes, or structure and agency, are each always active and reactive in the other, and the problem is to distinguish them. Ambivalent opposites, such as desires for dependence and independence, tendencies to conformity and rebellion, liking and disliking a person, are each always present in a person but activated by different factors. Ambivalences produce disorganized data with sharp breaks.[1]

If one is studying a larger social system, the opposites also have to fit into the context of other opposites that influence the process or provide its preconditions. This provides another test of the presumed pair. To find the essential contextual factors, one can compare cases to find a consistent facilitator or blocker, such as ethnic differences in a capital–labor relation. Or a particular case might bring out a unique factor that shifts the whole process. How did that happen? This question helps clarify the process. Also, having identified a possible pair of opposites, one can look at the data from the perspective of each opposite—labor or capital, or the supply side and the demand side—to locate other contextual factors.

After that one can, if one wishes, move on to a larger context: other influences, interferences, conditions, interdependences. The larger picture may also give a different view of the original pair of opposites; this is the whole-and-part dialectic starting to operate.

Heilbroner (1980, 45ff) asks for a handbook of specific instructions on how to proceed with the above process and criticizes Ernest Mandel's six instructions (1975, 16–17) as too vague. But there is no handbook; the process is too messy. The test is whether the theoretical construct can produce the available empirical data sequences. Chapter 6 will provide an example. Conflicts between the theoretical and empirical aspects are what move the research process along.

The back-and-forth process of inquiry ends when the philosopher has abstracted the apparently essential sets of opposites and their relations from the data. That is, the process moves irregularly from empirical to abstract. The presentation of the results moves in the opposite direction, from abstract to concrete, or simple to complex.

The presentation must bring out the logical structure or essence of the case, step by step, and leave out the messier process of inquiry by which those results were worked out. Social scientists do that too. Thus, in the PR, the logical aspect of the philosopher's dialectic stands out, while the empirical aspect remains in the background. Bits of the empirical material show up in the comments and remarks added to the text, but the empirical research method is not mentioned.

In his chapter on "Marx's method" Ollman summarizes: "Marx's goal is to bring together the elements of his explanation as they are related in the real world and in such a manner that they *seem* to belong to a deductive system . . . [Marx comments:] 'It may appear as if we had before us a mere *a priori* construction!'" (Ollman 1979, 177). But actually the relations have been discovered empirically by examining the actual context of each pair.

We turn now to the presentational aspect of the philosopher's dialectic, as it appears in a published work. The task is to present the essence or structural processes of some social system and show the interconnections between its parts. Hegel's procedure is to start with one very simple, abstract pair of opposites, show (not deduce) their relations to each other, then bring in another pair that is already implicitly present in those relations, show its relations, and so on. Each new pair is part of the context of the previous pairs of opposites. As more and more context gets filled in, we gradually move from the original abstraction to the complex concrete whole. All of the abstract items are present in the concrete essence, but in a complex context, not in abstraction. Consequently, as we move from abstract to concrete, we can look back at some earlier abstraction and realize that we now have the context for that item, so we can understand it better.

For example, he starts the *Phenomenology* with a sensation, expressed as, "It's dark." Presumably that is the simplest kind of sense experience. But not simple. There are two universal concepts, "dark" and "is," that express the particularity of the sensation. So we study how the universal and particular need each other. Presently we recognize that "I" am having the sensation, and the focus shifts to the subject–object relation; and so on. The *Logic* starts with the concept of Being, which negates its opposite, nonbeing, but carries the opposite within itself as its own potentiality: Anything could stop being and, conversely, has come to be—that's Becoming, which we look at next, in its two opposite aspects. Hegel starts the PR with the concept of free will, and its opposite: things. Things are *not* free. Then from things he moves to property, that is, things that are worked on by a person with free will.

Marx starts *Capital* with the commodity, that is, property that can be exchanged or sold. Then he moves from property that has exchange-value to the labor that created the value. Thus, he moves in the opposite direction from Hegel, from property to person.

Could philosophers start with any old abstraction and move around systematically until the whole picture gets filled in? No, probably not. In their empirical studies philosophers have worked out the relations among various processes, and they have to bring out those relations of interdependence one by one. Also, they have picked out the basic process, the one that influences, and is influenced by, all the rest; this is the goal they wish to reach in their argument, so they have to pick a route that will get them there. In the PR, the abstract starting point, free will, is also the conclusion Hegel wants to get to, concretely of course. "The will is free, so freedom is both the substance of right and its goal" (PR ¶4). That is, Hegel wanted to get to the political institutions and processes by which people make themselves actually free and maintain their freedom by managing their own society.

Marx, in contrast, writing forty-five years later, wanted to focus on the dynamics of the capitalist economy, such as the short-run circuit of capital, more intensively than Hegel did, and especially on labor as the source of economic value and as itself a commodity to be sold. So he starts with the central and most abstract concept: commodities. Hegel mentions the sale (alienation) of labor in passing (¶67) and warns of the danger to freedom, but he then moves on to contracts. He travels a different route. Also for Marx, labor is the ultimate agent who will establish a free society, the end he wants to get to, whereas Hegel wanted to get to present self-government.

Back to Hegel. In PR, as the philosopher's dialectic moves along and gets more concrete, actual social institutions gradually show up and, with them, their objective dialectic or dynamics. So the philosopher has to sketch their objective dialectic too. At that stage, things get complex because we have two dialectics going along together. This combination occurs in part 3 of PR: "Ethical Life." The two dialectics should mesh because Hegel is trying to describe the social dynamics of his own time. However, the two dialectics move in different directions, so there are breaks. The culture he is studying moves from the past toward the future, whereas his own thought is moving from abstract to concrete. Consequently, he has to take leave of some institution like property or family or social class because he has to get to some other institution that includes these within it; he has to get more concrete. The result is a semi-static picture that can be misread easily as a static nonhistorical account of the "modern state," rather than as an impressionist portrait of a constantly changing target.

Here again, Ollman summarizes: "Marx sought to reproduce the concrete totality present in his understanding in two ways, by drawing the interaction of social relations in the present and displaying their historical development" (1979, 177). The same summary applies to Hegel.

In the next chapter we shall work through the philosopher's dialectic in PR step by step. After that, in the following chapter, we shall return to the objective dialectical processes that Hegel describes in passing and see what they might look like when taken in a past-to-future direction. And since these processes did not stop in 1821, we can trace their later developments to get a clearer picture of them.

Incidentally, the movement of the objective dialectic into the future does not necessarily represent progress for Hegel. There is progress in history for Hegel in the very long run, but not every short-run dynamic is progressive by any means. There will be examples in Chapter 4. So be careful.

Now we reverse course. "It's about time," some readers may be thinking. Up to now, the objective dialectic has been dominant; the goal of the philosopher's subjective dialectic has been to discover, understand, and describe the dialectic of society. But once the philosopher–social scientist has uncovered and described the presumably basic dynamics of current society, it becomes possible to move into those dynamics and perhaps shift them or help maintain them. At this point the subject becomes at least active, and perhaps dominant. As mentioned before, for Marx, the subject was future labor; for Hegel, it was the self-governing community as of 1821. Kojève's dialectic, in which work, activity, was central, has returned as very important too.

The active subject can still use the objective dialectic that the philosopher has described, but not just as a description of the present. Since the dialectic moves into the future, it can point to a potential future that might be encouraged or counteracted. Thus, Hegel could see the growing individualism being produced by the economy and could hope that some government would counteract it somehow. Ollman (1998) in particular has emphasized this potential-future aspect of the dialectic.

However, I believe that this aspect can be useful only in dealing with near-future, short-run processes, not with the long-run future of a whole society. A whole society contains a number of interacting processes, each of which can dampen or redirect or encourage other processes over time, so that the potential future becomes more complex and indeterminate.

Notes

1. George Gurvitch has described a considerable number of such dialectical relations (Bosserman 1968, 232–239). In addition to the above, he points to opposites in social science: quantitative and qualitative methods; opposite theories, such as the wave and particle theories of light in physics; reciprocal perspectives on data, such as an entrepreneurial maximization-of-utility perspective and a labor perspective, or a public-goods government or community perspective versus a private-goods individualist perspective. Each method or theory or perspective produces rich understanding of empirical processes and empirical confirmation, such as the wave and the particle theory; but each opposite contradicts or supplements or reinterprets the other. If one could partly combine such opposites the result would be an enriched theory or method. But Gurvitch has gone considerably beyond Hegel here.

4

The *Philosophy of Right*

We will go through PR, Hegel's main political text, a logical step at a time. This will bring out Hegel's dialectical method, as he moves from abstract to concrete, and also will describe the interdependence of 1820 social institutions. The dialectical movement also will reveal the essence, the essential contradiction of modern society.

But before we start, let us consider the translator's comments about the translation, as well as Hegel's own brief summary, first in his preface and then in his introduction, of what he will be doing. That way we won't be wandering off into unknown territories.

The translator begins with a warning: The PR was written in German. So we must get the meaning of various hard-to-translate words from the context or from ordinary German usage.

1. *Recht* has been translated right, law, right and law. So don't distinguish the two sharply.
2. *Wirklich* carries a German connotation of working OK, doing the job, which you have to read into "actual"; it works, it "acts." "Real" would mean, in contrast, "it exists."
3. *Moralisch* has a subjective connotation, like conscience; *sittlich* refers to social customs, rules, expectations. But the two overlap.
4. You can think of "Estates" as Parliament, if you remember that each House represented a different Estate in Hegel's time.
5. Thought, Concept, Idea. These are three stages of subjective thinking, which move from abstract to concrete. "Thought" appears in ¶5; the will is free because it can choose anything. That's abstract; it specifies the *form* of freedom, choosing, but no *content*; just the universal: anything. "Concept" appears in ¶7; it includes content, choosing something, and form: could have chosen anything else. "Idea" appears briefly in ¶1, ¶2, and ¶21;

it is the actualization of the concept in society. That's concrete in thought.
6. Development. The translator is here referring to the development of a philosopher's thought, from abstract to concrete. This is the subjective dialectic that we took up in Chapter 3; it tries to comprehend the structure of an actual totality as it exists at one point in time. The move from thought to concept to Idea is part of that process. The actual totality, in contrast, has developed over a long time and continues to develop according to its objective dialectic.

Preface

Page 1, bottom. Method. Hegel is referring to the subjective dialectic, which is "philosophy's mode of progression from one topic to another." He says he's going to use it in the text. The goal of the philosopher's dialectic is to bring out, make explicit, the objective dialectic or dynamics of the structure being studied. The particular structure being studied is content; the dialectical way of studying it is form, as Hegel explains on page 12. And since the subjective dialectic (form) should bring out the objective dialectic (content), "content" is essentially bound up with "form."

Skip to page 10. "It is just this placing of philosophy . . ." Here Hegel asserts several times that he is going to describe the actual structure of contemporary European states. He is *not* going to construct an ideal state. "Philosophy is its own time apprehended in thought" (p. 11). It has to be. Since philosophers' ideas, and everyone else's too, come out of their own culture and its past, they necessarily think in terms that are relevant to their own time and its problems. It is incredible to me that so many commentators ignore this point and assume that Hegel is arguing for some kind of ideal state that ought to exist. But it shouldn't be incredible to me; that's the way *they* think, in *their* culture, a culture that distinguishes "is" and "ought," social science and philosophy.

"*What is rational is actual and what is actual is rational.*" "Rational" means having a dialectical structure; "actual" *(wirklich)* means that it works. If it's constructed correctly it will work. That is, Hegel will describe the essence or structure of the 1820 state, the inward pulse beating in the outward appearances, that makes it work. He won't fuss over the endless, varied appearances that he has studied to get at the essence. He will bring out the immanent substance that produces the temporal and the transient. Put differently, he will describe the Idea, the unity of form and content, as actualized in 1820 society. Form is the rational, the structural relations of the 1820 state, as described in the philosopher's dialectic; content is the actual, how those institutions work in practice.

Notice that on page 12 he describes the essence as "the rose in the cross of the present." Think about that dialectically. To understand the rose one must look also at the not-rose, the cross and thorns that make the rose look so beautiful. That is, one must understand what works as the correction or adjusting of what doesn't work, the consistent sources of trouble. The political state works *insofar as* its institutions redirect or counteract those tendencies. This does not mean that we have to look at *all* the manifold empirical troubles; we need only the dialectical tendencies, the structural dynamics that are always tending to produce trouble. We will see how Hegel does this when he gets to the political state, government. Chapter 7 will provide further examples from contemporary states.

One further implication of pages 10–12: If the philosopher can use only the ideas of his own time and its past to locate the rational essence of his own society, he will be able to comprehend only those structures that are fairly well developed. He will not be able to extrapolate to some future fulfillment, correction, transcendence, replacement. Philosophy can only describe, not predict. "As the thought of the world (as a culture studying itself) it appears only when actuality is already there cut and dried after its process of formation has been completed." Here Hegel differs most sharply with Marx.

Avineri (1972, 128) draws an interesting implication from the above: If philosophy is the wisdom of ripeness, then the state that Hegel described in 1821 was finished, on the way out. And, as Avineri adds (130) and as we shall see later, Hegel did see how his own society was already changing into something else unknown and unpredictable, in a variety of ways.

The argument that philosophy cannot give advice as to what the state ought to be has bothered some commentators: If Hegel is only describing his own time, which is now in the deep past, why should we bother with him? Chapters 5–8 below give my answer to this question.

Introduction

¶4. Our starting point is free will, which is subjective. The system of right is the objectification of free will. The consequence and goal of the system of right is again freedom, so that freedom is both the start and finish. Obviously, though, the final freedom is going to be very different from the initial one: The initial one is abstract, and the final one is concrete and objective.

¶5. Now we start the philosopher's dialectic. "Free will" means that you can choose anything you like. That's a universal, then: anything at all, but nothing specific.

¶6. Not good enough. To have a will, you have to eventually choose something. If you keep mulling over the endless possibilities, that isn't will; that's imagination. You have to will. That's a particular.

¶7. Not good enough. If you just choose one thing you may have been coerced into it. So we say, you choose one thing but you didn't have to; you could have chosen something else. That's a unity of particular and universal, that is, individuality, a very common concept in Hegel. It's a synthesis of the two opposites. The translator explains it nicely in note 35.

¶8. Now we have a concept of free will, our starting point, so let's look at it some more. First, it's subjective; deciding is something you do in your head, privately. Notice the implication: We will have to get objective eventually.

¶9. Next, let's look at the specific things we choose, the content of choice.

¶10. Contents are specific, immediate, particular. "It is the will in its concept." So we still have to get to the Idea.

¶11, 12. Ideas are all sorts of things, and thus, are different from the will that chooses one of them. The particulars are different from the universal will, the contents are different from the form. This point repeats the point of ¶10: content has to get bound up with form eventually; that would be the Idea.

¶13, 14. From our concept, ¶7, the will could have chosen any one of those impulses, desires, inclinations, and not chosen all the rest; but why? How do you choose?

¶15. It seems arbitrary. In addition, ¶15A, the content seems arbitrary too. Why did those desires show up as possible choices, and not other desires? Where does the content come from? If we are stuck with a particular list of desires to choose from and not another list, then we are not really free. For example, if our desires and opinions are selected and strengthened by advertising and public relations, and if we are taught by media commentators and economics professors that we have consumer sovereignty and voter sovereignty, then we can believe we freely choose some cigarette or candidate, but we are not free to choose (Rayack 1987; Coleman 1990, 633–634). We have been hoodwinked. Such free choice "may indeed be called an illusion."

¶16. Changing our mind and choosing something else doesn't help, contrary to ¶7, because that would be equally arbitrary.

¶17. One solution is to have some principles for choosing among available options, for instance ¶20, the principle of maximizing some sort of happiness.

¶18. But principles vary. The principle of maximizing satisfaction of desire assumes that desires are good; other philosophers have argued

The Philosophy of Right

that natural desires are evil and have urged different principles. We'll have to deal with that.

¶19. To return to the topic of ¶15A and ¶16: What we need is some way to make the impulses, desires, inclinations among which we choose come from ourselves, instead of just having them show up somehow. That is, our desires should come from our personality that we have ourselves developed, not from advertising. Then form, our will, and content, our desires, will match; we made them both. That sort of freedom is what PR is about.

¶21. Freedom then will be self-determination, making oneself, ¶22, developing one's potentialities, ¶23, self-related choice.

¶25. Now we move to the opposite of free will. Hegel reminds us of ¶8: The will that chooses is subjective, one-sided; its choices have to be carried out in the objective world to be actual. (The three subheads express the universal, particular, and individual aspects of the will.)

¶26. A dialectical reminder: Everything subjective tends to get objectified somehow, and everything objective gets taken in subjectively. The free will is an instance of this.

¶27, 28. So self-determination, the developing of one's potentialities, takes place in the objective social world. It involves remaking society in such a way as to promote self-development.

¶29. That is, it involves remaking or adjusting the system of right(s) so that it promotes self-development. That will be freedom as Idea, the actual unity of form (free will) and content (institutions).

Summary. Hegel has set up and analyzed his starting point, free will. He has then shown how abstract that starting point is. First, it is subjective, so we have to move to objective conditions starting in ¶34. Next, it doesn't say where the alternatives from which we choose, and the principles by which we choose, come from. They have to come from ourselves. That leads to the first definition of freedom: Freedom is making ourselves into a free, self-determining society, so that our choices come from ourselves. This definition is asserted in ¶27–29. "Mind's purpose is to be explicitly, as Idea, what the will is implicitly." Thus, we have moved from the starting point, abstract free will, to the goal, concrete free society. The goal is still abstract, of course; it will be filled in step by step, beginning with ¶34. ¶33 lists the main steps.

Notice that we *end* this discussion of free will, ¶¶5–29, with a sort of definition. The deductive logic of the Understanding, in contrast, *begins* with definitions and then makes deductions. So you can think of dialectic as a heuristic that one uses to develop a rationally and empirically adequate definition of some subject matter. The move from thought to concept to Idea is part of this process. Note also that freedom is defined as a process, making ourselves, not as something static.

Abstract Right

¶34. Hegel reminds us where we are: free will as initially conceived in ¶5–7 and located as subjective in ¶8. So our first move will be into its opposite, the external world.

¶35. First, we look at subjectivity. That's I. I choose; I am free. ¶37. What I choose is irrelevant; I am free to choose anything. ¶35. Where the alternatives come from is irrelevant, as of ¶7; I do the choosing. I am a person.

¶36, 38. Persons have rights. This makes no sense now because we don't know what rights are. Hegel is merely connecting the two for future use. This section is called "abstract right," so now we know that abstract persons are the subjects who have abstract rights.

¶39. The person as subject faces the world out there. But when I choose to do something, it has to be done in the world, not just in my head. So I have to move into the world out there.

¶41. That is, if I decide to eat a carrot, I have to have a carrot, or money to buy one. If I decide to plant a garden, I have to have ground plus seeds, or money to buy them. That is, I have to have property. Otherwise the choices are mere fantasies. To be a person, I must have property, so I can carry out my choices.

¶42. The world out there, the carrots, soil, seeds, consists of things. Things don't choose; they are not free; they don't have rights. Things become property. So you see, you can't have persons who are free, unless there are things, which are not free. Personality requires its opposite to be itself. That's dialectic.

¶44. Here's our first, most abstract right: The right to own property.

¶51. How do we get property? That's the next topic, starting in ¶53.

¶55. The simplest way is to grab it, but that doesn't get us very far because we have only two hands.

¶56. A more basic way is to work on it, that is to put my mind, my plans, into it; for example, cultivating a garden. Here subjective mind is objectified in things and becomes material culture, gardens, a synthesis of subject and object.

¶57. The most important thing we can work on and cultivate is our own body. We can learn techniques and skills for doing things.

¶57R. In the modern state we can't take possession of someone else's body; that's slavery, which is wrong, illegal. Slavery prevents a person from taking possession of his/her body and mind and developing it into a full person. Slavery existed in the earlier stages of history. Here Hegel for the first time touches on the objective dialectic of history, the movement away from Oriental despotism through imperial and feudal times to modern representative government. This movement involves the gradual recognition, supported by the requisite economic and political and religious developments, that all persons have a right to their own body.

¶58. The most general way to take property is to mark it. What's a mark? A sign, "Private, no trespassing," a sticker, "Property of . . . ," a license plate, a deed. Here Hegel hints again at the more concrete context in which we are operating. The context is a legal system, including a license bureau and a recorder of deeds. A mark is a legal device. Note that we have moved from particular, grabbing, to universal, a mark, in ¶55–58.

¶59. Next, when we have some property, we use it; that is, we use it to do whatever we have decided to do. We carry out our choices with it, make our freedom real. That's what property was for.

¶63. Now we move from property as particular, that carrot, to property as universal. The universal that all things share is their value, that is their usability, use-value. Note 47 expands on this. Value is quantitative and is measured by money. When you sell a carrot, you get its value in money, and you can use that money to buy something of equal value, equal price. Notice that the universal, value, depends on the particular: A thing sells because someone can use it. But you can't have both universal and particular at the same time; they exclude each other. When you're using the carrot, eating it up, you can't sell it, and when you sell it you can't eat it.

The context is pretty obvious by now. First, value requires other people to buy from and sell to; this will become explicit in ¶71. Second, the decline of feudalism is closely tied to the fact that feudal ownership was of use only, not of value. The duke couldn't sell his property (¶63R, end of ¶63A). He was stuck with it. This was a limitation on his freedom of choice; he couldn't use the value to pay his soldiers or banker, and so on. Consequently, the dukes were raising money by taxing the towns in their area, which the towns didn't like and tried to avoid. Meanwhile, in the city, people were buying and selling, hiring labor, manufacturing, and prospering. They were free; the duke wasn't. So the objective dialectic of feudalism and capitalism is mirrored in the movement of the text.

¶65. We move on to alienation, selling or abandoning property. The right to property is essential to freedom; but the right to get rid of it is also essential, as the dukes learned. If you're stuck with some property, you cannot get a hold of its value, and you probably have to maintain it as well.

¶66–70. Some things you can't sell, because they are essential to your freedom: You can't sell your body into slavery, for instance. Note the warning in ¶67: Selling your labor power is OK up to a point, but selling too much of it makes you a slave. If someone else controls all your work, you're not free. So informal slavery has returned since 1820.

¶71. Now Hegel makes explicit what was implicit in ¶63: We need other people to be free. Other people showed up in ¶58 to read our "no trespassing" signs, and then left, but when we want to sell the property, we welcome them with a "for sale" sign.

When we sell something we have reached agreement with the buyer on the price; that is, we share a common will, the contract. To be sure, a contract is the most abstract, smallest common will possible. We'll get to more concrete, complex ones.

¶81. As you must have suspected, sooner or later "wrong" would have to show up as essential to "right," just as "things" are essential to "persons," and "use" is essential to "value."

¶82. Here Hegel explains. A contract is an arbitrary agreement between two people; but what seems to be an agreement may be a misunderstanding or even deliberate trickery. You may think you're getting tuppence for that carrot, but the buyer may give excuses and promises to pay later. You may sign a contract to get a house built for $80,000, which you pay on demand, but the builder drags it on and on, giving various excuses. So you go to court and the contract gets enforced. Now it's not just an agreement, but a legal judgment backed by the law and the police. The right to property (value) has negated the negation of itself, and thereby become actual, enforced by the state rather than just by a handshake. That means that it applies to everybody; it's universal. So the other house-builders or carrot-buyers will know that they can't get away with such trickery. ¶82A and ¶83A explain it further. So wrong makes right actual.

¶90–104. Now Hegel goes over wrong a bit more deeply. No contract need be involved here, just property. In crime someone takes away your property by force, thereby negating your freedom to use that property. Then the criminal is punished, coerced, in order to negate the negation. But the criminal's family or tribe may regard that coercion as wrong; they may think that the taking of property was justified on some ground, as in Hebron, and that the wrong punishment in turn must be punished. So you get a feud. The solution is to have the punishment imposed by an impartial will, ¶103, a judge who is concerned only with enforcing universal rules impartially.

That's the definition of morality. So morality is necessary for freedom. If both contracting parties are moral and follow established rules, contracting becomes much easier, though not perfect.

Summary to here:

1. Free will, which is subjective, requires property, which is objective, to be actual.

2. A person must also be able to get rid of property, in order to get a hold of its value.
3. Value is the universal in property; getting it requires exchanges with other people, that is, contracts.
4. Contracts are particular agreements between two people, so they could go wrong. They must be enforced by courts and police; this rights the wrong and establishes contract rights and rules universally.
5. The two parties may disagree on which one of them was wronged, so mere force won't settle that. We need an impartial judge applying impartial rules to establish what's right. That's morality. So morality is necessary to enforce contracts, which are necessary for owning value, which is necessary for objectifying free choices.

Morality

¶105, 106. We have now moved from the objective world of property deep into subjectivity. But it's a different layer of subjectivity than where we started, a "higher ground." At the start, a person thinks, "I like that; I'll do it." Now the person thinks, "Looks attractive, but is it right? Is it the best thing to do? Ought I do it?" That's self-related negativity: We negate our own desires, impulses, and inclinations by reference to established rules of contract. When people do that, contracts work, are actual.

¶106R tells us where we are heading next, but you could have guessed it: We're heading for non-morality, evil, "sinking deeper and deeper into itself." See Note 2.

¶107–112. Examines the thought of this layer of subjectivity. Here the will that decides what to do is individual, separated from other individuals, separated from the good that ought to be achieved, and also separated from the eventual carrying out of the decision. All these separations have to be overcome somehow.

¶113, 115 set up the moral situation to be examined. The thing to be evaluated morally is my action, and the issue is whether I ought to do it (or ought to have done it). There is a court and judge of some kind in the background now, and other people who are affected by my action.

First, how much of it is my action, how much of what happens is my responsibility? Consider the builder who has contracted to build a house. What if certain materials don't come in because of a strike? That's not his fault, ¶116–118. Or suppose the buyer of the carrot finds that his tuppence has slipped through a hole in his pocket somewhere. He couldn't help that (or could he?). He can pay the next day when he comes back for his next carrot.

¶116–120. Responsibility is based on what your purpose was, what you intended to do. So you evaluate an action—yours, or someone else's if you are a judge—by what its purpose is or was.

Second, how does a moral being evaluate an intentional, purposive action? What standards does one use? Hegel mentions two: good and conscience. By "good" he means, Will it achieve the maximum good for everyone involved? If so, it is or was right. By "conscience" he means, Ought I do it? Is it my duty?

The trouble is, everyone always thinks they are intending to do good, ¶133–134. As for duty, what is my duty? Kant's rules won't get you anywhere. They can perhaps tell you not to do something, but they can't tell you what to do. ¶136–138. If duty is doing what your conscience tells you, people have all sorts of consciences. A religious fanatic might think it is his duty to kill the infidel or the abortion doctor (expressed in Kantian terms as: It's right to kill any person who deliberately kills one human after another, for money). Does that make it right? ¶139. Consequently, the moral person doing what he thinks is right might intentionally produce evil results.

¶141. Consequently, we need objective rules and standards. A subjective morality that depends on the individual's conscience to evaluate proposed actions gives different results for different people; the universal right is missing.

Ethical Life: Approaching the Concrete

¶142–156 is a general introduction to "Ethical Life." The German term is *Sittlichkeit*, which can be translated "custom" or "culture." This is the realm of objective *Geist*; we were in subjective mind in the section on morality. That section ended in indeterminacy: Individuals on their own have no way to work out universally valid moral principles. But remember, those were abstract, "state of nature" individuals, persons with free will and property, and nothing else. We now move *gradually* to concrete individuals who have grown up in society.

The general idea is expressed in ¶153A: To get a truly moral person, you bring him or her up in a state with good laws. "Good" doesn't mean "perfect"; it means laws that work well enough to enable a system of contract and exchange to continue functioning fairly well.

¶142. This is the Idea of freedom because it has both a subjective and an objective aspect: Customs are embedded in people's personalities and consciousness but also in social institutions, including grocery stores and offices and factories. Each of the two becomes meaningful in conjunction with the other.

¶143. Each is included in the other: The institutions are actual in people's habits, and people are in the city, working and shopping.

¶149. Living in a culture, a city, liberates people (presumably the abstract, isolated people in the section on morality) from the indeterminacy of ¶141. ¶154 makes an important point that will keep returning: People also have their private, particular interests, skills, living spaces, personalities, and so on that make them unique. Each particular person is different, though all persons share the same universal culture. That's how the particular and the universal always (universally) relate in the dialectic, though each particular time it comes out a little different.

Consequently, ¶155, when you act properly, follow the rules, you are simultaneously doing your duty (following the rules) and exercising your right to do as you please. For instance, you know the rules of driving: Stay in the right lane (or left lane in some countries), observe the speed limit, stop at stop signs, signal a turn, don't follow too closely. These rules enable you to exercise your right to drive anywhere, safely. Without rules, roads would be a disaster. The universal, rules, safeguards the particular, individuality. Duty is the basis for exercising right. We are getting more concrete: We need other people to be free (contracts), so we have to get along with those other people, and that requires rules, duties.

Family

How did we get to family? Think back to ¶141, where we found that the abstract moral individual had trouble deducing generally valid moral rules. Actually, individuals begin to learn their moral rules, their conscience, as children. So we begin with the family in general, semi-abstractly.

¶158. The family is a type of community, that is, a unity of differences. The basis of the unity is love.

We start with the parents. Go to ¶165–168. Marriage is a unification of two opposites, with different backgrounds, ¶168. These opposites agree to merge their personalities into a permanent partnership based on love and expressed in sex, ¶162–164.

¶166, 166R is the crucial paragraph. It is written from a masculine perspective: Men have lots of troubles; women don't. A man goes out into the world, works, gets things done, thinks about politics, and gets involved; he struggles with himself to do better, get better organized, get more efficient, plan ahead and be prepared, don't make *that* mistake again. Trouble, trouble. Then at the end of the day he goes home to his loving wife, who soothes and comforts him, feeds and relaxes him. Woman, on the other hand, takes care of the home and children and waits for him.

If we bypass Hegel's one-sided masculine perspective, we can recognize the two equal but opposite leaders in Parsons and Bales's successful problem-solving groups (see my discussion in Chapter 2). The husband is the task-oriented leader, focusing on getting things done on time, efficiently and effectively; the wife is the person-oriented leader, focusing on people's feelings, such as anger, jealousy, withdrawal, shame. That's why she can soothe her husband, recognizing that he's torn apart and exhausted after an acrimonious committee meeting. One difference is that for Bales gender was irrelevant to the leadership structure.

Incidentally, the same opposition is expressed in Mozart's *Marriage of Figaro* in the opening duet between Figaro and Susanna. Mozart expresses the opposition in feeling; Hegel and Bales express it in concepts.

But remember, Hegel was trying to describe the patriarchal family that was still standard in 1821. The musical expression of patriarchy was the sonata form, standard for symphonic first movements in Hegel's time and earlier.[1] He was trying to bring out the essence that made even a patriarchal family successful at raising children. He knew that marriage didn't always work and reminds us, ¶176, that if the marriage fails they get a divorce. In ¶179 he criticizes the patriarchal rule that made the father the sole owner of family property. So we can hope that in the 1800s some men put aside their public patriarchal status and privately developed a more equal partnership. Such marriages would work.

Now let us look at the dynamics of love, its objective dialectic. Hegel doesn't say much about this topic; he wishes to move on quickly to other institutions with his philosophical dialectic. So we will have to move beyond Hegel to more recent developments and psychological studies when we take up the objective dialectic in Chapter 5. But Hegel does present the basic contradiction in ¶158A. Each partner rejects his or her independence as something defective and incomplete and becomes dependent on the other. Through this dependence the partner is gradually liberated from defectiveness (¶162) and becomes adequate and complete.

We can give this process more content by reference to ¶166. Why would both men and women reject independence as defective and incomplete? For men, the answer is obvious. The struggle to make one's way in the world, learn skills and develop a career, control and organize oneself, is difficult and threatening to self-esteem. Men need comfort and care, belonging; they have feelings, even though they learn to hide them from themselves. Women, as of 1820, presumably needed someone to care for, someone with whom to make a home and family. Perhaps a woman could also need a man to take her out into the impersonal world, show her its ways and dangers, and protect her.

Next, how would this process, of giving up a defective independence and finding oneself in the other, develop over time? First, the newlyweds would tend to specialize their roles according to the special abilities of each partner. The husband would focus on tasks to be done: finding and maintaining a place to live, finding a job and source of income, managing finances, scheduling tasks, and travel. The wife would focus on caring for the husband and, later, children, and maintaining friendships and neighborliness. The same role specialization occurred, rapidly, in the Bales problem-solving groups.

Role specialization produces a whole, interdependent family. But it also produces recognition and respect for the abilities of each partner, since each contributes to the family's completeness. And this respect in turn produces self-esteem: "I count for something in the other" (¶158A).

Second, respect for the other also gradually produces an opposite effect: Recognition of the other's abilities implies recognition of one's own inadequacy in those areas. This recognition tends to produce a desire to learn from the other ("find myself in an other") and thus to become a more rounded, adequate whole person. Women can learn their way around the world of work, finance, and travel from their spouse; men can learn the techniques of friendship and neighborliness and caring, a little bit at least, from their spouse.

Both processes together change defective and incomplete personalities into more rounded, whole, adequate personalities.

Where do we move to next? Children? No! furniture! ¶169–172. When a young couple finally decides to form a life-long partnership and say "I do," what do they do next? Shop for furniture or a furnished apartment. Living together requires dishes, wastebaskets, chairs, a bed, and so on. That's dialectic! Everything internal, like love, gets externalized, and everything external gets internalized. So love implies its opposite, furniture, *our* shared capital. The family is actual, the Idea of the family, when it lives in its own property, estate, capital, *Vermögen*. In other words, furniture and housing are the material base of the family. The family uses this base to live together and develops the base to express and facilitate its unique lifestyle. The family and its material base change together.

¶169, 170, N25. Since the family hopes to be a lifelong partnership, the important aspect of family property is its use, not its exchange-value. The kind of use is the one described in ¶56 and 56R, shaping property to express the unique characteristics of this family. The shaping process continues throughout the life of the family; thus the "estate" is the objectification of love (and conflict) and continues to express the whole past life of the family to its members.

¶173. Children. The unity of opposite personalities exists as an actual unity in each child; that is, the opposition is internalized and continues to exist within the child's personality. Normally, girls identify basically with their mother, and boys identify basically with the father (and rebel against him), but the opposite side is also there, hidden but seeking an outlet. And apart from basic personality structure, each child can also pick up particular skills and interests from both parents. This happens because both parents participate in educating their children, each in his or her own way, ¶174–175. Education at first consists of simply doing things while the child is watching and later involves tutoring and supervision. Both mother and father do things around the home: play the piano, tend the garden, cook, fix things, read, clean the floor. The child is thus presented with a variety of activities and interests and selects some for further study and development.

¶177, 181. Children grow up, leave home, and get married; that is, they move from dependence to independence. To be sure, the dependence side of the opposition is still there, repressed or subordinated to the independence side (Chapter 5 below).

"This is the stage of difference." Everybody wants to be different, unique, particular, though they still carry the past family unity inside themselves, and, of course, the conscience they learned as children.

Leaving home means getting a job. Getting a job means working for someone, or opening a store, or playing music or acting ... In other words, one becomes independent by becoming interdependent with others in the economy, ¶182. So we move to the economy, the context of the family.

Civil Society

This is *Bürgerliche Gesellschaft*, bourgeois society, city life, the big achievement of the modern world. By now we have gotten fairly concrete, so the objective dialectic will be the main one operating here. Still, Hegel will want eventually to move on to the state with his philosophical dialectic, so he will drop the objective dialectic at some point, as he did with the family. In Chapter 5, we will build on his further hints on the objective dialectic.

¶182, 182A, 183, N41. The first step in the objective dialectic is the "mediation of the particular by the universal." The particulars are the grown up children becoming independent, on their own, each wishing to develop their own unique career. The universal is the market, which mediates between all the particulars, adapts them to each other; that is, in order to be able to demand what they want they have to supply what others want, in order to produce what still others want, in order to anticipate what prospective buyers will want . . .

¶184, 184A. This interdependence here is external, and this contrasts it with the internally related family members. That is, people in the market don't care who their customers or employees or suppliers are; value, not use, governs their relations, unlike the family. This external relation is what the former children want (and don't want); it facilitates independence.

¶185. The interdependence produced by mediation of the universal, the market, works both ways. People have to supply what others demand in order to earn money, so they learn to cultivate the necessary productive skills. But they also learn to demand what others are supplying; it's available. So both their skills and their tastes gradually adapt to the market. Nobody demanded computers in 1820. 1) Demand side. The result of adapting tastes to what the market makes available is both extravagance and want: If they have the money, people can buy all sorts of things they never heard of before; if they don't have the money, they can want the things but not have them. This theme will return later.

¶185A. The freedom to develop individuality, which the market provides, is the modern world's contribution to freedom. But notice that this freedom, buying whatever you want, "measureless excess," "ethical degeneration," sounds very much like the arbitrary free will with which we started, only magnified enormously. So we can suspect that the concept of freedom will be developed some more yet.

¶186. 2) Supply side. "The principle of particularity passes over into universality" = people adapt their skills and resources to the market. "This unity is present . . . as necessity" = they have to adapt their productive skills to what the market demands, or they won't earn anything. They can try to anticipate future demands, or try to cultivate demand, but if people don't buy, they lose. That's necessity. Freedom appears on the demand side, once people have money; necessity appears on the supply side.

¶187. Here Hegel sums up the positive aspect of mediation. Participation in the economy teaches people to "determine their knowing, willing, and acting in a universal way"; that is, to adapt their abilities and their needs and their lifestyle to the "market," to other people. They have to take themselves in hand, educate and develop themselves, learn to get along and be sensitive to what other people want. This is freedom in the sense of self-development, though helped by much nudging and pushing (mediation) from the economy. ¶187 points to the theory that Hegel is negating: the theory that people are by nature rational and fully human (Locke, Rousseau, etc.). No, Hegel is saying; people develop themselves in society, according to the opportunities and inducements that society presents.

¶189. Now Hegel goes into more detail. First, he observes that the "market" is a universal separate from its particulars. When we make a sharp distinction like this we are no longer thinking dialectically; we are in the sphere of the Understanding. This is the logic that characterizes the classical British economics of Smith, Say, and Ricardo, a deductive logic. It also characterizes neoclassical general equilibrium economics. This logic assumes the existence of both a market and rational (value-maximizing) particular people with given wants and resources. Because people are rational they will look for those market exchanges that maximize the value of their property. From these assumptions we deduce the laws of the market, later adding marginal utility, rational expectations, and transaction cost assumptions.

Hegel appreciates the work of the economists; they have discovered general principles operating in the mass of daily life details. But notice that these principles are a "show of rationality"; they deal with appearances, market transactions. Hegel wants to go beyond these transactions, though without rejecting the work of the economists. He wants to see how the universal mediates the particulars, changes them by inducing them to adapt to one another and become more and more interdependent. (¶182, 183, 185). Dialectic looks at how particulars change in relations with their opposites. In this case, the particulars are buyers and sellers, and their differences are mediated by the universal: exchange-value. The market also develops, gets more complex, during this process; it doesn't just exist.

¶190–195. Now Hegel looks at changes on the demand side, changes in needs and desires. ¶190–191, 190A, 191A repeat the observation in ¶185, namely, that increasing interdependence multiplies and differentiates needs indefinitely. As the market expands, more products are for sale and more variants of each product appear. The experienced consumer learns to evaluate quality and appreciate specialized products. As better products appear, one's expected standard of living, "comfort," rises. The fashionable consumer is being educated by "those who hope to make a profit" by selling quality products at a higher price. You won't read about such changes of desires in neoclassical economics texts.

¶192–193, 192A. Consumers also educate each other by displaying and observing each other's consumption. This conspicuous consumption sets social standards that people try to meet and surpass. Increased demand in turn induces suppliers to increase their production, productivity, and product quality.

¶194–195, 195A. Thus needs are increasingly produced socially rather than biologically. This would seem to be a liberation from nature, savagery, and its replacement by civilized consumption based on educated tastes. But this liberation is abstract (remember, "abstract" is a bad word), since the needs are produced arbitrarily by the market process, and by conspicuous consumption, rather than by deliberate self-development. So there is no limit to the process, which multiplies needs indefinitely. Consequently, most people are doomed to lose the race to be the most luxurious consumers. They are not liberated; they are caught by the market process.

¶196–198. Now we shift to the supply side.

¶196, 196A, 197, 197A. The basic resource that young people entering the market can supply is work. Work transforms natural resources into useable goods, thereby conferring value on them. Notice the labor theory of value here. But conversely, working educates people: They learn to be active and efficient; they develop particular skills; and they learn to keep busy at some standard job. Notice the tiny triplicity here.

¶198. As the process of production becomes more routinized and standardized (and as market competition induces greater efficiency; Hegel knew Adam Smith's work well and probably got ¶198 from Smith, as H. S. Harris comments in Stepelvich 1983), the division of labor (interdependence) increases, productivity increases, and work becomes more mechanical. Finally, one process after another can be mechanized.

In his early Jena manuscripts, Hegel discusses the effects of mechanization in more detail (Dallmyer 1993, 55–58; Cullen 1979, chap. 6). Mechanization means loss of skills, "stupefying, unhealthy, and precarious labor," alienation from work, exploitation, and finally unemployment as the machine takes over completely.

¶199. Having looked at the interdependence process from the demand side and the supply side, Hegel sums up the whole institution of interdependence: the economy. First, the economy converts individual selfishness into general well-being. Conversely, the economy provides the opportunities for individuals to promote their own well-being. Then Hegel calls this system of interdependence, which provides opportunities for all, the "universal permanent capital." Calling the economy "capital" suggests that these production and exchange facilities are shared by all the interdependent producers-consumers. The analogy is to family capital, which is the material basis for family life. Family capital, like the economy, provides resources and role-openings for children to develop their personalities, and for family members to live together.

Now is there some community like the family that has the economy as its material base? If so, this community would manage and maintain the economy for itself, just as parents maintain and improve the family capital for the well-being of the family. The obvious community would be all the members of civil society, because they use the economy; but they are not a community. So we need to look some more.

We begin by moving from the "stage of difference" to its opposite: similarity. People in the economy are indeed different, but the universal mediates these differences and produces similarities too, not accidental, chance similarities, but structured similarities based on the essential structure of the economy, ¶201–202. We already noticed the similarities on the demand side, produced by advertising and conspicuous consumption; now we see them on the supply side, namely, classes. N55: The three classes form another triplicity, so they fit together.

As we look over the three classes, ¶202–207, we notice that the family discussed earlier was not an agricultural family but a bourgeois family, living in the city. That would include the business class and the civil servants. By "agricultural" Hegel means mainly the feudal nobility (¶305–307); and their children would grow up on the family estate or, in England, get appointed to a secure Anglican Church position (MacGregor 1992, 25). As for the serfs and small farmers, their children would continue working on the farm; they would value family more than independence, ¶203. Also, ¶204A, the sense of freedom and selfhood, selfishness, has arisen in towns, so the children of city families would pick it up from their parents and look forward to becoming independent. So the shift from dependence to independence would occur in the city.

The three classes are objectively there in the economy; but as everything material becomes internalized, people would gradually become conscious of their class membership. Feudal nobles would recognize their similarity to other nobles and their difference from the boorish money-grubbers in the city; craftsmen in the city would recognize other craftsmen. Their particularity would become conscious to them as class consciousness, ¶206.

One aspect of class consciousness is a consciousness of the rules or procedures (culture, *Sitten*) that a proper member of one's own class follows. And of course a person will strive to follow these rules in order to be recognized as a respectable member of that class, ¶207. Nobles are supposed to be dignified, always properly dressed, very polite to other nobles but curt with serfs, and are to provide lavish receptions for visiting nobles. Craftsmen are supposed to fill customers' orders promptly with good quality merchandise at a fair price; traders are expected to honor all contracts and be honest and fair in all trades.

The latter, bourgeois, norms develop along with the development of town markets. But they are also an essential precondition for an actual market economy (Bogdandy 1989, 67–73). Bogdandy (1989, 71) quotes Hegel: "*Das System der Bedührfnisse kann gar nicht bestehen ohne das Recht*"—the system of needs cannot develop without rights. Presumably, business people would recognize gradually how important the rules were for their own business, so they would move to get rules made explicit and enforced as laws, ¶208, 210. So right becomes law, enforced by courts. Now everybody, not just respectable business men, must follow

The Philosophy of Right

the rules; no free-riders allowed. In addition the laws, as the "interpretation of bourgeois society" (Bogdandy 1989, 79, 80) reflect back on the rules of the market economy and reinforce them in class consciousness.

Here is another little subjective–objective dialectic, similar to the love–furniture–living together process. The objective contract and exchange practices get subjectivized, made conscious, as the right way for respectable city people to act. People learn that they share the same moral principles, and these rules are important for successful business dealings. So they objectivize the rules as laws, which feed back on business life and give it a stability and a basis for development. ¶209A: "It is only after man has devised numerous needs and after their acquisition has become intertwined with his satisfaction, that he can frame laws for himself."

So now we look at law.

Law

¶208–228 take up in more empirical detail a topic that has already appeared in ¶103. We found there that a system of contract and exchange rights logically requires an impartial judge applying a universal law in order to right a wrong and thereby establish contract law as actual. ¶210 takes us back to that point. The actual economy, which is built on contract, will require an actual legal system of this sort.

Actual or positive law has two aspects (of course!), ¶211–213. The universal aspect consists of rules, ¶214. The particular aspect consists of the judge applying a rule to a specific case. The objective dialectic is now ready to move.

¶211A, 215–217. The rules should be codified and systematized so that everyone can know them and obey them, and also so they are readily available for enforcement. But ¶224 notes also that all the particular applications of each law should be codified and made available, because each application sets a precedent that may be relevant to a new case. Remember those rows and rows of legal volumes on the shelves in the lawyer's office? They contain the precedents that keep accumulating. ¶216A: "A big old tree puts forth more and more branches." Also ¶222 the court procedures must be fixed and publicly known, so people can present their case properly.

Given the complexity of codified laws, precedents, and procedures, a layperson needs lawyer(s) to present his or her case in court. The lawyers are specialists in law, so they can make a better case than the layman, ¶228R, last paragraph. Second, since opposing lawyers will present different cases, a jury is needed to decide the facts of the case, ¶227, 227A, 228. Third, the judge has to make the final decision, thereby adding another precedent to the law code, ¶226.

The effect of a continuous succession of legal cases is, first, "the further determining of general laws ad infinitum," ¶216. As a result, ordinary people increasingly lose track of what the laws imply for particular cases and have to depend on their lawyer(s). And of course the lawyers on each side will be able to cite precedents that favor their client. Second, ¶223, the lawyers can complicate court procedure indefinitely with technicalities and appeals.

Here we see how the particular gradually destroys the universal *on which it depends*. Thus, it destroys itself. That is a new kind of contradiction; we can call it a self-contradiction. The law gradually becomes the professional property of lawyers, whose goal is to win by any means, any kind of technical trickery or knowledge of precedents. The really skillful lawyer who usually wins can charge higher fees. As a result, particular court cases become legal contests, entertainment, or tragedy, rather than the righting of wrong. Law disappears, both in its universal and its particular aspects. However, this disappearance is a continuous process that is never completed.

Hegel calls this an evil, ¶223, and mentions arbitration as a good way to stay away from courts. But what happens to right as law in the process? The highly abstract solution to wrong, ¶103, seems to have silently evaporated, not completely but gradually. Notice the contrast between the abstract treatment of justice in the philosophical dialectic, ¶72–103, and the more nearly concrete treatment of justice in the objective social dialectic, ¶219–228. Note also that the objective dialectic does not stop where Hegel abandons it; arbitration, for example, has its own political dynamics (consider the National Labor Relations Board), and lawyers tend to accumulate (wealth).

Public Authority

Here Hegel runs through a number of areas in which public authority needs to correct or supplement or regulate the economy. The economy, the universal, makes people more and more interdependent (mediates the particulars) and thus enables each person to freely pursue his/her own aims by helping others to pursue theirs. However, it doesn't work perfectly. Nothing does, for Hegel.

¶232. Crime requires policing to prevent it, if possible. Also (¶232, last two sentences) legitimate exchanges and productive activities sometimes have "neighborhood effects" or "externalities," as economists call them, such as noise, smoke, and pollution from a factory. ¶235. Public goods such as utilities, street lights, bridges, and public health, ¶236A, are not optimally produced for private sale because of free riders, so they are more optimally produced by a public authority. ¶236. Price fixing by oligopolies, which Adam Smith described, makes the dependence of customers on the oligopolies too one-sided, so such prices should be regulated. Also, safety inspections in factories are more efficiently carried out by the public authority than by individual workers and consumers; safety is another public good. ¶238. Children without families need public care. ¶239. All children need education. ¶240–242. Poor people need welfare, charity, and sometimes supervision.

¶243–248. The topic of poverty takes Hegel back to his earlier description of the objective dialectic of interdependence, ¶184–198. ¶243 is a very brief summary of the earlier paragraphs on demand-side and supply-side dynamics. On the demand side, needs multiply and differentiate, as a result of the continual expansion of consumer goods. On the supply side, the push for greater profits increases the division of labor, the routinization of labor, and mechanization. Routinization of work means alienated, meaningless, mind-numbing work—loss of "intellectual benefits"—and lower wages; mechanization means unemployment. ¶244. Combined lower income plus rising standard of living produces poverty, loss of self-respect, and indignation against the rich, society, and government, ¶244A.

¶245. There is no solution to this problem. The problem is that civil society is not rich enough (to deal with unemployment and poverty) because it is too rich; it overproduces. Another contradiction! The interdependent opposites are workers and employers. The employers increase their profits by a) encouraging ever higher consumption standards and b) reducing their labor costs. So in the process of getting rich, they push more workers into socially defined poverty. But these workers are also consumers! So, by impoverishing more workers, the profiteers also reduce their own wealth; as wages fall, demand falls, production falls, and profits fall. That's the self-contradiction: They do it to themselves, collectively.

The reference to "poor rates" in ¶245R probably refers to the 1795 English Speenhamland antipoverty law (Piven and Cloward 1971), which didn't work either.

¶246. The (temporary) solution to this inner dialectic, this self-contradiction, is exports and, ¶248, 249A, colonies. The exports sell the excess products and thus temporarily eliminate overproduction and falling profits. The colonies provide a home for the surplus labor. As a result, seaports and, earlier, rivers have been the most fertile ground for the development of capitalism. The modern world is built on seaports; Hamburg, Bremen, Amsterdam, Antwerp, London, Oslo, Copenhagen, and so on.

This inner dialectic obviously did not stop in 1821; we shall return to it in Chapter 5.

What is going on in this section on the public authority? I believe Hegel is developing the concept of the economy as the universal permanent capital, which he introduced in ¶199. Capital, like family capital, requires maintenance and repair; and here we have a list of maintenance and repair needs. Repair needs include the reduction of negative externalities, control of price fixing, welfare, child care; maintenance includes public goods, education, and crime control.

Poverty is a special case that goes beyond ordinary repair. All the other repair problems are rather marginal, but poverty is a consequence of the central contradiction of a capitalist economy. It belongs to the essence of the economy; it is produced by a well-functioning, effective economy. Consequently, it cannot be fixed, but only counteracted temporarily. The two remedies of encouraging exports and colonization serve to treat the symptoms but not the cause of the problem.

The legal system is similarly unrepairable, because the problem is the self-contradiction built into its essence. Hegel mentions bromides: recodifying the laws, providing arbitration and mediation facilities.

The maintenance and repair, and the bromides, are carried out by the "public authority," which suggests that the whole state will turn out to be the community whose material base is the economy. Government, as the agency that maintains the base, would be analogous to the parents in the family.

If, as we suspect, the state is going to be described as a community analogous to the family, then we need to return to subjectivity. The subjective aspect of the family is love, sharing, and conscious, deliberate interdependence; but in the economy the interdependence is unconscious, objective only. Subjectively, the participants in the economy start out selfish, concerned only with their own career. But if government is going to maintain and repair the whole economy, the legal system, and international trade, members of government will have to rise above selfishness and become conscious of the complex interdependence of civil society. They will have to become concerned with the well-functioning of the whole system, just as parents are concerned with the whole family. So we need to see how consciousness can be raised to that point. Hegel takes up this topic next.

Corporations

The issue here is, How does objective interdependence become subjective, conscious? Hegel introduced this topic in ¶201–207, which dealt with class consciousness. Now Hegel asserts, ¶250, that class consciousness occurs in everyday life in only two of the classes, the feudal lords and the civil servants. These two classes of people are not especially in-

The Philosophy of Right

dividualistic, so they can easily accept their similarities to one another. The nobility, and small farmers, are similar to one another, share the same occupation, so they readily feel solidarity with one another in contrast with other classes. The civil servants also share a common education and occupational experience and a common interest in politics. But in the city there are all sorts of occupations and interests, and people treasure their individuality. Consequently, class consciousness scarcely occurs. Instead, people identify with others in the same occupation, at most. ¶251, N92: This sense of shared interest leads to the establishment of occupational associations—banking, small merchant, machinist, garment worker, nursing ... These associations or "corporations" look after the interests of their members, ¶252. ¶253–254. The associations provide training and skill guarantees, and consequently good employment prospects, but also public recognition and, therefore, self-respect. ¶255. In short, they provide mutual care somewhat like a family.

In ¶270R, Hegel expands the concept of corporation by adding churches to the list. In ¶288, he adds municipalities to the list. Here is a different kind of community, a kind which Bosanquet (1899) has discussed. Note that Hegel was *not* referring to business corporations, which did not exist in 1820.

But occupational consciousness, or neighborhood consciousness, is still much narrower than class consciousness. The material base of occupational consciousness is a single occupation, a small segment of the whole interdependent economy. Consciousness of interdependence is missing or minimal. So we need to expand bourgeois consciousness considerably. And since the economy does not perform this function, it will have to be performed in the political process.

¶256R. Now Hegel makes it explicit: We are moving toward the state, including government. "The state is not so much the result as the beginning." In the philosophical dialectic, which moves from abstract to concrete, the state is the result at which we have now arrived. But in objective empirical society, the state is the whole within which all the other institutions—family, law, corporations, economy, churches, classes—develop. The state combines 1) infinite differentiation, that is, individuality, the moment of difference, and 2) universality, laws and institutions in which we all participate. Consequently the state, as the whole, is also the beginning point of the philosopher's empirical investigations.

To review: The economy is the material base of the state; the economy is the universal permanent capital. The institution that maintains and repairs the economy is government, the political state, ¶267, N9. Government, then, is the subjective, conscious, decisionmaking, active aspect of the state. But in the modern state all citizens are supposed to participate in government. Consequently, if the citizens are to be involved in the political process their consciousness has to be somehow raised to universality. ¶265A: "Stability is secured when universal affairs are the affairs of each member in his particular capacity."

Now, suppose that the political process does raise the consciousness of the members of government, the citizens (wow). Then they can participate in the political decisionmaking about the repair, maintenance, and improvement of the economy. What would we have then? We would have a free society, freedom objectified. This was the goal that Hegel laid out at the beginning of the treatise. ¶4 "Freedom is both the substance of right *and its goal.*" ¶27: "The absolute goal . . . of mind . . . is to make freedom its object . . . in the sense that this system shall be the world of immediate actuality." In the modern state the citizens participate in the process of managing the economy *that makes them what they are.* Thus, they make themselves. Agency manages and modifies structure, which conditions and constrains agency. The abstract free will with which we started was the ability to choose among seven different kinds of bran flake cereals, but objective freedom is the ability to participate in repairing the institutions that shape us.

¶260 summarizes all this once more. We have: 1) Individuality achieves its complete development (in the economy); 2) individuals also know and will the universal, the maintenance of the economy and other institutions; they take this as their aim and end.

Now that we have reached our goal, objective freedom, let us pause and look at it a bit. Hegel describes it in ¶21–23 as self-determination, developing one's potentialities. What's that? First, we can see now what self-determination is: It's participation in managing the economy that provides materials and channels for our desired career paths. The economy provides various kinds of education, job and business opportunities, financing, rules and procedures and standards, law enforcement, and so on. Managing the economy would consist of correcting hindrances to various career paths: making education more available, lowering or raising interest rates, reducing unemployment, encouraging foreign investment and foreign trade, improving transport and communication, and so on. People with different careers would have different priorities for improvement, and these differences have to be discussed and mediated in the political process.

Second, how do we discover our potentialities and decide which ones to develop, that is, which career path and lifestyle to move into? This process begins in childhood, ¶175. Parents act out their lifestyle in front of their children and help them learn the same things: play the piano, cook, repair things, entertain friends, and so on. Neighbors and friends provide more examples, and education continues the process. Through practice children find that they have certain skills and not others, and then the economy beckons with a range of opportunities to try out. This topic will return in Chapter 5.

Third, how does one develop potentialities? One learns by doing: By working with parents, in school, and in the economy, ¶207, 207R.

Notice that this objective freedom occurs in society and through social relations. Social beings develop themselves collectively through participation in the political process. We have moved from the abstract individual free will of ¶4–7 to the concrete member of society. "Self-determination" does not apply to an abstract, isolated, state-of-nature individual; it does not mean freedom from society.

Charles Taylor has developed this point nicely (1979, 154ff). He shows that an individual self-determination apart from society would be as empty as the Kantian rules. Apart from society the self would have no content, so "complete freedom would be a void in which nothing would be worth doing. 'Rationality' or 'creativity' cannot specify any content for our action outside of a situation that sets goals for us, which thus imparts a shape to rationality and provides an inspiration for creativity" (157). Hegel's "situation" is civil society and family: economy, corporation, and parents.

Now a warning, ¶258A. "The state is no ideal work of art." Also ¶270A, first paragraph: The state that Hegel will describe is the essence of the modern state, that in virtue of which such states work at all. Sometimes they don't work at all, for example, the eighteenth-century French monarchy. Other times they work somewhat, after a fashion. The modern state works insofar as it makes freedom actual *(wirklich)*; that is, insofar as individuals can achieve their own development somewhat but also participate in maintaining the whole state.

But according to Avineri (1972, 161, 164, 188) Hegel's state was far from being actualized anywhere in Europe as of 1821. Walsh remarks that "the European states of Hegel's day were ludicrously remote from satisfying the ideal he sketched" (in Pelczynski 1971, 194). The Prussian monarch was still absolute, without any constitutional limits on his power (D'Hondt 1988, ix). The Prussian state had censorship, no public debates, no trial by jury, no assembly (Taylor 1975, 452). The idea that Hegel was defending the Prussian state "is based on lamentable historical ignorance."

How then could Hegel claim to be describing an essence that barely existed in various states? The answer is suggested in ¶274, 274A; a constitution develops over centuries as part of the whole culture of its citizens, including their consciousness but also their laws and manners. Each state gets the constitution that fits its culture. This takes us back to Hegel's philosophy of history, Chapter 2 above. As Ritter observes (1969, 223–224), Hegel believed that the main dynamic producing modern culture and the modern state was the irreversible development of the capitalist economy. The sense of individual responsibility cultivated by the Protestant ethic also contributed; but this subjective sense required a material base for its full development in daily life. The material base was provided by the growth of cities with their manufacturing and trading and banking facilities and their bourgeois morals and laws. Living and working in the city strengthened a sense of individual freedom and responsibility; and this change of consciousness produced a growing demand for both legal changes and more participation in local and national politics. The growing productivity and wealth of cities, and the declining economic relevance of the nobility, gave the business class increasing political influence and led to demands for constitutional changes in various countries, including Prussia from 1807–1819. ¶298A gives several examples of earlier gradual changes.

So Hegel lived in a period of revolution, conflict, and change. He was describing a state that was coming into being through conflict and turmoil, not a state that simply existed. The main conflict was between the rising business class and various declining groups, such as the nobility and the "rotten boroughs." Michael Petry (in Jamme and Weisser-Lohmann 1995) describes the commotion and unrest in England and Prussia at the time and shows how the 1830 Reform Bill was an attempt to compromise and pacify and prevent revolution in England.

Hegel believed the development of capitalism was bringing his state into full being. It would be most fully developed where the manufacturing and business economy was most advanced; and as capitalism advanced in other countries their constitutions would change too.

Steven Smith offers a more sober interpretation: Hegel idealized certain progressive political tendencies of his time (1989, 135); that is, if these tendencies came into full being in some state, that state would be rational and would work well. Other existing (real) states could be fairly rational and would work more or less.

In either case, to understand Hegel's state empirically, we have to turn to the nations with the most highly developed economy in 1800–1821, namely England and Holland. We wouldn't look at Spain, ¶274A, or Russia, ¶297A. Russia was a mass of serfs and rulers, with almost no bourgeois class, so its constitution naturally was medieval: an emperor and feudal lords. Since Hegel's examples in PR all come from England, and since English institutions of the time fit his model fairly well, we shall take England as our example.

To be sure, Hegel had no idea of what changes the further development of capitalism would produce in the modern state; that belonged to the future. He could suspect troubles ahead with the continuing increase of individualism and of poverty, but he could not say how things would turn out. This topic will return in Chapter 7.

The Philosophy of Right

The Constitution

¶272, 273. Here Hegel gives us the subdivisions of the government: legislature, executive, and Crown. The judiciary has already been discussed in ¶209–228; there is no separate supreme court in England. The legislature deals with universals, the laws. The executive, including the courts, deals with particulars; that is, the executive applies and carries out the laws. The crown, an individual, makes the ultimate decisions that speak for the whole state. We have seen these three aspects or moments of a whole before. But ¶272 asserts that each of the three contains the other two within it; there is no separation of powers, as in the U.S. Constitution, and certainly no hostile opposition, ¶272A. The doctrine of the separation of powers comes from the Understanding, for instance *The Federalist Papers.* Remember, the Understanding deals with surface phenomena, considers them abstractly in separation from each other, and keeps making distinctions. No dialectic there. For Hegel we can think about them as separate, but actually they are part of a whole. They "abide in their ideality," that is, their separateness exists in our thinking only, not in reality.

So now we look at the three parts.

¶275. What's this? Hegel got it backwards. He starts with the third moment of government, the Crown. Why? Commentators have speculated over this. One possibility is that Hegel didn't want to offend the Prussian king, who already had strong doubts about Hegel; he knew that the king wouldn't understand his book, but might take offense at being put last. Another possibility is that Hegel wanted to exalt public opinion by putting it last, at the apex of the state. In any case, we have now nearly completed our journey from abstract to concrete, so it doesn't make much difference which moment we take first. Perhaps it would be better to start with the legislature, since it connects directly with our previous topic, the corporations. So we skip to ¶298–319.

The Legislature. ¶298. The legislature deals with the universal, that is, with laws and domestic policies, such as budgets and taxes, that affect everyone. Sentence 2, clarified in ¶298A, says that the legislature does not write constitutional amendments; it has no such power. This repeats the argument of ¶274. Note that the British constitution has never been written down and codified; it just grew in practice.

¶300, 300A. All three branches participate in legislative activity, and the whole executive cabinet of ministers sits in Parliament. This makes for somewhat confusing terminology. We are concerned here with the third "moment" of the legislature, the "Estates"; in simpler terms, Parliament.

¶312. There are two houses of Parliament, the House of Lords, ¶304–307, and the House of Commons, ¶308–311. The Lords consist of the landed nobility, and the Commons represents the business class. The third class, the civil servants, is in the executive branch. So the Commons is the house in which all the associations, communities, and the corporations are represented; each corporation elects its own representatives, ¶308, 309. Here the deputies talk to each other; they deliberate, instruct, and convince each other. Also the civil servants from the executive branch are constantly there, talking about what's happening all over the country. The result of all this talk is consciousness-raising: The deputies get the big picture of which their corporation is just a part, ¶289R. They hear about maintenance or repair problems that bother some other corporations but haven't yet come to affect them, and through such experiences they gradually learn to understand the interdependence of different parts of the economy. So they come to realize, after a fashion, how the well-being of their members is connected, sometimes, to the well-being of other groups; and if sacrifices are called for, they should be distributed fairly. We are back to the original meaning of dialectic: dialogue. Through dialogue the occupational consciousness is raised toward universal consciousness, a little bit at least.

But there's more. The House of Lords acts as a mediator between the Crown and the Commons, ¶304, 305, 312, 313; that is, it explains the Commons' thinking to the monarch, and the monarch's thinking to the Commons. This helps corporation deputies get the big picture from the top down, but it also sympathetically presents corporate viewpoints at the top. The Lords are fitted for mediation because they share hereditary nobility with the Crown, but also because they are there constantly talking with Commons members.

Similarly, the executive, ¶304—I presume he means the cabinet ministers, who are in Parliament but also in direct contact with the monarch—mediates, talks, between monarch and Commons.

But the Commons delegates also mediate—between their constituents and the government as a whole, ¶301, 301R, 302, 302A. Of course they bring the views of their corporations into the Commons and thence to the executive and the monarch, ¶311, 311R; but they also bring government affairs to the attention of the electorate. They do this by publicizing their debates, ¶314, 315–318. The debates educate the public, or at least corporate officials, about the affairs and problems of government and thus produce public opinion, ¶319. A free press is crucial to this educative process and, therefore, fundamentally important in the modern state. It's also quite harmless. (Remember that the Prussian censor would study ¶319 very carefully.)

Of course, public opinion is a mixed bag in which the various individual and occupational consciousnesses give many varied interpretations of public affairs. Commons deputies have to select from this bag the ideas they will present to the executive and the monarch as the "will of the people," ¶318, 301R, 302.

The Crown. ¶275. Again, all three moments or parts of government are present in the Crown: the laws, which are known to the monarch; advice from the executive; and the ultimate decision, made by the monarch, following the laws and the advice. ¶276 repeats the assertion that the parts of government participate in each other; they are not separated and certainly not opposed.

¶279, 279R, 279A, 280A. Here Hegel tells us what the monarch (king or queen) does. If the constitution is working OK, he or she signs the bills. This signature symbolizes that the state has made a decision; the state has free will. The end repeats the beginning, but of course goes beyond it (*aufgehoben*). This free will is not arbitrary; the options come from itself, from the corporations, and the goal is self-making. It is the whole state working on its own material base, making itself free. More generally, the monarch symbolizes the unity of the state.

Of course, no constitution ever works perfectly, so in practice the monarch has more to do: participate in the mediating process, try to resolve persistent conflicts, discuss problems with the prime minister, check over legislative and executive actions for soft spots (dot the i), ¶297. An example would be Emperor Hirohito in 1941, listening in on the cabinet's discussion on how and when to attack the United States and quietly asking one admiral how long it would take to defeat the United States. The answer came: "It's not a question of how long, but whether we can win at all." Well, then, why . . . But the emperor said no more. Perhaps he should have (Butow 1961). Hegel mentions another example, ¶295R.

¶283. Here are the people who advise the monarch: the cabinet, starting with the prime minister. Presumably members of the House of Lords also have access, ¶312, N67. The monarch appoints all his advisors and also, ¶292–293, the whole civil service. But note that the British monarch normally makes appointments on the advice of the prime minister or other top advisors.

The Executive. ¶287. Note: The judiciary and the public regulatory authorities are part of the executive and, more specifically, ¶289, of the civil service.

¶288–290. The civil service is the location of another mediation process parallel to that in the legislature. The civil service is decentralized, ¶290,

290A, N60, and in direct contact with the corporation heads, including mayors. So the corporations can press their concerns on their civil service contacts, who in turn selectively pass them up to higher officials. Consequently, "The Corporation mind . . . finds in the state (the civil service) the means of maintaining its particular ends." ¶289R. But conversely the civil servants can pass the bigger picture on to their corporate contacts, who thereby acquire a somewhat more universal consciousness and concerns.

¶295–297. Now Hegel presents an opposite kind of mediation. Civil servants are bourgeois, middle class too; they live in the highly diversified cities, experience the "stage of difference," and thus could have private, "subjective interests," ¶296. They might even form cliques to hide their misuse of power from higher ups, ¶295R. Or, more likely, they could develop a Weberian functional rationality, a concern only with the assigned task of their own department. An example from California will occur in Chapter 7.

But their corporate contacts can keep their mind alerted to the complex public problems that should be their concern, while the top executives and the monarch can remind them of the bigger picture and enlist their help in working on it. Thus, ¶297, the corporation representatives and the higher officials together can help maintain the universal consciousness that tends to come with the civil service occupation, but doesn't always.

In summary, "The Constitution is essentially a system of mediation," ¶302A. When you put all these mediations together, you realize that Hegel's government is kept very busy. The theological version of such politics is the Holy Spirit, who is in us and who mediates between the Father and the Son.[2]

One thing is missing here: political parties. There were two British parties in the 1800s, the landed gentry Tories and the manufacturers' Whigs. Aristocrats dominated both parties, according to MacGregor (1992, 230–233). Hegel ignored the parties; feel free to speculate on why he did. However, Avineri's suggestion (1972, 163) that political parties can fulfill the mediating role that Hegel assigned to corporations seems strange. He should have studied Bosanquet (1899). Political parties tend to promote conflict, at least in two- or three-party systems like those in the United States and the United Kingdom. Such systems do not promote the shared universal consciousness that Hegel said was essential in the state as of 1821. Besides, corporate and neighborhood consciousness are grounded in one's daily experience, so they have both stability and empirical content relevant to government policy. But party ideology in a two-party system has no occupational or neighborhood material base to check its flights of fancy, so it is subject to rhetoric and propaganda, fantasies, crowd-consciousness at rallies, and party loyalty. Parties become a way to control public opinion from the top through talk and spectacle, acting, rather than a conduit to convey work and daily life experiences into the governmental process (Edelman 1964; Mitroff 1989). Hegel also made this point in his article on the 1930 English Reform Bill (Jamme and Weisser-Lohman 1995, 240, 243).

Foreign Affairs

¶320–329. Now we expand our view to take in the international context of the state. The context is other states. We have finally gotten concrete. Other states are *not* this state; that is, they are its negation. The effect of looking at what the state is not, other states, is to treat the state as a single entity. Up to now we have been looking at parts—families, occupations, classes—and their relations, but now we see a single entity, the state.

¶324. The negation of this state by other states is at its strongest empirically in war. As a result the unity of this state is forcefully brought into the consciousness of its citizens in war. In peacetime people focus on their own family, their own occupation, their own neighborhood; and the country appears as a vast plurality of different families, occupations, relations, cities, government agencies. But in war other states force themselves on people's attention, *they* are fighting *us*. So the petty differences over health insurance, safety regulations, tax policy, wages become insignificant, or worse, hindrances to our united efforts against the enemy. *We* must work together.

¶324R. Thus war is not an absolute evil; at least it temporarily unifies the citizens. It serves to strengthen the community consciousness that all those mediation processes probably produce only irregularly. In fact, ¶324A, a long period of peace would tend to fixate individual and corporation consciousness and thus weaken the community consciousness more and more. Apparently all that mediation isn't enough to get beyond the increasing individuality of modern life. We could use an occasional war too. "People . . . acquire peace at home through making wars abroad." Aristotle made a similar point.

¶329. Since the unity of the state is symbolized by the monarch, war also brings him or her into prominence. The monarch is properly in charge of foreign affairs, since these involve the state in relation to other states. But remember, ¶329A, the monarch acts only on advice.

¶330–339. In peacetime the "otherness" of other states is more subdued: States recognize each other; that is, they recognize their similarity to other states as well as their difference (notice the dialectical thinking). Such recognition is not exciting enough to affect popular consciousness; but within government it emphasizes the power of the Crown. Actually, ¶332, not much goes on diplomatically because states are pretty autonomous, as of 1821. They recognize each other and go their own way. But, ¶338, in wartime the recognition of the other as a similar state serves to moderate the war and emphasize the need to make peace and get along again. How times have changed since 1821!

The Federalist Papers and the United States

We end with a negation. According to Hegel, the United States, like Germany in 1821, is not yet a state at all (Brod 1992, 93–96, citing Hegel's *Philosophy of History*). The citizens' prime political interests seem to be the protection of their private property and the utmost reduction of their taxes. Their positive interests are private: making a profit and acquiring more property. They have laws, but businessmen seem to be dishonest when they can get away with it. Perhaps one reason for such individualistic consciousness is the open frontier, which beckons people to go West and find new wealth for themselves.

As for the government, Hegel notes that the president is simultaneously head of state (monarch for four years), head of the executive, and party leader. Thus party partisanship runs through governmental affairs right to the top, including foreign policy. The "state" is never a unity; it is always mired in conflict. Conflict is also encouraged by the separation of the legislative, executive, and judiciary, which Hegel calls a "monstrous error," ¶272A.

Electoral voting is by individuals, not by corporations, which do not exist. But since an individual vote is almost worthless, this system encourages indifference and nonvoting, ¶311R. Anthony Downs was not the first to notice this reason for low participation rates in U.S. elections. In addition, individual voting leaves the representation of the various group interests in the economy to chance.

We can raise the issue of the U.S. Constitution to a philosophical level by contrasting *The Federalist Papers* with the PR. In *The Federalist Papers*, individuals appear as fully formed, with adult interests, tastes, intelligence, and moral principles. (This abstraction would for Hegel be a mark of the Understanding, which makes sharp distinctions and ignores interdependence, over-determination, and development processes.) Individuals differ in their interests, called "passions," but share a common reason. Reason shows them a Lockean natural law, which applies to all individuals equally. Thus, it provides moral principles that ought to limit their selfish passions.

It turns out that reason is extremely weak, even among members of government (*Federalist* No. 49). A person's passions will usually prevail over his reason; and people with a similar passion, most importantly property owners or the propertyless (*Federalist* No. 10), will join to form a faction to get their way in government. Thus, the main function of government structure—separation of powers, checks and balances—is to enable the inevitable factions to check each other. In the resulting deadlock, passions are checked, and legislators will be able to agree only on what their shared reason tells them about the common good. No mediation or dialogue is needed here; everyone shares the same reason and the same natural law.

John Calhoun added a negative comment some years later: In a two-party system a majority party need only stay in power a number of years, say ten or twenty, to get control of all three branches of government. Thereafter, the passions of this majority faction can rage unchecked.

The U.S. Constitution (unlike the one in Britain) was written; but Hegel's critical comments about a manufactured constitution, ¶274A, 273R, 298A, seem irrelevant in this case. The Constitution was not imposed by Napoleon from abroad but was written domestically, and it seems to express the individualistic mentality of the frontier that Hegel noticed.

Obviously for the Federalists the United States was a state, and a very good one at that. It was based on natural law, and its main purpose was to check power and protect individuals and their property. The United States was also a good society because it was so large and diverse; it was "broken into so many parts, interests, and classes" (*Federalist* No. 51). Its extreme diversity prevented any majority faction from even forming (*Federalist* No. 10). So people could safely pursue their own happiness in their own way. Calhoun's objection was irrelevant.

For Hegel the Federalists were confusing the state with civil society, ¶258R. The movement from the individual consciousness of civil society to the community or the universal consciousness of the political state is missing. The individual's destiny was the living of a private, individual life, not a universal life. Consequently, the objective dynamics of the economy, including its market power, technological development, externalities, and so on, remained hidden to individual consciousness and, therefore, beyond any political management and correction.

Also for Hegel the Federalist "reason" was simply a philosophical expression of bourgeois individualism. There never was a state of nature or laws of nature; society evolved over thousands of years according to its own dialectic. Hegel's "reason" was a process of discovering and systematizing this inner dialectic of society.

To oversimplify, *The Federalist Papers* assumed individuality and a government in which many opposed interests checked each other so natural law could prevail, whereas Hegel wanted mutual balance and support between individuality and community.

How might we explain the philosophical differences between the Federalists and Hegel? Differences of philosophical tradition will not do, since both the writers of *The Federalist Papers* and Hegel were familiar with the same political philosophers. Indeed, both Hegel and Madison refer positively to Montesquieu, though to different parts of his theory (PR, ¶3R, 261R; *Federalist* No. 47).

One obvious difference is that between the well-developed manufacturing and commercial economy of European port cities and the mainly agricultural, hunting-and-fishing economy of the American colonies. The intricate interdependence that Hegel could see in cities like Frankfurt and London simply did not yet exist in the ex-colonies. Southern cotton planters who exported to Europe, Pennsylvania dairy farmers, and Boston rum producers had no connection with each other; their well-being depended on their own or their slaves' work. There were no market externalities; there was no price fixing, unemployment, and poverty; there were no unsafe factories and no public transport facilities (the Erie Canal came thirty years later). Consequently, the public authority functions of managing and maintaining the economy that Hegel emphasized scarcely existed in the United States. Individual families managed their own material conditions by moving west and starting a farm or shop or mill. Locke and Hobbes's concept of a state of nature made sense; there was plenty of nature out West for anyone who needed it.

Apparently slavery still made sense economically in the unskilled agricultural economy of the South and was accepted very ambivalently in *Federalist* No. 54. In No. 54, slaves were defined as [threefifths] persons and [twofifths] things: property. But in European cities slavery made no sense and had long ago become illegal (PR ¶57R), and serfdom was being abolished.

In addition, there was no monarchy or nobility in the American ex-colonies to provide a sense of spatial community rooted in the past and objectified in castles and cathedrals. And there were no corporations yet.

The United States has developed greatly since 1790; the frontier economy has disappeared, and most property now is corporate property (McDermott 1991). Consequently the U.S. political structure has changed greatly as well, and Federalist political philosophy hides or disguises these changes. This topic will return in Chapter 7.

In short, the Federalists expressed the mainly frontier society of colonial America, dependent on overseas trade, whereas Hegel expressed the post-revolutionary, developing, manufacturing capitalism of western Europe, expanding into colonies. Each philosophy was relevant to its own time and place.

Summary

Let us review the steps of the philosophical dialectic from abstract to concrete.

1. We begin with the concept of free will and move to its opposite, things. Free will needs things to actualize its decisions; it needs property.
2. Then we explore the will–property relation, moving from taking the thing to using it, to getting free of its use and thereby getting its value.
3. Getting rid of property requires other people and contracts, that is, a shared will. The social context of free will has appeared.
4. Next we explore contracts. Contracts can go wrong, so we explore the right–wrong opposition.
5. The negation of wrong and restoration of right requires an impartial judge and shared moral rules.
6. So we study the relation between shared (universal) rules and particular intentions that are judged as right or wrong according to the rules. People are responsible only for what they intended to do, what their purpose was, not for accidental consequences. So now the free will estimates and evaluates the consequences of its decisions; it is no longer arbitrary.
7. But everyone always intends a good result and can claim and even believe that they were aiming at the general welfare. Similarly, they can claim that they were obeying their conscience, as when a religious patriot bombs a government building.
8. Therefore we cannot depend on particular consciences and conceptions of good for the needed shared moral rules. We need a shared conscience (contrary to the Federalists).
9. Such a conscience exists in a society in which people share moral principles, which they have learned in childhood.
10. "Childhood" takes us to the family, as the transmitter of culture; so we look at the dialectic of the family. This is a thesis–antithesis–synthesis dialectic, the synthesis being children. The family is based on love, which is objectivized as furniture, family capital.
11. Children grow up and move from dependence to independence. They achieve independence by getting jobs, so we shift to the economy.
12. In the economy people are independent subjectively by being interdependent objectively.
13. This objective interdependence has two aspects, supply and demand.
14. Subjectively people are independent, that is, they intend to develop their own unique lifestyle. But objectively they are similar to others who have the same location in the economy. So we look at the three locations or classes.

15. A person's similarity to others in the same class becomes conscious as morality, the rules and practices that respectable people follow in that class.
16. The business class lives in the economy, so its morality consists of rules of how to do business, such as honoring contracts. The rules gradually are objectivized by laws and courts, which support the functioning of the economy.
17. The economy needs maintenance and repair in other ways as well, and this is done by a public authority.
18. One of the troubles of the economy, the dialectic of increasing wealth and poverty, can't be fixed. It's the essential dialectic of a capitalist economy. But the developing market can provide a temporary pain-relief pill, exports and emigration to colonies.
19. If government is going to be able to manage the economy, its members have to have a shared interest in the general welfare. This requires a community or collective consciousness, not the individual consciousness produced by the economy. Where can we get a community consciousness?
20. We return to the three classes. Two of them have a shaky class consciousness. The third, the bourgeois class, has a class consciousness of the rules for doing business, combined with an occupational perspective on the economy. Each occupation is organized as a corporation, which pursues the interests of that occupation and supports its members. The interests of each occupation differ, so on the subjective level the political process is full of conflict.
21. To develop a community consciousness, then, we need to include representation of the corporations plus the other two classes in government. Perhaps the other two classes can mediate the conflicts between the corporations and produce some kind of shared interest in the well-being of the whole economy. However, continuing conflict is essential to this mediated political dialogue.
22. The result would be, we hope, a government that repairs and maintains the economy well enough so most people can work out their own lifestyle and make themselves into self-developing persons. The others, the poor, can be exported, though this doesn't solve the problem. And since the poor are not organized, ¶290A, they unfortunately cannot contribute their outlook to government policymaking.
23. The government structure, to be rational, has three interdependent parts, representing the universal, the particular, and the individual.

24. International relations emphasize the unity of the country in contrast to other countries, so international conflict contributes to the community consciousness that government needs to do its work.

When we look over the steps of the dialectic in PR, we can see the movement from abstract to empirical that is characteristic of the subjective dialectic. The first step, items 5–7 above, is completely a priori. Free will could choose anything, chooses something, chooses something but could choose anything else. That's universal–particular–individual, Hegel's favorite. Any Kant-type philosopher could have written that; it's an instant thesis–antithesis–synthesis (T-A-S). The second step, person–thing–person uses thing, is another T-A-S but with minimal empirical content: Human–nonhuman. Step three, use-value, another instance of particular–universal, has no third phase and certainly no synthesis. Instead, the pair, use and value, are incompatible, contradictory. This is an obvious empirical fact; we are now dealing with empirical commodities. And empirically the contradiction is mediated by the purchaser, who enables the owner to have both use and value but not simultaneously. So now Hegel is adapting the universal–particular pair to specific empirical processes. He is also moving to the most abstract context of free choice: contracts.

Next comes wrong, the negation of right, and the negation of the negation. This is one of the triplicities that appears in the *Logic*. Why does it come now? Empirically, contracts between different people can go wrong and need maintenance. Expressed philosophically, the wills in a contract are particular and arbitrary and need to be united by a common (universal) will. The dialectic expresses the empirical situation but also points ahead to the need for common, shared rules of contract. So now we explore subjectivity, people's intentions when they make a contract, to find shared moral rules. Sociologically, people's moral rules, values, and conscience are learned as children in a family. So we move to family as the social context of morality; the movement is no longer based on dialectical implications but on empirical relations.

By now the empirical material is controlling the kind of dialectical process that appears. The basic dialectic is the objective social dialectic. The philosopher's subjective categories, such as universal–particular, are used to bring out the objective dialectic at each empirical step. So they have to be adapted to the objective dialectic.

In the section on family, there are two dialectical processes going on simultaneously. One is the masculine–feminine opposition or interdependence, and the other is the love–furniture interdependence. Where did these come from? I believe they express Hegel's experience with families, including his own. The masculine–feminine opposition expressed what men and women were like in those days, and Hegel then brought out the implicit dialectic in their relationships. Similarly, love–furniture, a subjective–objective opposition, occurs in all families. In these two objective dialectics the synthesis of opposites is a continuing process in which the opposition also continues, unlike the instant a priori synthesis.

Children, part of the continuing masculine–feminine synthesis, also embody a dependence–independence dialectic, characterized by a reversal of domination in which the two opposites continue.

In the next context, the economy, the opposites are supply and demand, and their movement involves continuing expansion, first domestically, then via ports to other countries and colonies. But later an employer–worker dialectic appears, and this opposition is a self-contradiction that also pushes for continuing expansion to solve the overproduction problem. The movement from economy to law and back is again an empirical movement, but the self-contradictory dialectic of law is expressed by the philosopher's dialectic. And so on. We keep getting more concrete.

But there is a deeper dialectic that moves consistently through the whole PR, from abstract to concrete. This is the individuality–community relation, which one might call the essence of a free society. The movement begins with abstract individual free will, then moves to exchange or contract, the simplest form of common will or community. Contract is a necessary condition of individual freedom. Next, contracts are damaged by individual subjectivity—intentions, desires, selfishness—so we need a larger community to control subjectivity. This leads us to socialization in the family. The family community promotes, permits, channels the growth of individuality in children, along with rules of proper conduct, and this individuality is expressed by leaving home, marrying, developing one's own skills, raising and supporting one's own family. This individual development requires a larger community: the economy. The economy is damaged by intended or unintended consequences of individual development: externalities, crime, impoverishment, exploitation, price fixing . . . So a still larger community, the state, is needed to maintain the economy as a facilitator of individual development. This community of discussion and policymaking is built out of diverse individual consciousnesses by much mediation—corporations, civil servants—so it is a continuing synthesis of individual and community consciousness.

Throughout this contradictory dialectic, individuality depends on community for its development but damages the community on which it depends; and community—family, corporations, state—also depends on individuality, on difference. The state, the concrete community–individuality dialectic, is not the end but the beginning of PR. It was there all the time.

One could go a step beyond Hegel by observing that an actual, effective political state would require an approximate balance between individuality and community. A deficiency of mediation and community would allow bitter disputes, continuing conflict and deadlock, and delayed, inadequate management of economic and social problems. A deficiency of individualist participation in politics and an unquestioning loyalty to the authorities by most people would encourage a narrow, authoritarian regime that was uninformed and insensitive to the problems of the economy and society.

Notes

1. Sonata form: After an optional slow prelude, the first theme comes on: loud, vigorous, rhythmic, assertive. It begins in the tonic key, the primary key. Then, after some development, it moves on to one or more other keys and expands, until it reaches the "dominant," secondary key. Here the second theme appears: soft, gentle, sweet, soothing. That ends the "exposition." Next comes the "development." The first theme, or sometimes both themes, moves around and changes, in various ways, ending in the tonic key. Next comes the "recapitulation." The first theme starts out as before, moves off to another key as before, but then returns home to the tonic key, where it is welcomed home by the second theme. Finally, there is an optional happy-ending coda.

2. Steinberger (1988, 234–239) misses the central importance of mediation, dialogue, consciousness-raising, in managing the continuing conflict between the "stage of difference," occupational or class consciousness, and community consciousness. He reads too much into ¶260, which summarizes the whole point of the constitution, and he thus overlooks the many detailed mediation processes by which individual consciousness is raised to universality more or less, ¶272–320. As Jean Hyppolite observes, "The Hegelian dialectic still preserves the tension of conflict at the very core of the mediation, whereas Marx's real dialectic works for the complete suppression of that tension" (1969, 116). This point is my only disagreement with an otherwise excellent book by Steinberger.

5

Dialectic of Society

This chapter deals with the various objective social dialectics that Hegel describes briefly in the PR. These dialectics move over decades and centuries, whereas Hegel wishes to focus on his present time, so he does not follow out their development. From our vantage point we can look back and observe their development more extensively than Hegel could. Indeed, we can even watch them continuing at the present time.

Use and Value

Our first instance comes from ¶63, 72, and 73. At this point the philosophical dialectic is still highly abstract, so there is only a hint or two of the corresponding objective dialectic. In ¶62 the particular is use and the universal is value. Use is always of a particular piece of property by a particular owner or renter for a particular purpose at a particular time and place, whereas value is what all property shares, ¶63. The source of all value is labor, ¶196, 196A: "Through work the raw material directly supplied by nature is specifically adapted to these numerous ends. . . . This formative change confers value on means and gives them their utility."

The use of property is essential to freedom; we use things to do what we have decided to do, ¶41, 59. But property also limits our freedom insofar as it is suitable only for certain uses. We may have enthusiastically used a child's small bicycle for two or three years; but as we grow older the bicycle becomes too small and becomes useless. The solution is to exchange it for a larger bicycle of the same value. Thus, the value of property is also essential to freedom, because it vastly expands the possible uses of particular property through exchanges for other property.

Though both use and value are essential to freedom, each excludes the other, ¶72: You have both when you own property, but you can't have both at the same time. You can't both eat the carrot and sell it. This contradiction is the key to the objective dialectic.

Hegel starts us off in ¶63A by observing that feudal property could not be sold; such property "is not in accordance with the concept of property." That is, property is an instrument of free will, but feudal property didn't fit that concept; it could be used but not sold. Consequently, such property is mostly disappearing.

Let's look at the stages of that process. In the first stage land was used by the lord and the tenants to provide food, building materials, heat, recreation (fox hunting), and so on. The market value of the land and its products was unknown, nonexistent. Use was actual, value potential. Since the land had limited uses, lifestyles were quite limited; there was little freedom. In a second stage some products—food, lumber—could be informally exchanged in town for clothing or tools made by craftsmen. This is Adam Smith's "truck, barter, and exchange" stage, the simplest kind of market economy. The items exchanged were commodities, that is, properties with both use and value.

As such exchanges continued people would learn to estimate in advance how much some item was worth, that is, how much of some other item it would bring in, based on past performance. But if the exchanges were among a variety of items, the estimates would have to be made in money terms, since money is the general measure of value, ¶63A. Money estimates make value more explicit, more conscious. Next, such explicitness suggests the possibility of selling items for money and then buying other items. At this third stage, value is the dominant aspect of property in the town marketplace, whereas use still dominates at home on the land. There is an alternation of use and value.

Hegel hints at a fourth stage in ¶203A: English agriculture is becoming like a factory. Here the property is used to produce food and other products for the market; that is, it is used to make money. Value is now the goal, and use is the means.

This stage probably developed out of the feudal lords' need for money to pay off their debts. Raising taxes on the towns didn't work so well; the alternative was to chase the serfs off of their tenant farms and use the land to grow crops for sale. Thus some dukes gradually became agribusinessmen, hiring workers and making their feudal domains useful and productive.

Note that at this stage labor power is being bought and sold, both in the factory and on the farm. Labor has become a commodity; we have arrived at full capitalism.

We know what the fifth stage was, after Hegel's time: A market for agricultural land developed, as feudal rights disappeared. Now people would calculate whether they could make more money buying or constructing a factory, or buying a large farm. (The purchase money would come from a bank loan.) The value of land became the amount of profit that could be made from it. Similarly, one could estimate whether the land was worth more as agricultural land or as a housing development. In other words, the value of an investment is measured by the expected value it will produce; investment value produces profit value. Here use and labor have faded into the vague distance. There is an ultimate consumer of the carrot or the apartment, hopefully, but consciousness of the investor and the banker is focused on capital costs, producing and marketing costs, and returns measured in money. Use is encouraged and promoted by advertising, as Hegel observed in ¶191A, because somebody has to buy the products in order for the investor to realize the value, the profit.

At a sixth stage, Hyman Minsky's money manager capitalism, investment banks and pension funds and mutual funds calculate the potential profit from investing in housing development companies or shopping mall developers or oil or steel or hospitals . . . Calculation is based on the potential profitability of the various corporations, which in turn is based on the profitability of potential stores, homes, malls, and so on. Investors in turn buy or sell mutual funds based on their estimates or on conflicting professional advice as to which funds or stocks will perform better in the near future. This has been called "casino capitalism." Use is now vaguely potential.

At the sixth stage, and somewhat already in the fifth stage, the market is located in the future. Banks and investors make loans and invest and buy stocks in order to gain future profits—interest payments, dividends, capital gains. For example, in 1998 there was a market for the euro, which did not yet exist. People bought euros for future delivery at a specified price, in hopes that the actual price on that date would be higher. Conversely, people or banks sold euros for future delivery (and immediate payment) with the opposite hope. People also sell pounds or bahts for future delivery at a lower than current price in expectations that the currency will fall sharply.

But since there is little information about the future, decisions must be based on extrapolated past occurrences, including information on how other investors and banks are behaving. Those investors might know something. This is a positive-feedback system in which future prices go up and then down again. For example, the Hong Kong financial market rose steeply in the period before June 30, 1997; financiers were obviously expecting the Hong Kong–China connection to open new opportunities in the Chinese economy. When that didn't happen immediately, Hong Kong markets plummeted 50 percent. So equilibrium at the sixth stage is nonexistent, even as a possibility.

The future-oriented market of the sixth stage requires corporations not just to make profits, but to make continually higher profits. At the fourth stage producers have to make some profit to tide them over the next recession, or to expand production to maintain market share if demand increases, or to pay for newly invented capital equipment. However, such need is limited. But in finance capitalism investors are looking for future profits, and a corporation's record of rising profits provides evidence that it is a good investment, because its profits (and the investors') will probably keep rising. Such a corporation can issue stock at a good price and borrow from banks or issue bonds at a low interest rate. A corporation with stationary or falling profits will have difficulty attracting any investment. So there's trouble ahead when the market changes, as it always does.

The fifth and sixth stages also raise questions about the adequacy of the labor theory of value. Incidentally, Hegel was probably not subscribing to the whole labor theory when he remarked that labor "confers value" on raw materials, ¶196. He didn't add that the value equals the value of the labor power used on the materials. That would have been undialectical, looking at the supply side but ignoring the demand side. Dialectically, value is an interaction of supply costs and demand intensities. If nobody wants a laboriously produced ugly art object it has no value.

In any case, the supply side of the labor theory is most plausible at the third stage, Hegel's time. But starting at the fourth stage other factors enter the picture. By the fifth stage the value of land has become explicit; there is a market for it. Land value can depend on the fertility of the soil, the amount of timber on it, the amount of coal, for example, under it and the thickness of the mine seams, its location in relation to population centers and transport routes, its degree of slope, and even the view from it. All these factors affect the amount of value that can be produced from the land and therefore affect the value of the land. To be sure, labor will be required for realizing the land value, but the realized value depends in part on the qualities of the land.

And if land has potential value because of its qualities, it is also necessary for someone to discover those qualities and invest money in realizing their value. For instance a developer might notice that land with a certain slope and height might make a good ski resort and then invest money to develop it. Whether or not the developer's investment planning can be called labor, it certainly contributes to the realization of land value.

Next, labor productivity is increased by technical schools, engineering schools, and some industrial engineers. Some engineers, the Taylorizing ones, are mainly arranging the increased exploitation of labor (Chapter 6 below), but others, such as line balancers and production layout arrangers, increase overall productivity. They may even be making work more challenging and less alienated (Chapter 8 below). And if engineering and training increase productivity, then investment in production R&D (research and development) and in training is also effective. To go one step farther, mutual fund investment in corporations with high R&D, such as Microsoft and IBM (Chapter 6 below), also contributes somehow to productivity. To be sure, there are also many nonproductive participants, such as lawyers and security guards, the modern equivalent of the knights who protected the castle and the serfs.

In short, as value becomes more and more central in the fourth to sixth stages, its production becomes more complex. Labor is still central in "conferring value" on raw materials, but various other factors are also involved. Some factors determine how much labor is "socially necessary," and some determine the potential value of the raw materials or land.

As the production of value becomes more complex, and as use fades into vague potentiality, the measurement of value in money becomes vaguer and more speculative as well. What does the price of stock in a ski resort construction company measure? In the stock and mutual fund market, prices change by the minute; investment is a form of gambling, based on estimates of how many other people will be buying or selling the stock or fund in the near future. Somewhere in the speculative process there are vague estimates of the potential value of the future ski resort, based on even vaguer estimates of its distant future use. But use, value, and price have moved far apart.

What sort of dialectical process occurs here? It is obviously a *reversal of dominance*. In the first stage value is nonexistent, potential. In simple market exchanges use dominates, causing the exchanges to occur, and value appears vaguely as the equivalence of the two exchanged commodities. In the third stage, when money appears, the value of commodities becomes explicit and precise; they have a price tag on them. Consequently value is dominant at the time of sale, especially for the merchant, but use then takes over for the buyer, while value moves back into implicitness. In the fourth and fifth stages, use is produced by advertising, and maximization of value, money, is the goal. Money is now dominant; the desire (and the need) to accumulate money stimulates the production and marketing process. In the sixth and later stages—stock markets and mutual funds—even production fades into the distance. Money is the means and money is the goal.

The basis for the reversal is the incompatibility of use and value, though value depends on use in earlier stages. And, at a later stage, use of a factory or land or labor depends on the value that can be obtained from it. Each is dependent on the other, so you always have both, though you can't actually have both. Consequently, one tends to dominate, that is, stimulate the production and exchange process. In principle the two could balance, as in the third stage, but the balance is unstable.

Remember that we are still at an abstract level, so the objective dialectic will certainly turn out to be more complex than a simple use-value reversal.

Family

We begin with Hegel's patriarchal family as of 1821, when men were expected to go out and work and women were supposed to take care of the house and the children. Hegel's account, ¶158–181, is still fairly abstract; the concrete context, economy and state, comes later. When we place the family in this context we realize that Hegel was describing the bourgeois family. His family was nuclear—no grandparents living in the house, no nearby aunts and uncles, no inherited family farm to pass on to the children. Children were expected to go out and get a job or start a business or enter a profession. Consequently, the development of the capitalist economy would strongly influence the development of the bourgeois family.

Specifically, when the children grow up and leave home, get a job and become independent, which children leave home? Just the boys? Or girls too? The pattern of available work or entrepreneurial opportunities would strongly influence the answer. MacGregor (1992, chap. 5) observes that even in 1821 many women entered the work force, and opportunities have expanded and diversified since then.

The dialectic of the family moves from parents to children. Children are the objectification of love; they represent the unity of mother and father in a single person; they are a unity of opposites; that is, both parents are internalized in the child's developing personality. As Carol Gilligan (1982) observes, in the traditional family, where the father goes to work and the mother stays home with the children, baby boys tend to identify first with the mother who cares for them, then gradually realize that they are different, then struggle to identify with the father and reject (repress) the earlier feminine identification. As a result, their masculinity is precarious and needs to be recognized by others. Having a job, like other men, is the best basis for recognition and self-esteem; unemployment is a crushing blow to self-esteem. In addition, more caring and loving and playing together by the father early in life might make the masculine identification more secure.

Another barrier to masculine security and self-esteem is the macho-masculine culture image and its supporting institutions, like the military and sports. If men are expected to be powerful, domineering winners, youngsters will have a harder time accepting and incorporating their feminine or "sissy" side.

Conversely, little girls have a more secure identification with the mother from the start. The father gradually shows up as the other who provides adventure, excitement, and protection, and who shows the girl how to do things, like tend the garden. Such skills provide the basis for a secondary masculine identification: I can do A, B, C. Of course, the girls also learn skills from their mother, including caring for the baby.

Next, children grow up and become parents, "a process which runs away into the infinite series of generations," ¶173. Little girls become mothers, and mothers have learned both a caring and a doing side from their parents, which their daughters can internalize in turn. In each new generation the mixture changes; boys can learn gardening or cooking from their mother, and can pass their skills on to son or daughter.

If the mother has worked for a time, or simply works, as in the early 1800s, the daughters can internalize that as, "I can work, and/or I can have children." If the work involves caring for people—for instance, nursing or teaching or being a receptionist—the two sides of work and children can easily combine as feminine. If the daughter inherits her father's small business because no sons are available, or because the daughter has learned skills from the father, work can be regarded as her masculine side. If both father and mother work, the working self can be internalized as masculine or feminine, or both ambivalently.

The kind of work available to women will affect, via the mother's work, the little girl's self-concept. For a long time, women's occupations were predominantly of a caring type, like nursing, or a sewing-machine-type fingerwork, like textiles or electronic chip assembling or typing. But more recently a large range of occupations has been opening up (Gottlieb 1987, 144–147).

When the daughter grows up and marries a man who expects to work, like his father, a struggle for recognition can develop. "I am the breadwinner, the head of the family!" "No, you're not! We both are!" The intensity of the struggle depends partly on which sort of occupational range the wife has internalized as feminine—or masculine, since she is masculine too. A caring occupation will facilitate acceptance of a dual role of caring for the husband and children and also for schoolchildren or patients or customers; a management self-concept will produce more challenging, difficult results. The intensity of the struggle will depend also on which sort of feminine side the husband has picked up from his mother and how fragile his masculine self-concept is as a result.

The struggle for recognition can end in death, as Hegel observed in the *Phenomenology*—death of the wife in this case. Wife-beating is another result, and divorce another.

What enables the wife to escape the marriage struggle? The availability of work related to her self-concept. Work enables the woman to develop a "mind of her own," skills and self-respect, plus money. When no work is available (coal mining won't do for most women), the wife is caught. "I am the head of the household!" "Yes, master."

Consequently, as the number of occupations psychologically open to women has increased, we have gotten more divorce and shorter marriages. A counteracting factor would be the increasing acceptance by men of their feminine side, and this becomes easier as the feminine side includes working in a hospital or office. They need not fear such a feminine side.

At this stage it is perhaps misleading to describe the synthesis or opposition as masculine–feminine, since both women and men have internalized both in varying ways. Both men and women have several sides to them, and different sides can dominate at different times and stages of life. Men can rebel against what they perceive as the authoritarian father and try to suppress their own internalized patriarchal tendencies, which keep coming out anyway. Once their masculinity is recognized they can let their passive, listening or caring side come out and develop. They can pick up cooking and caring for children from their mother or father. Women can rebel against the "submissive" mother, resolve to assert themselves, and despise their own contrived, artificial "feminine" charm. So, rather than speaking of masculine–feminine, we can follow Hegel and Bales and describe the interdependent opposites as task-oriented and people-oriented, or more concretely as work-oriented and family-oriented. Or, following Gilligan, we can speak of the externalizing and internalizing cognitive abilities; both men and women have both, in varying degrees (Diesing 1991, 280–293).

Notice that the synthesis of work and family is a process lasting for centuries, and never completed. In particular, the core opposition continues in all the changes. One basis for the continuation of the opposites is the continuing set of objective needs of the family, or any small group. A successful family needs to deal effectively both with people (the family members and relations) and with things, such as furniture and housing maintenance, income and garden. These needs provide an opportunity and a demand for one or both parents, or group leaders, to develop their opposite potentialities and get them recognized and respected. Another basis is the continuing conflict between the two opposite orientations, even while they recognize and learn from each other. And perhaps there is also a genetic difference, though this would not explain Bales's data; his subjects were all male.

Thus, a synthesis over time in the objective dialectic is very different from a synthesis in the philosopher's subjective dialectic, which is an instantaneous logical step in thought. Readers trained in Kantian logic will have trouble conceiving such a "synthesis"; instead they can think of it as an increasing intermixture of opposites in which the opposition continues.

As we look over the synthesis developing in the past two centuries we see that Hegel's account of the masculine–feminine opposition is abstract: It deals with the universal, men and women in general, not with particular intermixtures, which vary endlessly. Gilligan's account is thus also abstract. Over time, as children pick up personality characteristics from (or against) both parents, in the context of changing opportunities, the mixtures become more complex and varied. A dialectical thinker should include both universal and particular in her theorizing. Some feminists, like Gilligan and Nancy Chodorov, have emphasized a basic difference; others have furiously insisted on similarities. Both are correct, from a dialectical perspective.

We can vaguely discern a new stage in the masculine–feminine "synthesis" in recent years. For many years more occupations have become socially open to women through feminist pressure and through the expansion of service occupations involving direct contact with customers. But recently the expansion of computer communication has changed the picture again. Women's work is moving more into the home again, via the computer. A wife can spend most of her day in her study, editing or writing or consulting by fax and e-mail or managing finances. Conversely, a husband can take his child to his office, an office well-stocked with toys; in between appointments he can play with or hold the child. As needed the wife or secretary can take over temporarily. Here both parents share the people-oriented and work-oriented aspects of the family.

Many other arrangements are occurring. For example, one woman opened a graphic design studio in her home office shortly after her son was born (*Bradenton Herald,* October 16, 1995). She works regular hours there and sharply distinguishes office and home. When her son returns from school he does his homework at a desk near hers. Some years ago she hired her husband, who quit his engineering job to join her. There was a bit of a power struggle over who was boss, and she once threatened to fire him, but now they divide the work amicably.

This new stage seems to be a *reduction of dominance*, a shift toward equality of the marriage partners. In Hegel's time the father was obviously the head of the patriarchal family, ¶171, 178, the one who earned the money, controlled and administered the family capital, apportioned the family tasks, and gave the orders. But as the opposite roles have become subdivided and mixed in each partner, dominance has declined. Both partners can earn the money and share or distribute the family financial planning in various ways. The husband is still dependent on the loving and caring wife, but the wife is less dependent on someone to take her out into the world and get things done; she can go out on her own.

Children Grow Up

The shift from dependence to independence is a reversal of domination inside the personality. Dependency dominates at first. Insofar as the infant's dependency needs are satisfied, it can make some independent, self-asserting moves. Gradually it learns to become a different, independent person inside the enveloping, comforting family. But as self-assertion, "doing it my way," develops, it begins to entice the child out of the family home, and this threatens one's sense of belonging, especially if independent moves produce family conflict. During adolescence the conflict reaches a peak; the youth wants to be out in the world but also at home with the mother, and each desire threatens the other. Adolescents struggle with this conflict in many different ways, but usually they learn to set up their own place or join a sorority or other group or, eventually, start a family of their own. The conflict continues within the new family: Getting married gradually provides independence from the parents, emotionally and financially; but conversely, dependence on the marriage partner replaces the earlier dependence. At this point the contradictory process that Hegel describes, in which dependence gradually produces independence of personality, begins to operate. Meanwhile the dependent cushion of the old family continues in the background; if there's trouble one can always return for help.

That's the subjective aspect of independence: Moving out emotionally into a family and living your own life together; but objectively, independence is really interdependence. To live one's own family life in the city, it's necessary to get a job, or make money somehow by providing what other people want; that is, objectively, it is a synthesis of independent decisionmaking and dependence on others in the economy, whether customers or suppliers. This synthesis, like the other syntheses we have noticed, develops over time. On the independent side, planning one's own lifestyle develops as one learns more about the multiple opportunities available in the city and then becomes more deeply involved with other people in various ways. On the dependent side, the interdependence expands as the economy expands, until one's job or business can disappear because of developments in Korea. The kind of subjective decisionmaking required varies with the kinds of objective dependency networks—financial, house construction teams, musical performance, management, and so on. The degree of dependence and independence also varies; with the continually increasing unemployment that, as Hegel observed, is normal in a capitalist economy, workers must be quite subservient to the boss or they will get fired, whereas the boss doesn't depend much on any one worker because he can easily hire another one. With highly skilled labor or work teams the proportions are different again.

Notice that the subjective independence and the objective interdependence do not match. Consciousness doesn't match its economic base. This mismatch is the main problem that the political process has to solve.

Economy

For Hegel the 1821 economy was characterized by a vanishing feudalism and an expanding capitalism. In past centuries feudalism dominated; in the near future feudalism would be *aufgehoben* and capitalism would dominate: a dialectical reversal. We look first at the reversal and then at the internal dynamics of capitalism up to now.

The reversal has already been described more abstractly in the section on "Use and Value" above; it is the shift from use to exchange-value and money. In feudalism, property was used, not sold, ¶63R, and this was a sharp limit on freedom. The indebted lord could not sell property or its produce to pay his debts; the serf could not do anything but try to survive on his small plot. So some lords chased off some serfs by enclosures and tried to produce food for sale in the city; some serfs moved to the city and learned a trade or opened a produce market, and so on.

The result was a gradual shift from the agricultural community, where extended families lived together in the same location for generations, to the individualistic city, where nuclear and subnuclear families move anywhere in the world as markets and job opportunities shift. Hegel praised this development as a great increase in freedom; but it also involved the decline of community. According to Charles Taylor (1975, 454–456), Hegel recognized how the growing manufacturing economy would gradually wreck the precarious balance of individualism and community in the English state of 1800, and he hoped that the government would somehow check the growth of privatization. And perhaps they would have tried if they had read Hegel. The individualism–community dialectic will be considered further when we look at current political states in Chapter 7 below.

In an agricultural or neighborhood community, exchange occurs mainly in the form of gifts, not as monetary transactions. Thus use dominates value, though some vague calculations of value occur, as Marcel Mauss observed long ago. As of 1821, use still dominated exchange value in family capital as well, ¶170. Since the family is an enduring entity, it requires "permanent and secure" property for long-term use and the preservation of the past in the present. In other words, the 1820 family was a form of community, not a profit-making partnership. As a community, it returns in ¶255 as one of two roots of the state. More recently, more marriages have become "marriages of convenience" that dissolve when one spouse gets transferred to Singapore or Toronto, or when a more suitable partner shows up. In such cases the value of the partner, and of the family property and its location, is important in calculations of whether to dissolve a partnership.

We turn next to the dialectic of capitalism, described in ¶190–198 and ¶243–248. The dialectic has already been analyzed in the previous chapter. The basic process is a self-contradiction. Employers need to make a profit to insure against hard times, or to expand production in expanding markets, or to provide investment capital. They do this by using Fordist principles: Increase the division of labor, simplify each step in the assembly line, and finally mechanize production, ¶198. The effect is to increase productivity and output and decrease labor costs. More profits! Thus the employers get richer and the employees get poorer, especially those made redundant by mechanization. But the employees are also consumers, on the demand side. So as they collectively get poorer, demand falls and there is an overproduction crises and a fall in profits. Employers reduce their profits collectively by increasing them individually.

There are two phases of the overproduction process, a short-run and a long-run phase. In the short run, overproduction produces the business cycle, as studied by Keynes, Wesley Mitchell, Howard Sherman, and others. As unsold inventories accumulate, production is cut back and workers are laid off, leading to decreased demand, decreased production, and depression. At this stage some employers go bankrupt because they have not made enough profit in the previous expansion phase to tide them over the recession phase. Their fixed capital is devalued and abandoned or bought cheap by employers who have made more profit. As the next expansion occurs, these employers have more fixed capital and credit, so they can expand production and profits to a higher level than before. Thus over a series of business cycles a few of the most efficient or farsighted or lucky employers will get quite rich, while others, including newcomers, will stay small or fail. Perhaps this is what Hegel is referring to in ¶244 when he speaks of "conditions which greatly facilitate the concentration of disproportionate wealth in a few hands." According to A. S. Walton (1984), Hegel in class lectures described how monopoly capital crushed small businessmen.

The long-run phase is mentioned in ¶246–247. The positive solution to overproduction and unsold inventories is to export them. Capitalism has been expanding markets in this way for centuries as a solution to overproduction. In the sixteenth century the Baltic sea was a locus of expanding trade, for instance of north German manufactured goods and Polish farm produce (Denmark and Thomas 1988). Earlier, Venice was a trade hub between north Italy and eastern Mediterranean ports. Later, trade routes to Africa and America were activated.

Since trade moved through port cities, the economy in and around those cities always had a readily available solution to overproduction: Export! Consequently, those cities and areas were always the most advanced economically and the richest; and the countries with prominent ports—Holland, England, Lower Saxony—were leaders in capitalist development and colonialism. Ports are the main material base for the development of economy and culture.

Those philosophers who think of Hegel as some sort of idealist should concentrate intensely on what a port is made of: water, a nearby sea, lots of sand, docks and warehouses. That's as material as you can get. To be sure, the docks and warehouses and dredged harbors have been made according to a conscious plan, and thus are objective *Geist* for Hegel. A port is a synthesis of mind and matter, developing over centuries; but the crucial facilitating condition is matter. This synthesis in turn is the basis or condition for the development of culture.

Compare ports with the forces and relations of production in Marx. The forces of production, technology, are developed by human inventiveness and embodied in machinery, spatial production layouts, and transport facilities, including ports. Hegel refers to the forces of production in ¶198, again, an objectification of mind in matter. Relations of production are objectified in culture, habits, and are thus more "idealistic" than ports. But a dialectical philosopher should not be either an idealist or a materialist. Each opposite requires the other for its development (Norman 1976). The issue is rather the materialist–idealist dialectic: How do the two opposites interact and which is dominant, substance or subject, structure or agency (reason)? In the *Phenomenology* and the *Logic*, subjectivity, consciousness, is dominant, but in PR I believe objective material structure and its dynamics are dominant. J. M. Bernstein (1984) makes the same point, as does Hans-Dieter Bahr (1971).

So one could say that Marx turned Hegel upside down in the sense that he reverses the idealist dominance of the *Phenomenology*; but this does not apply to PR. Lucio Colletti (1973, 51) suggests "that Hegel is *half idealist, half materialist*; that his entire philosophy is divided and disconnected by a deep contradiction." Maybe so.

If one thinks of "materialism" as an emphasis on the economic base, the forces and relations of production, and "idealism" as an emphasis on political superstructure, then one can say that both are present and interact for Hegel. The base constrains and facilitates superstructural development, which in turn maintains and adjusts the base. Heilbroner (1980, 82) criticizes a one-sided materialist "economism" by observing, "The challenge rather lies in defining the material sphere itself without introducing elements of idealism; or, if you will, in distinguishing activities in the base from those in the superstructure." Each requires and implies the other. But Hegel and Marx agree that the development of the economic base, capitalism, is the crucial historical determinant of the modern state. The economy, especially in port cities, has produced a bourgeois class that gradually acquired political power and transformed the state.

The dynamic that Hegel describes—accumulation and concentration of capital, expanded impoverishment, and colonial expansion—continues. But the situation has reversed itself in one respect. In 1848 the *Communist Manifesto* asserted that workers have no country; that is, they can always emigrate to America, Argentina, New Zealand, and so on. Capital, in contrast, was embodied in specific factories and warehouses in Europe. Now, workers can no longer emigrate to new, undeveloped lands, whereas corporations are multinational, and capital in the billions of dollars can move around the world in a second. Capital has no country. Indeed, cities, states, and countries compete with one another to attract new auto, electronics, or chemical plants. For example, the Korean electronics giant, Lucky Goldstar, was recently lured into building a $2.6 billion electronics plant in Wales by an offer of $310 million in development grants. The competitor, Scotland, lost its bid to host the plant.

Conversely, for many workers the chief threat seems to be cheap labor in the former colonies, and cheap labor immigrants, the reverse of the situation in 1821. As a result, in France, for example, LePen's anti-immigrant National Front has become the main working class party (*Manchester Guardian*, October 15, 1995, p. 7). In Austria, the anti-immigrant Freedom Party got 28 percent of the votes in the most recent election, and 42 percent in Carinthia, a border province.

The reversal has greatly increased the power of capital relative to labor. Hegel and Marx were describing the dynamics of manufacturing capitalism, whereas the continuing accumulation of capital has moved us into finance capitalism with its stock and bond markets and constant shifting of investments.

How has the capitalist dynamic of overproduction produced this reversal? To begin, the colonies had to pay for their industrial imports; they paid with raw materials and with agricultural produce such as cotton and rum from the United States. Capital goods exported to the colonies provided the machinery for mining and transporting the raw materials and exporting them, and the profits went back to the colonizing country (Gunder Frank 1967). The ports gradually developed industrial facilities—shipping maintenance and repair, construction, steelmaking for railroad lines and mining machinery, and so on. Industrialization and cheap skilled labor provided inducements for manufacturers to shift some production to the colonies and ex-colonies. For example, shoe production in Sao Paulo could use nearby Argentine leather.

So, capitalism and its class structure and culture of contractual rights gradually developed in the colonial ports—Hong Kong, Singapore, Capetown, Buenos Aires, Sao Paulo, Santiago, Sydney . . . Hegel supposed, ¶247, that such commerce was "the most potent instrument of culture"; it would gradually bring some backward countries, but not landlocked ones like Egypt and India, into the modern capitalist world of freedom.

But with the development of future-oriented finance capitalism after Hegel's time, the process got speeded up. In finance capitalism profits must always be re-invested for future profits, so now finance capital as well as specific capital goods went to the "developing" countries. The banks pressed industrial development loans on the ex-colonies; the World Bank started loaning in the 1950s (to provide purchasing power for buying U.S. steel and other capital goods), and many other banks flush with OPEC cash joined in the 1970s. Later, Japanese banks had to reinvest the huge profits from the successful Japanese economy. All developing countries were now targeted, not just the ones with well-developed seaports.

Accompanying this urgent export of surplus capital was a justifying ideology, such as that of Walt Rostow (1960). The theory was that all countries advance inevitably through the stages of growth that end up with pure capitalism (not pure communism), but at varying speeds. But a "modernizing elite," the vanguard of the bourgeoisie, could speed up the process greatly if they had access to sufficient loan capital. This vanguard would know, or be taught, how to invest in infrastructure, basic industry, education, and comparative advantage niches and would thus develop a modern culture in a few decades.

This ideology seemed to be justified by the rapid economic development of the "Asian Tigers" and other countries. Construction booms, surging construction employment, expanding export corporations, and agricultural mechanization showed that capitalism was succeeding. Consequently the loans and investments continued and intensified.

But if some country succeeded in rapid industrialization, Hegel's dialectic of developing capitalism would appear: exploitation of cheap labor, profits, underconsumption and overproduction: Export! Indeed, the push to export would be more intense than in Hegel's western Europe because most of the population in countries like Indonesia or Pakistan lived in a precapitalist agricultural economy. So industrial production would have to be export-oriented from the start. Japan and, somewhat, South Korea were exceptions; Japan had been developing a capitalist urban culture and middle class since 1880 or so. But Japan was also export-focused, especially after 1950.

Consequently a successful Third World economic development would have intensified world overproduction, business cycles, and the amount of surplus capital searching for investment outlets.

Unfortunately, many of these countries, such as Zambia, had little or no sea access and had a feudal or tribal economy and culture. So the governing elite consisted mostly of tribal warlords or military governments established with U.S. help or acquiescence as a Cold War policy. These elites followed traditional or military practices in distributing investment money (see for example Robert Bates 1981). They planned huge industrial construction projects, managed by their supporters or relatives; but without adequate infrastructure, management, repair facilities, and so on most were noncompetitive in the global economy. Much money also went to the military, of course, as in Nigeria and Zaire. The result was many bankruptcies or defaults, such as Mexico in 1982, hopeless indebtedness for other countries, and more desperate searches for new outlets for excess finance capital. The World Bank loans for the enormous Pergau Dam in Malaysia, which would flood a large agricultural area to produce electricity for industrialization, is an example.

However, some countries were fairly successful, especially those that already had a well-developed export economy based on good seaports, like Argentina, Brazil, and Chile. Another example is Taiwan. Here the military government from China removed the power of the feudal elite by land reform, encouraged small farming, built many roads that provided seaport access to most of the country, encouraged small manufacturing, and so gradually built up a capitalist culture.

The near bankruptcy of the other countries, beginning with Mexico, brought the IMF into the action. The IMF's new task was to protect the banks and big investors from insolvency, since if they declare bankruptcy due to nonperforming loans the effects will spread through the interconnected international banking system. The IMF solution is the same one they used 40+ years ago to help developed countries with *temporary* balance-of-payments deficits: Offer a huge loan to the debtor country's government to pay off some loans and restore investors' confidence; require the government to stabilize its currency, stop inflation, by reducing spending and raising interest rates. The effect is to protect the banks against inflation and bankruptcy, but also to produce a huge recession, unemployment, and impoverishment. And of course, the IMF debt must be repaid in future years by more budget tightening. So the banks are protected, but farmers, workers, and small businessmen are impoverished.

Other factors also contributed to Third World impoverishment. In Africa, as Bates (1981) describes, some governments exploited the small

Dialectic of Society

farmers; the collapse of inefficient steel and manufacturing plants in other countries, including Brazil, left growing unemployment; mechanization and expansion of large farms displaced peasants; and deforestation and exhaustion of soils displaced more. Population growth intensified the problem.

So there was no more room for exporting the surplus poor from Europe. Instead, the increasingly desperate surplus poor from the Third World tried to migrate to the developed countries, thereby threatening the gains that labor had made. The temporary solution to poverty and overproduction that Hegel had observed in the 1800s has disappeared. Consequently, the dialectic of increasing overproduction, wealth, and poverty has intensified. (The above is a highly simplified account.)

We can return now to the use–value dialectic and place it in the larger context of the economy. The context shows us the source of the pressure for the increasing domination of value over use; the source is the central economic dialectic, the capital–labor self-contradiction. The capitalist needs profits to beat the competition and stay in business. So to make more profits than their competitors, employers exploit labor, Taylorize production, invest in new technology, and mechanize. The result is overproduction and market expansion but also increased profits. Next, the profits must be reinvested to make more profit. The result is a continual expansion of investment, which gradually moved the capitalist economy from manufacturing to finance capitalism: banks, brokers, investment companies, holding companies, leveraged buyouts, mutual funds, the World Bank, and continuing globalization of investment.

More recently the profit-driven domination of value over use has moved in a new direction. In Hegel's time the overproduction problem was managed by expanded trade overseas, thus bringing more people into the capitalist economy. Later, in finance capitalism the surplus capital was invested overseas. More recently market expansion has moved increasingly into daily life in the city. More and more household activities can be bought; thus household labor becomes a commodity with a calculable value.

Producers are constantly devising new substitutes for household labor—take-home meals, baked goods, child care, window-washing, lawn maintenance ... They also sell machines that may increase productivity—machines for peeling and chopping carrots, bread-making machines, exercise machines ... So people can calculate whether to buy the activities they used to do themselves, such as walking, and whether to mechanize them.

An important part of the calculation, and the value, is the time that is "saved." "I can chop a whole week's worth of carrots in a few seconds with this machine!" one friend boasted to us. Time becomes a valuable commodity to be "spent" only after careful calculation (Diesing 1962, 24–28). The efficient use of time increases one's home productivity. The result is what Ben Agger calls "Fast Capitalism" (1989; one of three excellent books he published that year; he got a promotion immediately).

The continual appearance of new, more efficient household products (and new theories) also implies its opposite, the increasingly rapid obsolescence of older products (and theories) (Albert and Hahnel 1978, 144–145). The consumer can never be satisfied because a better product soon appears and shows up the deficiencies of her recently purchased product. Computers, cars, children's toys, clothing, and so on rapidly become obsolete and must be replaced to maintain one's self-respect. Consequently, one can never stop purchasing; and if one's finances are running low, credit cards are always being urged on people by the banks.

As a result of internal market expansion forces we produce more, consume more faster, discard the leftovers faster, and use the earth's resources faster, driven by the capitalist need for ever-increasing profits and their reinvestment.

Law

There is little new to add to Hegel's account of the self-contradictory dialectic of law. The particular court cases gradually diversify and complicate the universal law on which they depend, making expensive lawyers a necessity for those who cannot avoid going to court. Courts become a setting for unpredictable contests. Hegel mentions arbitration as a way to avoid the expense and uncertainty of a court trial; nowadays, plea bargaining is another way. Both prosecutor and defendant have to estimate the probability of conviction, based on differing legal advice. For the prosecutor, a guilty plea solves his problem of getting a conviction; for the defendant, a lesser and certain sentence at less legal cost must be weighed against a greater and probable sentence at greater expense. Thus, the two bargain it out. Is that justice? Probably.

Also the increasing complexity of the legal process requires more and more time for completing a case. First, the lawyers need ever more time to search out the relevant precedents and evidence and witnesses and possible bargains. Courts get ever more overloaded, which requires longer delays. Appeals courts are impossibly overloaded and must dismiss most appeals offhand to avoid the complex judicial process and the writing up of the legal reasons.

Another source of uncertainty has developed since Hegel's time, as laws and regulations have become more numerous. Parliament makes laws (universal) but the executive has to implement them (particular).

Implementation depends on current governmental policy, including the policy of a particular department or agency, and also on the size of the agency's budget. A new administration or agency head can change policy, suddenly or gradually. Thus a corporation that would be taken to court by one administration could be left alone by the next administration, or vice versa.

For example, Neil Fligstein (1990, chaps. 5–6) describes the continuous change in U.S. enforcement of antitrust legislation from 1938–1981. In 1938, the Roosevelt administration decided that large corporations were partly responsible for the length of the depression; the administration decided, therefore, to enforce the Sherman Antitrust Act more vigorously (Fligstein 1990, 162). The Antitrust Division budget went up from $400,000 to $2 million and the number of court cases increased from 13 to 105 in three years. In 1941, the War Department intervened to protect military-related companies, and lawsuits dropped from 105 to 25 by 1945. Then in 1948, enforcement went up again . . . In 1981, the new Reagan administration dropped enforcement entirely.

Fligstein summarizes the current situation:

> For business, the problem has usually been that the laws are too vague. This point of view is understandable since the antitrust laws do not specify what constitutes a tendency toward monopoly or an anticompetitive effect. The courts and antitrust officials have to interpret when a violation has occurred. The interpretation, in turn, depends on the composition of the FTC, the Antitrust Division of the Justice Department, and the Supreme Court. For firms, the environment has seemed inconsistent, ever changing, and contradictory. The Supreme Court in the 1960s, for example, took the view that almost any horizontal or vertical merger was anticompetitive. The Supreme Court of the 1970s decided the opposite. (213)

Consequently, the large corporations have depended on their legal departments to predict how the Justice Department might react to some planned buyout or merger. The lawyers in turn depend on informal contacts between the Bar Association and the Justice Department, and on legal publications, the business press, and law school experts to predict how the Antitrust Division will react.

Another example of implementation uncertainty is the Environmental Protection Agency. Some environmental laws were passed in the early 1970s to satisfy public pressure, but business objected strongly to EPA and OSHA regulations, so the Nixon administration enforced them very slowly if at all (Useem 1993, 20–21). Environmentalists took to suing the EPA in an attempt make the agency enforce its own laws, and these lawsuits moved irregularly and slowly. Then in 1981, the Reagan administration stopped nearly all EPA enforcement and shifted to a bargaining and compromise strategy.

The accumulation of capital has added one factor to legal contests. The really shrewd, experienced lawyers charge high fees and are hired by the rich and the corporations, whereas the poor people are represented by overworked and inexperienced public defenders. Similarly, the environmental organizations, which had little money, had to pick their lawsuits against the EPA very carefully. In corporate civil law, where both sides have plenty of money, the issue becomes which corporation can better afford the millions of dollars that a lawsuit will cost. A threat by one corporation to sue another is a move in a bargaining game; if the other corporation cannot afford the legal fees, it will have to give in. If both can afford it, the threatener's bluff is called, the suit goes on for years, and the lawyers win.

For example, Philip Morris and RJR tobacco companies announced a $10 billion lawsuit against ABC, the American Broadcasting Company (*Manchester Guardian*, September 3, 1995). ABC had reported that the cigarette industry added nicotine to their tobacco, which the companies denied. "But legal experts note Philip Morris was required to prove the network acted with malice in airing a report it knew to be false. Anybody with half a brain would advise [ABC] that at the end of the road they will prevail." On the other hand, the lawsuit was brought in Richmond, Virginia, where the trial judge, who had several relatives who worked for Philip Morris, had made rulings favorable to tobacco companies. ABC settled out of court with a public apology and agreed to pay the preliminary legal fees of the two tobacco companies, amounting to millions of dollars. It decided that it could not afford the enormous costs of a protracted lawsuit, win or lose, so the tobacco companies won. CBS later canceled a short program segment on tobacco, in fear of another lawsuit. Is that justice? No.

Government

The basic opposition here is between community and individuality. This opposition runs through the whole PR, moving from abstract to concrete. In ¶182–183, children grow up and move into the economy, approaching the political arena. Individuality appears as "the concrete person, who is himself the object of his particular aims," ¶182. Community is the economic and social structure that provides opportunities for individuals to develop: schools, offices, stores, banks, streets, communication networks, and factories. At this stage, individuality is subjective and particular, "his particular aims," and community is objective. But as individuals develop, their individual lifestyle is objectified in furniture, housing, clothing, occupation, and daily schedules.

Community and individuality are contradictory: Individuality needs community to develop, but individuality tends to undermine and destroy community. Ex-children need schools, job opportunities, mortgage banks, and economic growth to become "independent." Merchants and manufacturers need the public authority to maintain the social conditions for a prospering economy: control of crime, maintenance of streets and other public goods, education, welfare, low inflation, and so on, ¶249. But maintenance costs money, taxes, and individualists resent paying taxes that they perceive as vanishing into government coffers. They also resent safety and price and zoning and environmental regulations, which they perceive as interference with their pursuit of profit with their own property, plus much annoying paperwork. But the same people also demand control of crime and improved highways and schools and recognize little connection between these public goods and taxes. Consequently, an excess of individuality results in government deficits and a tendency toward inadequate maintenance of public goods; thus the development of individuality for some people is stunted.

The central political problem that Hegel discusses is, How can an adequate community consciousness be developed in individualists, so that they willingly pay taxes out of their concern for the maintenance of community institutions? Hegel recognized, or constructed, two consciousness-raising processes: classes and corporations. First, the objective lifestyle similarity of people in the same occupation tends to promote occupational or class consciousness, which is maintained by the corporations. Second, dialogue among corporate representatives in government could develop a sense of community and a better awareness of the community repair and maintenance problems. Insofar as these two processes are successful, the community–individual conflict is temporarily held in check.

In Chapter 7 we will see how Hegel's two processes work in various contemporary states, as well as what sorts of problems come up when the two processes don't work so well. We will also notice other factors that help or hinder the maintenance of community consciousness in particular states.

Another problem that Hegel barely touches on is, Who is included and who is excluded from the political community? Hegel, in his optimistic moments, hoped that "all" would be free participants in government, as the modern world got fully established; but he admitted that the poor were not (yet) included as of 1820. To participate, they had to be organized or included in some corporation, and they were not. However, in many countries the central employer–worker dialectic of the capitalist economy has operated to keep the poor, and other marginal groups, excluded since then. The dialectic produces increasingly concentrated wealth and increasingly distributed poverty; but wealth is a source of power, and power gets people into government. The topic of who participates in various contemporary states will return in Chapter 7.

Summary

Let us review the kinds of dialectical process that Hegel has described:

1. Use and value. Here use is the particular aspect of property, and value is the universal aspect. The universal depends on the particular, in the sense that a thing's value depends on its usability to someone. The relation between the two is one of incompatibility: A person cannot simultaneously use and sell property. One must dominate the other at a particular time; one is actual, the other potential. The historical process is one of reversal of domination. In ancient and feudal times property was mostly used, and its value was usually indeterminate or vaguely estimated. In modern times, value and its measure, money, are at the core of the economy, while use has been pushed to the vague fringes of the economy. The reversal has occurred over several centuries.

2. Family. Here we have a gradual synthesis of the two opposites, which occurs between a married couple and also via the children over many generations. In this case, each opposite needs the other for its own completion; they each depend on the other. But the synthesis has been accompanied by much conflict, as Hegel noted, in part because of varying degrees of incompatibility, and in part because of struggles over domination. Throughout history there have been both patriarchal and matriarchal cultures, including cultures that practiced polygamy and polyandry; but the Western culture that concerned Hegel has moved from patriarchy toward approximate equality, in large part because of technological development in the economy. The synthesis consists of gradually fragmenting both masculine and feminine personalities into several parts, with each child taking in and adapting different combinations as its own. Each succeeding generation then receives a different mix of masculine and feminine parts, redefined and transformed.

3. Dependence to independence. Subjectively, a reversal—dependence to independence; objectively, a gradual synthesis of dependence and independence, producing interdependence.

4. Economy. Here the main opposites are worker and employer, though workers also play two opposite roles as supplier and demander. Again, each needs the other for its own completion. However, here the conflict of opposites reaches the stage of self-contradiction. In order to make more profits employers do things that result in less profit; a self-

contradiction. The consequence of this continuing contradiction is a continuing pressure to expand markets in all directions, to bring more and more of human life and the earth into the market.

Here again, there is domination by employers over workers, which varies in intensity; but there has been no reversal (yet?).

5. Law. Here is a really severe self-contradiction. The particular court judgment and the universal law each need the other, but all the particular judgments and government implementation decisions endlessly complicate and render unknowable the universals on which they depend. Thus law and government policy gradually become the domain of lawyers and an arena of conflict and bargaining among corporations and other powers.

6. Government. Another contradiction between the particular, individuality, and the universal, community. Historically the particular has tended to gradually undermine the universal more and more, thereby weakening itself, but in Hegel's time there was apparently an uneasy balance.

So we see that opposites over time can either accommodate to one another by absorbing aspects of each other and developing a division of tasks (synthesis); or one can undermine the other and thereby weaken and damage itself (self-contradiction); or each can mostly support the other and thereby itself, but one gradually gets stronger and the other weaker (domination and, sometimes, reversal). The three processes need not be sharply distinct and exclusive, and cooperation can continue along with conflict and contradiction. The optimum arrangement is a temporary balance of opposites, but that is probably rare.

6

Dialectical Research

Next we look at an example of a dialectical process in the economy. This will illustrate the working of the philosopher's subjective dialectic, outlined in Chapter 3. Chapter 5 has examined a number of dialectical social processes, but these were all extensions of processes that Hegel described in PR. Now we study a new process that probably had not yet occurred in Hegel's time. Of course this new process occurs in the context of the larger processes Hegel described, but we will postpone that complication.

To review: One starts with lots of time series data and looks for somewhat regular patterns. Then one digs into appropriate locations in the data with qualitative techniques like interviews and case studies to find the processes, cross-pressures, and contradictions that might be producing the changes, breaks, reversals, and so on; that is, one tries to move from the appearance to the essence. Then one tests the suspected pair of opposites against the data to see whether they could produce such data. Finally one brings in the context bit by bit, and this will probably revise one's interpretation of the proposed essence.

The last paragraph of Chapter 5 has summarized the types of dialectical processes that Hegel briefly described. Each process produces its own kind of data series. Although the list is not comprehensive, it is a good start. It shows us some of the kinds of data that can be studied dialectically. There are three processes in Chapter 5:

1. Synthesis, for example, family. The opposites develop a division of labor that makes them more interdependent; and each absorbs or at least appreciates some of the other's characteristics while remaining opposite. This process produces Bales-type data: increasing role specialization, positive communication, reduction of conflict, alternation of, or lack of, domination . . . One might find such processes in partnerships or cooperatives. A brief example will appear in Chapter 8. Of course the data could also reveal breakdown or decay of the synthesis.

101

2. Self-contradiction, for example, law and policy implementation. Here the opposites are universal and particular, and the particular undermines the universal and thereby itself. The data would show increasing variety and complexity of implementation, decreasing or fluctuating implementation, increasing complexity of bureaucratic or legal processes, increasing complexity of policies or laws.

3. Increasing domination and sometimes reversal, for example, use and value. Here the data are long run and consist of a continuing increase of some quantity, with short-run fluctuations. For example, the increasing distance between wealth and poverty, the top 1 percent and the bottom 10 percent of a population, respectively.

We will look at a fourth kind of data, cyclical data. Such data are short run, several decades in length, and relatively easy to collect. With cyclical data one looks at the peak and trough of the cycle to see what forces might be producing the reversal.

Business cycles are the best known example of cyclical data, and they have been studied quite extensively. However, these studies have shown business cycles to be a complex mixture of several factors, not just a simple capital–labor contradiction. A recent brief summary of business cycle theory (Sherman 1995, chap. 8) mentions five interrelated factors operating at the peak and trough cycle reversals and then adds several more.

Falling profit expectations, which Keynes called the marginal efficiency of capital, led to decline in investment, production, employment, and demand, that is, a cycle reversal at the peak. But profit expectations are affected by past profit levels, and profit is squeezed on both the supply side and the demand side. On the demand side, falling employment and demand near the peak feed back on declining production and profits; on the supply side, rising raw material and production costs, as 100 percent of production capacity is approached near the peak, reduces profits or profit rate increases. The type of investment, whether for capacity expansion or cost-cutting technology, also affects the cycle. Capacity expansion, as in Southeast Asia, tends to produce overproduction, declining investment, and so on, and a cycle reversal. But investment is also reduced by increasing costs of borrowing money, from banks or new stock issues. Borrowing costs in turn rise with rising interest rates, based on the inflation-control policy of the Federal Reserve or on rising demand for money near the peak; borrowing costs also rise with lower stock prices, based on declining profit rates. Rising demand and supply of money in turn are influenced by previous rising profit expectations; and the resulting rise in the stock market feeds back on bullish expectations. Other relevant factors include international financial interdependence, in which a reversal in one country encourages a reversal in other countries, and government budget policy, as Keynes especially emphasized.

There is also an interrelated merger-buyout cycle, moving from a debt-reduction and cash-buildup phase (1970s), which encourages leveraged buyouts (1980s), to a debt-increase and poison-pill phase to discourage buyouts, which reduces profits.

So matters have gotten much more complex since Hegel's description, ¶243–245: The desire for more profits induces employers to increase productivity and lower labor costs, which reduces employment and therefore purchasing power and demand, which produces overproduction and lower profits (and a recession). By now several dialectical processes are interacting in the business cycle, and an adequate account requires a large volume (such as Sherman 1991).

Consequently, we shall take a much simpler example for study in this chapter. We shall look at oligopoly–competition cycles in particular U.S. industries. Such cycles also have been studied extensively, but the topic has remained fairly simple up to now.

The Oligopoly–Competition Cycle

In the U.S. economy there has been a great deal of variation in the number of firms in a particular industry, ranging from one to hundreds. One firm, or one producing 80 percent or more of a product, is called a monopoly. Three to six firms, or so, producing 80 percent or more of a product is called an oligopoly (or oligopsony, as when three or four firms buy nearly all agricultural products). When no firm produces or buys more than 15 percent or so of a product, and there are many smaller firms, that is competition, whether perfect or imperfect.

There have been many shifts over time in particular industries from competition to oligopoly and back again, from near-monopoly to imperfect competition to near-oligopoly, and so on. What causes these shifts? Is any dialectic operating here, and if so, what are the interdependent opposites? Oligopoly and competition are not interdependent; the terms simply designate the number of firms in an industry. So we have to look beneath the surface of the data to find some dynamic that produces the shifts.

We begin with oligopoly and then look at competition. How does an oligopolistic firm act? To begin with, each firm has a large share of the market, so it must be a large corporation, with several divisions or branches located in different cities or countries. In the case of the 1970s agricultural oligopsony, three corporations—Continental, Cook, and Cargill—had purchasing branches all over the country, with several central processing locations. In oligopolies, organization is hierarchical, with a central board locating funds for R&D, production, advertising, and new production or sales branches. Production planning, including new models and techniques, is either centralized or assigned to the top board of each branch. Since these three to six corporations dominate the market, they know who their competitors are and what they are doing, so they can communicate tacitly to manage or shape the market: They can manipulate base prices, labor pay rates, or quantities to be produced.

In the United States, where cartels are illegal, planning is tacit and will take the form, for example, of price leadership by the largest corporation (as was the case in the steel industry for many years) or of agreements to avoid other firms' main transport routes (as formerly with railroads and now with airlines). There also can be tacit agreements to avoid overproduction and a ruinous price war in a cyclical market. For example, in industrial equipment markets demand rises rapidly at the end of a recession and falls rapidly at the beginning of a recession. Falling demand can induce a short-sighted firm to lower prices; the other firms will be forced to do the same, and all will lose. One or two such experiences should teach the short-sighted firm that lowering prices as a recession begins doesn't work; so the next time it will not lower prices. The other firms will notice this move and keep their prices steady as well. The result is a tacit agreement, which prevents the price war. Notice the game-theoretic thinking here. In a game each move is a communication to the other players, so tacit collaboration is not difficult. Conversely, where cartels are legal, they can assign production quotas to each member and set a base price, as with OPEC. Government can also participate in industrial planning, as with MITI in Japan.

In the case of competition, there are too many firms to permit agreement, tacit or explicit, on prices, wages, quantity, and protected sales areas. Firms are large enough to require complex production planning, R&D, and marketing. However, all such planning is guided by estimates about future market potentialities, future demand, and price curves for current or potential new products. Then the market process aggregates the results of all these plans by suppliers and demanders. The market also punishes bad planning, such as overinvestment in capacity expansion and underinvestment in productivity improvement, for example Brazilian steel in the 1970s.

Here we may have our interdependent opposites: plan and market. We are studying markets, both oligopolistic and competitive; and markets, historically and logically, imply planning. That is, the nineteenth century expansion of markets has produced the expansion of corporations that produce for the market, and corporations must plan increasingly as they get larger. Production planning, including price and quantity, is based on estimates of future market potentialities, and each market process aggregates the results of these plans. Conversely, planning influences its markets, as we saw with oligopoly. So each influences the other.

In recent years the direct influence of production and financial planning on the global economy has become approximately equal to the influence of market processes. Various quantitative studies conclude that from 36 percent to 90 percent of international transactions occur within a multinational corporation or within internally related corporations, rather than between separate corporations (Hasnat 1998, 338; Yaghmaian 1998, 251–253); that is, the transactions are non-market. Of course, both plan and market are ultimately involved in all transactions somehow.

Normally, in the cases to be considered, one of the two dominates the other. Planning dominates market in oligopoly; that is, the top firms tacitly decide prices and perhaps other factors—transport costs, approximate quantities, labor costs, protected niches or sales areas. Any small firm in such an industry simply has to work within the given market. In a monopoly, planning dominates market even more directly.

Market dominates planning in competition; that is, all the many firms are price-takers. They can compete by lowering prices, improving quality, introducing new products, more service, tricky advertising, but the anonymous market determines the payoff for them. They must accept the market's decision.

The characteristic, but not inevitable, dialectical change is one of reversal of domination. If planning dominates its markets too much or too long, it produces a resurgence of market processes, especially innovation by new firms, which shakes up planning and restores competition. Conversely, a period of intense competition produces oligopoly and a return of planning. Readers not used to thinking dialectically could express the reversal process as: Intense competition, and also oligopoly, "carries the seeds of its own destruction."

Notice that the domination of planning over market appears in the quantitative data as oligopoly or monopoly. Conversely, the domination of market over planning appears as competition. Thus, the essential planning–market dialectic appears as an oligopoly–competition cycle.

There are several kinds of markets, each encouraging a different kind of planning (Prasch 1995). The present analysis applies only to industrial and raw material markets involving large corporations. In contrast, open-air farm produce markets require a minimal, rather routine planning as to how much to bring each Saturday and how much to charge. Such markets are probably understood adequately by means of an equilibrium-seeking model: An oversupply of tomatoes one week will induce suppliers to bring less or charge less next week. No dialectic there. Stock markets, which change by the minute, are different again.

I begin with four recent examples of the planning–market dialectic and then induce some characteristics and contexts of the process.

Automobiles

Competition. Sources: Epstein 1928; Gelderman 1981; Keller 1989.

The first automobile factory, preserved in the Greenfield Museum near Detroit, consisted of three stationary platform-like jigs. Workers assembled one vehicle on each jig, working on three in sequence; then when the three were complete they were removed and another three set up. With such technology, entry into the industry required little capital or organization, and many firms soon appeared. Autos are a consumer durable, and since they were a great improvement over horse travel, demand was huge and increasing, and the industry prospered. A great variety of cars were designed—the Hupmobile, Willys, Hudson, Nash, Morris, Simplex, Deal, Essex, Terraplane, Reo ... Almost any new firm could prosper in the short run. However, demand could not increase indefinitely, and when it eventually stagnated, price competition would be intense. The long-run competitive issue, therefore, was how to increase productivity and output enough to underprice the competition and survive when the market got saturated. Thus, the market called for some far-sighted planning.

During the early 1900s there was indeed much technological innovation of various sorts. By 1913 Henry Ford had devised and developed the basic solution: an assembly line producing a cheap, standard car, the Model T. Willys-Overland started a similar assembly line in 1913–1914 (Epstein 1928). The parts were produced by specialized plants located elsewhere in Michigan—fender stamping plants, gear and axle plants, and so on—and delivered to the main assembly plant in Dearborn. Each part was delivered to one spot on the line, and the jig moved to each spot in sequence. Each worker, except the delivery people, was rooted to one spot and repeatedly performed a single task. The result was an enormous increase in productivity, which, given the intense competition of the time, was reflected in lower prices. The Model T was priced at $950 in 1909; $490 in 1913, with the fully operational assembly line; and $290 in 1924.

Over several decades this new technology was steadily improved by Ford, Willys, General Motors (GM), and others. The specialized parts plants were integrated into production planning by vertical mergers. Each plant was assigned a single part to produce; the components came from other plants; and the finished part was sent on to a subassembly plant. Gradually the specialized parts plants were organized into about three concentric rings around Detroit. The simplest parts were produced in the outer ring—Saginaw, Lansing ... and sent on to subassembly in Flint, Pontiac, Jackson ... with final assembly occurring in Detroit or Dearborn. Industrial planning had triumphed.

The new technology (Fordism) produced huge economies of scale. A fully competitive corporation had to be huge; a whole set of specialized parts, subassembly, and final assembly plants was required. Each model required its own final assembly plant and set of feeder plants. Alfred Sloan, at General Motors, developed the basic management system for such an organization: decentralized production planning and centralized financial planning, plus production coordinating committees. The basic collection and allocation of resources was decided at the center, based on the performance of the various units, but the units managed their own production process (Keller, 45).

As a result, those producers who could not achieve the required size, by mergers or other means, gradually failed. In 1927 Ford, GM, and Chrysler produced 59 percent of U.S. cars; by 1933, 87.5 percent (Scherrer 1991, 211). By the 1950s there were, in addition to the Big Three, two smaller corporations—Studebaker-Packard and American Motors, the latter formed by a merger of three firms. Competition had produced oligopoly.

Oligopoly. The market situation in 1950 was entirely different from that in 1900–1925. Each corporation had two well-known competitors, and the entry of newcomers was almost impossible. Fordist technology was well-developed and shared by the Big Three (and the two smaller) companies. Any small improvement would soon become known and copied by the others. All three were so large that driving one into bankruptcy by a price war would be impossible. Consequently, the corporate goal became one of maintaining and improving market share and profits. Survival was no longer a problem.

What sort of market competition was still possible in order to achieve these goals? Price cutting was pointless because the other two would match the cuts and all would lose. In fact, small price increases would probably be matched as well, and all three would win; the game was Leader. Putting pressure on wages would not work because by 1950 the United Auto Workers (UAW) had developed pattern bargaining, in which an initial wage agreement with one firm would have to be matched by the other two to avoid a strike. In addition, the tacit social structure of accumulation agreement involved regular wage increases in return for no wildcat strikes and no interferences with management. The wage increases could be paid for with price increases. Costs could be and were reduced by speeding up the assembly line; one popular labor song went, "Please Mr. Foreman slow down the assembly line ... No, I don't mind workin' but I do mind dyin'" (Georgakas and Surkin 1975, 11). The occasional slipups that resulted from increased speed could be checked by a quick inspection at the end of the line and by a replacement guarantee for any defective parts. Speeding up could increase profits but not market share.

The increasing profits in the 1960s went into conglomerate and international expansion—auto leasing and loans, of course, but also real estate, chemicals, boats, air conditioners, and space rockets. Ford and Chrysler expanded into Europe and Latin America; later GM also moved into Europe.

The main form of market share competition that occurred was in styling. A dapper new model might catch the public fancy and increase sales. Elaborate ornaments, hub caps, tail fins flourished in the 1950s; in the early 1960s Dodge came out with "low to the road" seating; ever sleeker flowing lines suggested grace and speed. But mainly the Big Three tacitly collaborated in jointly increasing profits. Cars became larger and more luxurious, with corresponding price increases. Political power was used to increase demand by encouraging highway construction, first in Michigan in the 1920s and then nationally. Economic power was used to eliminate streetcars and reduce other public transport. Robert Moses was one ally in these projects.

In short, planning had triumphed and market discipline had moved into the finance background. Planning included a) the cost-minimizing management of a complex production process; b) continuous design of new, larger, more luxurious and expensive models; c) tacit collaboration among the Big Three and the UAW; d) demand management by reducing other forms of transport. Profits were still relevant for stock prices and the availability of investment capital, but successful planning had assured adequate profit for the foreseeable future.

Competition. About 1950 a new competitor appeared: The Beetle, also known as the Bug (Volkswagen). That's a car? Huh. Gradually other foreign cars appeared, but without a national maintenance and repair network not many would be sold. These small competitors could safely be ignored in a politically managed expanding market. Volkswagen and the Japanese could have the cheapie market; there was more profit in big, stylish cars. There the real competitors were the Big Three, or in GM, other GM departments such as Dodge and Chrysler (Keller, 51). Besides, if GM developed a really stylish small car to beat the Japanese, this would lure customers away from the profitable large-car market (Keller, 52).

Gradually the new competitors established national dealer and repair networks, and VW moved into the middle-priced market. In 1970, foreign cars were 14.7 percent of the U.S. market; by 1982 the foreign share had doubled to 29 percent. Only GM had increased its share, from 40 percent to 44 percent; Ford's and Chrysler's shares had fallen steeply. By

1987 GM's share had declined to 36 percent; as of 1997 it was 30 percent. Oligopoly had produced competition.

What happened? (a) The oligopolists' tacit collusion on cost-plus pricing, with steady wage and salary increases and more stylish, luxurious cars, produced a steady average price increase up to 1981. In 1972, the average price was just below $4,000; by 1981 it was about $8,500 (Source: U.S. Department of Commerce). The new competitors could undercut these prices more and more by postponing profits and by devising new techniques such as just-in-time parts deliveries. (b) The new competitors elicited labor cooperation through teamwork, profit-sharing, and decision-sharing, as in Sweden and Japan. The goal was a high-quality, low-maintenance car, in contrast to the often defective cars that the fast U.S. assembly line produced. (c) The new competitors made innovations that improved performance and safety, such as radial tires, disc brakes, fuel injection, and independent suspension, whereas U.S. innovations emphasized greater comfort, such as electronic window and door opening, automatic steering, higher horsepower, and air-conditioning (Galambos and Pratt 1988, 194). (d) The small and less powerful foreign cars got better gas mileage, and by 1979, with the second oil-price "shock" (part of another planning–market dialectic), gas mileage had become important.

The Big Three continued to ignore or dismiss the new competitors from the 1950s through the 1970s. "GM's arrogant we're-number-one posture, buttressed by a corporate culture that could not stand to hear the bad news about itself, set the company up for a fall as foreign competition began to make inroads. . . . General Motors was a monster, a smug and secure empire" (Keller, 50, 47).

By 1980 the handwriting was flashing on the wall, with Chrysler's $1.7 billion loss and near bankruptcy, and with falling profits for the other two. The U.S. Department of Transportation published a scathing indictment of the incompetent U.S. auto industry (Keller, 81). Big planning changes were needed immediately: price cuts, labor bashing, the development of small, higher mileage cars, the acquisition of foreign techniques, collaboration and potential mergers with Japanese or other firms, and most of all a speedup of the internationalization of production. The result was a period of intense international competition and turmoil, with changes in production, management, and labor relations—changes that included bankruptcies and mergers. The market had punished an overly routinized, narrow planning.

What next? The cycle continues. Collaboration and merger have continued since the early 1980s, including GM–Toyota, Volvo–Renault, Volkswagen–Volvo, GM–Opel, and Daimler Benz–Chrysler. American Motors has become a subsidiary of Chrysler. One prediction is that the international auto market will be able to sustain eight or nine multinational corporations (MNCs), or perhaps only six—an international oligopoly.

Steel

Sources: Tiffany 1988; Borrus 1983; Gondolf 1986, chap. 3; Lynn 1982; Strohmeyer 1986.

Market Context. Unlike cars, steel is a producer good, and in fact the basic good for industrial and military production. As such, any government in an industrializing country will want to develop and protect a domestic steel industry, and industrialized country governments will also be concerned with maintaining domestic capacity for both military and industrial purposes. In an industrialized country demand is cyclical and fairly price inelastic; that is, in a recession when production declines the demand for steel will also decline regardless of moderate price declines. But since steel plants have high fixed costs, a cyclical decline in demand causes large losses, and there is a tendency to cut prices below cost to cover fixed costs at least. In the resulting price war all lose; the game is Prisoner's Dilemma.

Oligopoly. Before Bretton Woods (1944) high steel tariffs were the rule. Governments encouraged exports during recessions, but import tariffs protected domestic steel from such unfair dumping by other countries. Domestically, steel producers recognized the futility of price wars and attempted to manage prices. In the United States, antitrust laws forced price cooperation to be tacit and informal; the solution was price leadership by U.S. Steel. In addition, the FOB Pittsburgh rule prevented competition on transport costs, since transport charges were the same from anywhere in the United States—the cost of shipping from Pittsburgh. This prevented steel companies from building new plants close to suspected future industrial areas, such as California, so they could sell cheaper. Instead, they located close to coal and iron ore sources so as to reduce production costs. Nor was there significant competition on quality, since all U.S. companies used the same open hearth technology.

In short, tacit cooperation in the U.S. steel industry, with government support, had essentially eliminated market competition before 1940. Individual companies could pursue higher profits via controlling raw material production and delivery, better customer service, and so on, but market share was not much affected.

In 1940, the U.S. government called for expanded production in preparation for war. The call for expansion continued after the war in order to rebuild European industry (to keep out the Communists) and to continue

TABLE 6.1 U.S. Steel in the World Market

	World Output (Million Metric Tons)	U.S. % of World Output	World Trade (Million Metric Tons)	U.S. % of World Trade
1950	190	46	16	16
1955	273	39	29	14
1960	351	26	43	7
1965	456	26		
1970	593	20		
1975	666	16		
1980	721	14		
1985	704	11		

SOURCE: Paul Tiffany, *The Decline of American Steel* (New York: Oxford, University Press, 1988); International Iron and Steel Institute, *Steel Statistical Yearbook 1987* (Brussels: IISI, 1987).

military production for the Korean war. The steel industry was reluctant, fearing surplus capacity when things quieted down, but government provided cheap RFC loans, big depreciation allowances (later reduced), and tacit approval for price increases. The resulting expansion of existing plants produced record profits by 1955, which convinced corporate boards that expansion was OK.

Shift to Competition, 1960–1980. European recovery was completed before 1960, and the European steel cartel, founded in 1952, was no longer interested in imports from the United States. Similarly, developing countries like Brazil had welcomed imports in order to build their own steel industry in the 1950s; but, having built enough domestic capacity, they no longer needed U.S. steel. One by one the foreign outlets for U.S. surplus capacity closed; the steel industry had produced its own competition. To add insult to injury, in 1962 President Kennedy undermined a price rise announced by U.S. Steel by inducing other firms not to follow U.S. Steel's lead. (See Table 6.1).

The long steel strike of 1959 provided an opening for new competitors, and several electric-furnace minimills opened about that time. These mills, such as Florida Steel—which opened in November, 1958—used continuous casting, mainly of scrap iron, to produce about 60,000 tons a year. Big Steel ignored these tiny mills (Strohmeyer, 73). Expanding demand was the goal, as the 1950s had shown, and the solution was to expand capacity and thereby profits. The tiny mills could have their tiny piece of the market.

More serious was the rise of imports from the new foreign competitors. Japanese steel companies, with government assistance, had built their postwar steel industry around a new technology, the basic oxygen furnace (BOF). This and other production efficiencies such as computer controls and transport minimizing locations enabled them to undercut U.S. steel prices, especially in California. For one thing, transport costs to California from Japan, Taiwan, and South Korea were lower than from Pittsburgh (D'Costa 1993, 111). In addition, Japanese steel produced 400 tons per man, per year, using 1,100 pounds of coal; U.S. steel produced on average 250 tons using 1,550 pounds of coal (Borrus 1983). U.S. imports in 1960 were 3 million tons; in 1968, 18 million tons. U.S. firms were annoyed at this government-subsidized "dumping," as they saw it, and pressed their ally, government, to protect them against unfair trade. The government obliged with a "voluntary" restraint agreement in 1969, orderly marketing agreements in the 1970s, and the celebrated Trigger Price Mechanism in 1978, scarcely enforced to avoid antagonizing anticommunist allies, and easily evaded by importing finished parts rather than raw steel.

As steel profits went down from 1955 through 1970, steel firms used their political power to reduce costs. They fended off attempts by "environmental extremists," as George Bush would call them, to establish smoke pollution controls in Gary, Indiana (Greer 1968; Crenson 1971). Every year in Lackawanna, New York, in the 1970s they pressured the city to reduce their taxes by threats of plant closing. When all political efforts failed they closed plants, beginning sharply in 1979, and used profits and government assistance to diversify out of steel. Steel industry employment fell from nearly 600,000 in 1979 to about 340,000 in 1983 and 230,000 in 1994 (Cleveland Federal Reserve Report, May 1994). U.S. Steel became USX. When the Lackawanna, New York, mills (Bethlehem and Republic) closed in 1983 a large vacant section of suburbs downwind from the mills experienced a housing boom that continues to this day.

Why didn't U.S. steel firms invest in BOF, continuous casting, and other efficiencies to compete against imports in the 1960s and 1970s? They did invest somewhat but feared that a few more efficient mills would disrupt their price leadership arrangement. Their focus of attention was on their fellow oligopolists; they feared that a large cost-cutting innovation by one or two firms might induce a price cut that would set off a price war. Also they were still convinced in the 1960s that their mills were the most efficient in the world and that the problems were government anti-pollution controls, high labor costs, and foreign government-subsidized dumping. John Strohmeyer describes the steel tycoons in the 1960s: "They grew so smug that they became oblivious to what was happening in the world around them" (1986, 12). They thought that the solution to their problems was to continue their standard operating procedures of tough bargaining and political negotiation and pressure. By 1979 it was clear that this solution had failed.

Competition, 1980– . In 1982 Ira Magaziner and Robert Reich suggested that the only competitive U.S. steel firms were the small high-carbon electric minimills, which represented 13 percent of U.S. steel production about 1980. There were also a few high-tech firms producing specialty alloys. And NUCOR imported a new continuous-casting technique from Germany. Additionally, there were a few BOF plants that could compete with imports, such as the Burns Harbor, Indiana, plant which is now one of Bethlehem Steel's two main plants. According to the 1980 General Accounting Office report, world steel production capacity exceeded demand by 20 percent. As a result, plant closings, bankruptcies, foreign buyouts, and joint ventures with foreign firms that were exporting their surplus to the United States occurred in the late 1970s and 1980s (D'Costa 1993, 116–117). Big Steel has been dissolved by international competition.

Computers

Competition to Monopoly. Main Sources: *Der Spiegel,* April 5, 1993; Pugh 1995.

Computer technology has developed much faster than auto or steel technology, so the cycle under study also has moved much faster. For the first few years, about 1955–1964, a wide variety of programs appeared, and changes in these programs came every year or so. The programs were incompatible, untranslatable, except perhaps into the newer products of the same company. Thus the purchaser had a wide choice but gradually learned that whatever choice was made would soon become obsolete. In addition, each program was designed for a fairly specific data-processing use.

The change came in 1964 when IBM, the largest company, announced its new Model 360. This was a modular machine whose separate modules could deal with all current data-processing needs (hence, "360"). Here was the ultimate all-purpose computer whose modular structure provided flexibility, both for the purchaser, who could buy the specific modules needed, and for IBM, which could constantly add new or improved modules. When the 360 finally appeared it was a big success. Orders quickly exceeded expectations, and a new 360 factory had to be built immediately (Pugh 1995, 289). By 1969 IBM had produced 73 percent of the world inventory of installed computers (Pugh 1995, 296). Soon other firms (the "seven dwarfs") were designing software programs and products to plug into the 360 and were making their own new machines IBM-compatible. IBM research, therefore, became the leading edge; other firms had to wait and see what IBM was up to so they could adapt their new products accordingly. IBM profits went up from a few hundred million dollars in 1965 to nearly $6.6 billion in 1984, before dropping. A government antitrust investigation was launched in 1969 and continued until 1982, when it was ended without action.

Monopoly to Competition. IBM continued its R&D leadership with Model 370, which appeared in 1970. But research for the next new model, the F/S (future system) was quietly terminated in 1975. Meanwhile the small follower firms moved from IBM-compatible software to clones of 360 modules that could plug into a 360 but were cheaper. Other firms such as Hewlett Packard and Digital developed smaller and cheaper imitations of the 360. In 1977 a new firm, Apple, developed a tiny one-person computer. Technology had developed from the enormous ILLIAC of 1950, which filled a large room, to the approximately 12 foot x 12 foot IBM 360, to the Digital minicomputer, to the desktop Apple.

Soon PCs were taking over the market. A company's PCs could be networked to communicate directly as needed, leaving the IBM mainframes only the function of serving as data archives. Before long the desktop PCs could be connected to a company's mainframe for access to archives, and all the data processing could occur at the PC. In 1981 IBM brought out its own PC, with the help of two small firms, Microsoft and Intel, and quickly took over about 50 percent of the PC market. But their prices were higher, and with new models coming out of the smaller firms every six months, their technology lagged behind. By 1992 they had 12.4 percent of the PC market, barely more than Apple's 11.9 percent. IBM profits continued to fall after 1984, until in 1991–1993 there were huge losses (Pugh 1995, 324).

What happened? Nothing fails like success (for example, OPEC). In 1964 IBM had won the race. The task now was to stay ahead with ever better versions of the 360. Money was poured into research on improvements, including the 370. But discoveries that might lead to a quite different kind of computer were squelched by management, as any such discovery might compete with the highly profitable 360/370. The F/S was stopped in part for the same reason: It might make the 370 obsolete by moving in a different direction. And conversely, the F/S would not sell at first either; the leasing companies that were buying and leasing out 370s would refuse to discard their stock and start over, and owners would prefer to upgrade their 370 with the constantly appearing improvements (Pugh 1995, p. 310).

A more serious problem was bureaucratic conflict. Remember that the 360/370 was a modular machine, and the F/S was to be modular also. But each module was being designed by a separate research department, and all the research projects were occurring simultaneously, under high pressure for rapid results. Consequently it became impossible to coordinate the research and make the modules compatible: To make module A compatible with the latest ideas in Module B would wreck project A, and vice versa (Pugh 1995, 310, 313). The result was continuing conflict and lack of progress. The complex planning structure that had beaten the competition had developed gridlock.

The F/S failure induced management to focus even more on the goal of maintaining and protecting the 370's central position in the computer industry (Pugh 1995, 311). That's where the profits were; there were no profits in those tiny new computers. By 1980, when Microsoft people were hired to develop an IBM PC, IBM management seemed to have lost touch with new developments. They thought the new PC would encourage purchases of the 370 as a company's central processor, but actually mainframe sales continued to fall. They were living in the past, 1970: the golden times.

A similar process had occurred at Ford in the 1920s on a lesser scale. The Model T was the ultimate, cheap, mass-produced car, the triumph of the Fordist assembly line. It made Ford the leader in the new technology. Consequently management strategy was focused on continuing the Model T success, while other corporations developed more stylish models. Not until the 1940s, when Ford had lost much market share, did management realize it had to change drastically to stay in the oligopoly game.

Competition Toward Duopoly. The intense competition of the 1980s produced two big winners by 1995, Microsoft and Intel. Apple was nearly bankrupt by September 1997, and a few other companies each maintained smaller market shares (*Macworld,* November 1997). An antitrust lawyer recently commented, "There is absolutely no question that Microsoft has enormous power, that if you are in the computer business you are better off being a friend of [Microsoft]".

Airlines

Competition to Oligopoly. Sources: Meyer and Oster 1987; Tregarthen 1987.

The domestic interstate airline industry was controlled by planning until 1978. The planning was done by the Civil Aeronautics Board (CAB), which assigned landing rights at airports and regulated fares. The goals of the CAB were to insure that all airports had some service and to insure a healthy, profitable airline industry to service the airports. Profitability was protected by assigning landing rights in proportion to demand at each airport. A particularly weak airline could get a monopoly at some airport to improve its profitability. Conversely, service to some small, unprofitable airports was subsidized to keep the airports open.

This was a government-run market, managed competition, in which it was impossible to win or lose completely. Since prices were fixed, competition was limited to services such as in-flight meals, departure hours, and ticketing flexibility. New entries were permitted only if demand increased. In theory a totally inefficient airline would lose customers and eventually landing rights, but in practice that didn't happen.

Wild competition appeared suddenly in 1978 when CAB regulation was abolished. Any new domestic airline could enter the market; for example, Frank Lorenzo entered the competition with an investment of $35,000 in Texas Air and a good deal of leveraging. The result was many new airlines, much surplus capacity, and a ferocious price war. By 1982 the number of airlines had grown from twenty-eight in 1976 to sixty-one. In addition the sharp rise in fuel prices in 1980 and the recessions of 1980 and 1981–1982 squeezed the airlines and produced huge losses in 1981–1983.

Obviously survival was now at stake. Already in 1982 Braniff went bankrupt, and other airlines such as Continental were following close behind. Airline stock prices fell, and in 1985 only four carriers had high credit ratings: American, Delta, U.S. Air, and Piedmont.

One way to avoid bankruptcy was to increase productivity. A new airline, People Express, had entered the competition with a new scheduling technique, the hub and spokes. Small airports located on a spoke thus had access to a large number of other airports via the hub, and the number of flights on each spoke could be adjusted to the number of passengers. Soon other competitors could strengthen and extend the hub system by increasing the spokes and perhaps buying out the competitor. The spokes included some small local airlines, which developed scheduling agreements with the large line. The effect, in addition to fewer vacant seats, was to prevent competition from moving into the hub, because competitors could not provide the spokes and compact terminal space needed. Other cost-cutting tactics included reducing wages, flying longer hours before aircraft maintenance, overbooking, and dropping unprofitable routes. The other way to avoid bankruptcy was to have enough accumulated capital and bank credit to withstand losses year after year.

By 1991 three big airlines dominated the industry: Delta, American, and United. Discussions were under way with various foreign airlines. There were still many smaller airlines providing spokes with the hubs, plus some bankrupt lines that continued to operate temporarily. The price war intensified, and the industry continued to lose money: From 1983 through 1989 the industry's total annual profits ranged from $1 billion to zero, and from 1990 through 1992 the industry lost $10 billion (Cleveland Federal Reserve Report, August 1993). Since 1993, mergers and buyouts of the near-bankrupt lines have been in process or have been proposed. When enough marginal contenders are wiped out we can expect the price war to end and the Big Three to return to profitability, along with their dependent small-firm spokes.

The Dialectic

In these examples competition produces oligopoly, and oligopoly produces competition, in varying circumstances. Let us review the processes and contexts involved.

First, moderate, limited, controlled competition, as with the regulated airlines, does not produce oligopoly. This combination of plan and market restricts new entries and limits competition to certain areas. For the regulated airlines competition occurred at the large airports and was limited to departure times, comfort, reliability, and transfer opportunities. It is only uncontrolled, unlimited, wild competition with easy entry that destroys itself. The example is airlines after deregulation in 1978.

Wild competition can be produced by oligopoly; this process will be taken up later. But wild competition also can occur in the case of a new product with rapidly developing technology, a large potential demand, and easy market entry requiring little initial investment and experience. The auto and computer cases (1900–1925, 1955–1964, respectively) are illustrations.

A new product does not have experienced customers who know what they are getting, what to use it for, and how much it should cost. Nor does a new product have experienced producers who know what will sell and how to produce it. Consequently, production planning involves extreme uncertainty about what will sell, at what price, how to produce it efficiently, who the competition will be next year, what new products will soon appear, and how to deal with labor. In such circumstances the issue is survival under uncertainty. Tactics include the invention of new techniques that may reduce costs and increase output of some sort, the design of new models that may sell, price cutting that leads to price wars and bankruptcies, escape to a special-product niche, and mergers.

How do these tactics promote long-term survival? A new technique (Ford, GM, IBM) works if it produces a quick, massive increase in market share before most of the competition can pick up the technique. If the new technique is relatively cheap to set up, such as the airline hub, the competition will adopt it rapidly and the competitive advantage will disappear. Thus People Express, the developer of the hub, went bankrupt a few years later. A new model can work only until the competitors design their own new models, which they are already doing. Price war works if a firm has already accumulated a very large cushion of capital, perhaps by merger or technology lead, a cushion large enough to outlast the competition. It also works if the firm is already bankrupt and needs quick cash before selling out. A merger works if it facilitates either productivity improvement or cushion against price war, or both. Finding a niche works as long as the niche lasts; it is a way of escaping the competition.

All of the successful tactics, except the niche-escape one, involve size. Surviving a price war without a niche obviously requires massive reserve capital or diversification or banking allies. Developing or imitating a new technique usually involves large investment, both in R&D and in production facilities, or if it does not, as in the case of Apple and Microsoft, the success will bring in profits that expand the firm anyway. In either case the winners will be large.

In sum, uncontrolled competition with easy entry produces a few large, successful firms plus small firms clinging to niches or dependent on the large ones, as with airlines and computers; that is, it provides the setting for oligopoly.

We turn next to the topic of how and in what circumstances oligopoly turns into competition. The examples are autos and steel from about 1960 to 1980, and computers since 1970. These examples suggest that the reversal is not automatic but requires the removal of barriers to free entry, if such barriers exist.

In two of these cases, autos and steel, the oligopolists had long ago survived intense competition. They had done so by inventing or adopting the leading technology, developing the necessary large organization to plan and manage a complex production process, learning to limit and control their own competition with other large firms, and developing an uneasy collaboration with labor and national and local government. In the computer case IBM beat the competition by devoting its large capital and organizational resources to R&D, thus becoming the technology leader.

In all these cases the result was a large and smoothly running organization devoted not to survival—that was deep in the past—but to maintaining the production technology and organization that had succeeded so well. IBM was devoted to staying ahead of the competition in the large mainframe machines. Steel maintained its tacit industry collaboration with moderate innovation, moderate price and wage increases (ten of them from 1945–1962, Strohmeyer 1986, 79), dependence on national government for protection and financial support, and threat power over local government. The Big Three auto companies maintained their limited competition over new styling and comfort, limited collaboration with labor, and political pressure for more highway construction.

In all three cases the corporate strategies involved gradual price increases. Prices were determined by cost plus needed investment capital plus standard profit, to maintain stock prices and borrowing potential.

For IBM the large investment needed to maintain the technological lead was a price determinant. For autos and steel, the regular wage increases that produced labor peace were one determinant, and the cost of styling and comfort was another.

The regular price increases provided a market space that could attract potential competitors. In the case of computers, the competitors were already there or, like Apple and Microsoft, could easily enter, so competition intensified in a few years. In autos and steel the national boundary that set limits to competition was gradually removed after 1950 by rapid lowering of tariffs, new transport and communication technology, and the resulting internationalization of capital. In addition, from about 1960 on, world excess capacity encouraged attempts to penetrate national boundaries. In short, while oligopolistic price increases and quality stagnation provided an attractive arena for new competitors, surplus capacity plus new production techniques provided the resources for moving into the arena.

When new competitors gradually appeared they were interpreted in terms of existing corporate strategies. The Volkswagen Beetle was simply not stylish at all and so could be ignored; expensive Mercedes and Rolls-Royces called for upgraded, more luxurious Lincolns and Cadillacs. The electric minimills were too tiny to be a threat to Big Steel and could be ignored. Cheap steel imports were another instance of unfair trade practices, dumping, which required government protection. There was no profit in those tiny toy PCs; but perhaps they could be sold as a supplement to the 370s, an upgrading. Gas price increases in 1973 by OPEC were a temporary problem that could be ignored (Keller 1989, 51). Japanese lower prices were due to the low wages they paid; U.S. wages were much too high (Keller 1989, 82). "We don't talk about that in administrative meetings," said one corporate executive, referring to a report on the many defects in GM cars (Keller 1989, 50).

The new production techniques introduced by the new competitors were not copied at first either, in contrast with the wild competition phase. Roger Smith's plan for a joint production venture with Toyota, to learn Japanese techniques, enraged the GM executive committee (Keller, 88–89, 92). "They tell us we're number one in the world. So why are we getting in bed with the Japanese?" Later, managers were sent there to learn the new techniques; but when they returned to report on what they had (mis)learned, their ideas were rejected. "I don't want to hear it; it's a Japanese system of thought" (Keller, 133–136, 142–144). IBM's researchers were supposed to improve on the 360 and not move into new types of product that might compete with or outmode the 360. Research discoveries that pointed in new directions were squelched by management: Research had become a threat. When outsiders developed the microcomputer, it was at first seen as a threat—IBM tried to buy out Apple in self-defense—and then as a way of improving mainframe sales. Similarly, technological discoveries in the Bethlehem Steel research center were vetoed by board members. Continuous casting was tried out in the 1960s, succeeded, and was then abandoned (Strohmeyer 1986 60–61). Basic oxygen was tried in one newer plant, Burns Harbor, succeeded, and left there.

When competitors' new larger models sold well in the booming 1920s Henry Ford responded with his standard tactic: lower the price. For once it didn't work. So, lower prices still more. Edsel Ford and others had an extremely hard time over several years persuading Henry Ford to authorize the design of a new, larger, more expensive model (Gelderman 1981, 208, 256).

To simplify, successful planning had become systematized, organized, routinized, and departmentalized. Novelty was interpreted in terms of existing planning categories and responded to with existing defense mechanisms. Only after these had obviously failed did the organization experience upheaval, turmoil, executive turnover, reorganization; and by that time it was too late. The competition had established itself. (Incidentally, government foreign policy planning gets routinized in the same way; George 1993, chap. 3.)

Note that the oligopolistic corporations in these cases did not work like Joseph Schumpeter's idealized creative corporations; they didn't innovate. Innovation came from outside oligopoly, from small newcomers like Apple, People Express, or Nucor, or it came from developing corporations in other countries, like Toyota, which moved into the U.S. market. Innovation was encouraged by the market space opened up by routinized oligopolistic planning.

Naomi Lamoreaux (1985, 193ff) has induced a similar cycle or dialectic that sometimes occurred between 1875–1925. She distinguishes three stages: 1. A new product or a new technique with easy entry arises, along with many small, underfinanced and indebted firms and an uncertain and developing demand (pp. 59ff). The pervasive uncertainty plus high fixed costs of production produces a price war. This leads to bankruptcies and discourages new entries. 2. The managers of successful firms, in desperation, arrange mergers and then collaboration to end the price war. The collaboration is maintained in various ways, usually by a dominant firm (chap. 5) or by an industry association (such as OPEC). The leader or association sets prices, maintains discipline by threats of price war (as Saudi Arabia did in OPEC, 1982–1986), discourages innovation, perhaps allocates market share or controls raw material sources, or uses other tactics. 3. Foreign competitors, or a new product, enter the market from outside the cartel; and then a new price war begins.

The rapidly changing U.S. telecommunications industry is apparently another example of the planning–market dialectic. The process began with the ending of the AT&T monopoly, moved into intense competition and the development of the Big Three long-distance companies, and then entered a new stage with the 1996 Telecommunications Act, pushed in part by the Big Three.

We turn now to the question of what sort of corporate policymaking occurs in these cycles. The static choice model, which assumes adequate information and given alternatives, is not relevant; nor does the rational expectations assumption apply. We are dealing rather with decisionmaking under uncertainty. The uncertainty is most obvious in the period of wild competition. Here the corporation does not know the most efficient technology, what will sell, who the competitors will be in a few years, what price to charge, and how much to invest in R&D. The general rule is clear: Outsell the unknown future competitor by producing more efficiently and more cheaply what customers will want; but how and what?

Consequently, policymaking is a process of learning and searching for information over time, a process of seeing what works and what doesn't work. The Simon and Tversky bounded rationality models describe such a process, as does John Harvey (1996). One way to get information is by feedback: How did that choice work out? What went wrong? What did we overlook, and how can it be improved? Policy choices by Ford, Bethlehem Steel, and so on go on over decades, and the feedback is used to improve on the previous policy. One also learns second-order rules for detecting and correcting errors, such as making sure "we don't make *that* mistake again." For example, the Federal Reserve had learned by 1993 not to make the mistake of the mid-1970s, "when monetary policy appeared to react too little, too late and inflation accelerated to new highs" (Bauer and Carlson 1994). This time, 1994, the Fed would stay ahead of inflation. Similarly, one basic Cold War policy rule was "No More Munichs!"

The same process occurs in the "learning curve" in a production process; one gradually learns how to do some repetitive process faster, avoid specific errors, notice signals of trouble, and so on. The learning curve has an asymptote, however. Eventually one has mastered some process thoroughly and there is not much more to improve. At this point, routine gradually sets in. For example Henry Ford worked out a successful policy in about two decades: keep improving the assembly line, produce a simple standard car, and keep lowering the price. If the competition is catching up, cut costs and lower prices faster. Pay good wages to get the best workers. Don't let a bank get its fingers on you; cut costs rather than borrow. (Perhaps he learned that from watching the banks move in on the auto industry in 1903–1916; Keller 1989, 39–42.)

Similarly, the oligopolists learned over decades how to beat the smaller competitors and how to get along with the other oligopolists and with government and unions. The evidence that they had learned was that their strategy was successful year after year, with minor improvements. So the strategy gets systematized; enough information has been accumulated. The organization develops a shared belief, or myth (Hirschhorn and Barnett 1993, 180ff), that they know how to operate successfully. This gives them security and confidence. Then we add frame theory or schema theory from cognitive psychology: New information is interpreted in terms of the learned categories—up to a point. Then the frame collapses and a new learning process begins. The collapse occurred in steel, autos, and IBM around 1980, shortly before the apparently similar collapse of Soviet top-down, routinized planning.

In summary, in these four cases the corporate planning or policymaking process follows a cycle parallel to the wild competition–oligopoly–competitive cycle: learning–systematization and improvement of successful strategy–routine–crisis–collapse.

The Context of the Oligopoly–Competition Cycle

So far we have looked briefly at four examples of a hypothesized planning–market dialectic. The examples suggest that this is a short-run cycle: Each reversal took some ten to thirty years. The OPEC reversal took thirteen years, from 1973 to 1986. Obviously we need to study more cases, possibly including economic development planning and foreign policy planning, to get a more complex understanding of this process. Most of all, we need to examine the context of the process to see what factors are involved in making it happen.

One obvious prerequisite for the cycle is the modern industrial corporate form of organization. In all four cases corporations had to engage in complex production planning, focused competition, and then mergers, acquisitions, or cartel arrangements to end the price war. The Lamoreaux cases show that in earlier instances of the cycle, as far back as 1875, it took corporations to arrange the mergers and collaboration that ended the price wars. In addition the routinization of planning that characterized the oligopolies in our cases required a large, hierarchical organization with separate production divisions.

Modern governments also have the hierarchical organization that facilitates the routinization of policy planning described by Alex George (1993). Soviet planning was obviously hierarchical; also some hierarchical OPEC governments quickly developed a long-term plan that would require ever-increasing oil revenues: Iran under the Shah (among other countries) planned rapid industrialization, and Iraq under Hussein planned a rapid military buildup and then war, which called for more and more oil revenues. Accordingly, when oil prices went down due to increasing competition, these countries evaded their export quotas and gradually wrecked the cartel arrangement.

The post–Bretton Woods international monetary regime, including, beginning in the 1960s, the Eurodollar, is another important facilitating condition. The greatly increased speed and ease of money flows around the world increased ease of entry by foreign corporations into the U.S. market. On the other hand, it also facilitated U.S. auto corporation expansion abroad, as well as auto and steel exports; both factors helped maintain the oligarchic peace for decades. The same money flows, including World Bank loans, facilitated steel and auto plant development in Latin America, using U.S. steel and machine tool exports, thereby producing eventual world surplus capacity and intense competition. So international finance helped maintain oligopolistic planning but also strengthened and expanded the world market that gradually undermined oligopoly.

These two facilitating conditions, corporations and international finance, suggest that the general context for the planning–market dialectic is modern finance capitalism.

An important channeling factor for U.S. oligopolies throughout this period has been government antitrust policy and policy implementation (Fligstein 1990). Neil Fligstein studied changes in the organization and policy outlook of U.S. corporations since 1860. He observed that oligopolistic corporations, that is, those with a large market share, were always interested in restraining and limiting competition. They feared the destructive effect of wild price wars and overproduction. So they tried to cooperate with fellow oligopolists in planning a limited, regulated competition. But if a particular form of cooperation failed to limit competition, or if it was prosecuted by the Federal Trade Commission (FTC), the corporations shifted to a different form of cooperation. Thus the particular form of market planning was partly shaped by the FTC.

From about 1865–1898 many big corporations tried cartels, that is, OPEC-type agreements on prices and quotas. These failed because they could not be enforced, so the corporations shifted to trusts, especially in the years 1880–1890. A trust was a holding company that owned stock in each corporation and so could enforce the agreed prices and quotas. Then trusts were declared illegal by the Sherman antitrust law. So the corporations shifted to horizontal mergers, especially in the years 1895–1905. The Sherman Act as then interpreted did not prohibit mergers. However, according to Fligstein, 60 percent of these mergers gradually failed, perhaps because they could not be efficiently managed or perhaps because they could not prevent new entries (sounds familiar).

A fourth form of market planning developed in the 1920s. At this time production planning was taking the Fordist form of vertical mergers, which were not illegal, and the Sloan management form of centralized financial control of separate production divisions. Corporations had gotten much larger, partly through horizontal and vertical mergers. Market planning began to take the form of tacit price leadership, as in steel, and competitors shared cost-price information with each other. Also, in contrast with the earlier cartels, a price-cutter would be punished by a focused price war.

Still later, from 1950 to the 1970s, the FTC began to prosecute some horizontal and even vertical mergers, if they increased market share. During this time, ever-changing FTC antitrust policy was published and reported to the corporations, so they could avoid prosecution. The effect was to sharply reduce the merger tactic of market control and to reinforce the (legal) price leadership tactic.

Fligstein (1990, 304–314) also observes that different market control policies have been followed in other countries, depending on what policies have been permitted or encouraged by the various governments. For example, in prewar Germany, cartels dominated the economy. The U.S. occupation forces passed a law, with loopholes, prohibiting cartels. Later German policy encouraged selective mergers and cartel arrangements that would promote exports and economies of scale. In postwar Japan, competing corporations bought each other's stock, set up informal associations, and/or became dependent on banks for capital and informal regulation of competition. MITI also encouraged limited cooperation. And so on.

Fligstein's much larger sample of corporate market planning suggests that the planning-market contradiction has been a continuous process since 1860, taking varying shapes depending on governmental and cultural influences. There has been a fairly constant tendency of oligopolistic corporations to try to plan and manage the market in some fashion, and an opposite tendency of new firms (as in computers and air transport) or outsiders (as in autos and steel) to move in and disrupt market control. The reversal-of-dominance pattern would appear only when either corporate control of the market or unregulated competition had achieved effective dominance. At that point the dominating factor, planning or market, would gradually destroy itself and prepare for a reversal. At other times and in other industries there would be an unstable fluctuation back and forth.

Up to here we have examined the influence of three contextual factors on the market–planning dialectic. Now we reverse our perspective. (Remember, think dialectically.) The market–planning cycle in turn facilitates the development of corporations and an internationalized market.

First, surviving the period of wild competition required rapid corporate expansion in order to develop and adapt the latest technology: In steel and autos, this expansion occurred from 1890 to 1930 in the United States and since 1950 internationally; in computers it took place in the 1970s. Second, the large corporations pushed internationalization in order to export their surplus products and to invest their huge profits in international production. OPEC countries contributed surplus oil revenues in the 1970s, which banks vigorously urged on to developing countries like Brazil, Mexico, and Argentina.

The forces of production are another contextual factor that both influences and is influenced by the market–planning cycle. The competition phase of the cycle demands rapid development of new technology: in autos, the Fordist assembly line in the 1900s and just-in-time production in the 1970s; BOF in steel in the 1950s; the hub and spoke airline system in the early 1980s; and most spectacularly the rapid electronics development since the 1960s. The oligopoly phase of the cycle slows or even blocks new technology, temporarily. Conversely, the invention of modern telecommunication, electronics, internal combustion, open hearth steel production, and undersea oil drilling, set the stage for the ensuing cycles. Thus the forces of production are not a self-propelling engine that moves an economy along; they influence and are influenced by their context. Consequently, alternative technologies develop in different cultural contexts (Feenberg 1991). For example, the type of labor relations in a given country has influenced the technology of auto production, which differs in the United States, Sweden, and Japan.

The reference to Sweden and Japan suggests that differences in national industrial organization and labor relations are also relevant to the planning–market dialectic. This is indeed the case. World surplus capacity in steel had different effects in different countries. German, Austrian, and Japanese steel corporations adjusted flexibly to overcapacity in a variety of ways, in contrast to the rigidity-crash of U.S. steel. In the U.S. case the oligopolists believed they had control of a closed national market, whereas German and other corporations knew they were operating in a competitive world market. We will examine Austrian steel planning in Chapter 7.

Political culture also affects the style of planning, since planning is a political process. MITI in Japan, for example, had a quite different style of planning, which expressed the complex corporatist political culture (Magaziner and Reich 1982). In contrast, Soviet planning was based on the tzarist political culture that preceded it: The tzar gave orders prepared by his noble advisers, and the serfs obeyed. Soviet annual plans were prepared by the national planning office, then endorsed by the Central Committee, and then handed down and enforced by the bureaucracy

(Kornai 1992, chap. 7). "Implementation is compulsory" (p. 114). The lower levels of the bureaucracy could comment on the initial draft of the plan and also coordinate their suggestions with other ministries, but the Central Committee made the final decision.

This sort of planning excludes market processes entirely and thus is entirely undialectical. The purchase and sale of goods and services occurred in the "private sector" or "informal economy" but were usually illegal and in any case ignored by the planners (Kornai 1992, 85–86). Consequently, market processes could not influence planning, which became "extremely rigid; there are long delays and serious losses before it adapts to changes in needs, technology, the domestic political situation, or the outside world" (Kornai 1992, 118). (Sounds like Ford, GM, IBM, etc.) There was no internal monopoly-competition cycle; instead, planning gradually destroyed itself, for instance by preventing new technology, and produced a reversal of domination. And when the planning system finally collapsed politically, it was replaced by an equally abstract opposite, an idealized free market concept. In practice the same political structure continued in power: The nomenklatura barons like Berezovsky "bought" the industries that they previously ruled and then ruled them for private profit.

Obviously much more empirical study of various markets and corporate-government planning styles and structures is necessary to work out the planning–market dialectic and its contexts. We can also expect the process to change as corporate, financial, and world governmental structures develop further. This raises the question, where is the dialectic going?

We can perceive the general direction of change at this time: Corporations get larger and more multinational, and markets expand also. Ford has expanded from a small shop in Dearborn, Michigan, to an integrated fifteen-country production organization. Expansion is based partly on economies of scale, partly on the need to manage and/or devise the latest technology, partly on the need to stay ahead of the competition by reinvesting profits, and partly on the rapidly expanding market in which competition operates. Corporate expansion can occur by merger, as with airlines and some autos, by buyouts, and by new plants. It can also occur through collaboration between two or more corporations, for example the GM–Toyota NUMMI collaboration of the 1980s.

In recent years international collaboration and mergers have increased rapidly in order to keep up with the rapidly globalizing economy. Airline collaboration, for instance Northwest–KLM, is one leading example. The reason is the rapid increase in international travel. Collaboration, or merger through exchange of stocks, enables the airlines to share scarce landing rights at large airports like Heathrow and Frankfurt and to plan flight schedules that will enable travelers to use both airlines on a flight with minimum waiting time. The pressure to collaborate is so strong that the French Socialist government is planning to "sell off" (privatize? No! No!) its ownership of Air France. The reason is that potential partners like British Aerospace and German Dasa would be reluctant to go into partnership with a state-owned company, and as a result Air France would lose out in the international air flight market.

So the dialectic is a spiral in the long run, in Ollman's sense (1971, 58), not simply a cycle. Obviously this cannot continue indefinitely; some sort of qualitative change must occur eventually.

Throughout the planning–market spiral both markets and planning get more complex and varied in different countries. The causes include the expansion of corporations and markets, the development of information technology, and the enormous accumulation of world financial capital. As corporations expand, their planning process gets more complex and includes manufacturing, collaboration among mutually supportive corporations, contracts with relevant government agencies, careful attention to various financial and stock market prognoses, concern with international political developments that will probably affect the price and availability of raw materials as well as markets for their products, and so on. Government and bank involvement in planning has also gotten more complex and includes the provision of more and more GDP-type market indicators, regulation of unstable financial markets, Fed and central bank financial planning, allocation of capital to promising industrial sectors or locations and to education in needed industrial skills. One could describe such planning as a mutual coordination of a complex production process among diverse corporations, suppliers, banks, and government agencies.

As for markets, consider the increasing complexity and instability of financial markets, including various derivatives (puts and calls, hedges, options . . .), currency speculation, and international loan interdependence.

One advantage of thinking dialectically is that it counteracts the tendency to construct a static model of capitalism based on a particular time period. An example is the theory of the now-extinct Marxist parties of the 1970s, for whom the main, or only, dialectic was the relation between factory workers and factory employers. This theory ignored the enormous economic and political and family developments that had occurred since 1850, developments that brought huge changes to both labor and capital, and to their consciousness. Obviously the capital–labor dialectic is not the only dynamic in operation.

Another example is the Walrasian general equilibrium model, which idealizes nineteenth century manufacturing capitalism as a static free market economy. This model assumes that all later developments are simply new forms of market exchange. But the increasing complexity of production techniques has promoted the development of corporations, corporate planning, oligopolistic planning, investment planning, Fed planning, and government planning; the market has produced its own opposite. The model also assumes that a market economy tends toward equilibrium and generally is not far from it, but is thrown off by "shocks" and by government interference. But the development of banks, financial and stock markets, mutual and pension funds, currency speculators, and so on has produced chronic instability, which Hyman Minsky has analyzed so well. As a result, general equilibrium has vanished from this "post-Walrasian" world, except as an intricate professional technique for economists to display proudly. Veblen was probably the first to make this point.

Various economists have made similar criticisms of general equilibrium theory. Michio Morishima (1992, chap. 2) asserts that the "standard" Hicks-Arrow-Debreu model applies to precapitalist commodity production, with no bank credit, no capitalists, and little innovation—and no corporations and no market power, I would add. "The world of general equilibrium theory is in fact a dream world" (p. 198). Allesandro Vercelli (1991), Ingrao and Israel (1990), and Yves Balasko (1988) make other criticisms.

When economists construct a static, idealized model of the "free market" and of planning, for example Hayek's planning fantasy, the effect is to distinguish the two completely. One is good, the other bad. But in reality the two have continually changed each other through their constant interaction, and both have gotten more complex. Thus the static models have blinded such economists to most of economic reality.

However, the partial equilibrium assumption is still a useful device for studying the relational tendencies between a few variables in abstraction from their context, before bringing the context back in. It's a start.

I believe that a concrete dialectical study of current capitalist dynamics will help us understand their complexity.

7

Rational Political States Today

Now we look for transformed *(aufgehoben)* versions of Hegel's political state that may have appeared in recent years. According to George A. Kelly (1978, chap. 4) such a search is almost hopeless; Hegel's type of state scarcely exists today. But we can try anyway.

Hegel's explicit objective in PR was to systematically describe how the state of *his time* worked, more or less, to promote freedom. He also explicitly denied any reference to the future. The state he was describing, a state that involved a delicate balance between a decaying feudalism and a developing capitalism, had already reached maturity, at least in England, and had to change into something else before long. To be sure, less developed societies would still be catching up for a while as their economies matured. "When philosophy paints its grey in grey, then has a shape of life grown old" (PR, preface, 13). As Marx complained, Hegel's state depended on medieval survivals (Berki, in Pelczynski 1971; Marx 1970, 75, 96, 113–114).

The main survival was feudal property, which as Hegel noted (¶63A) was mostly disappearing because the inability to sell such property was a limitation on the duke's freedom. But Hegel asserts in ¶305, 306, 306A that such property tendentiously produces a national consciousness in the nobility because it keeps them out of the individualizing capitalist economy. Their lifestyle doesn't involve making money or working; they are above that and can get involved in larger causes, such as getting land mines banned. The same point applies to the monarch. But these two feudal survivals were crucial mediators in Hegel's constitution.

Consequently, we cannot simply apply Hegel's model of the 1820 state to some contemporary state, either to evaluate the contemporary state or to interpret its functioning. Instead, we can use Hegel's model as a guide that can show us how to look for the dynamics and interdependencies of a current state.

But to use Hegel's model it is necessary to be aware of the differences between Hegel's time and ours, of the changes that have occurred since 1820 and that continue to occur. These changes will alert us to the changes we will have to make in Hegel's model to adapt it to the present. For instance, since feudal property and the nobility have become irrelevant we will need to look for something new that performs a similar function; and if no substitute can be found we can expect, and look for, a deficiency in the promotion of community consciousness in Hegel's sense. And if the deficiency does not appear, we can infer that the feudal nobility were not as important as Hegel thought they were. Something different was promoting community consciousness.

We begin by reviewing the main changes in the capitalist economy and class structure since 1821, because the economy and its class structure supply most of the materials that are available for constructing a government. These changes will suggest the sort of changes we need to make in Hegel's model to study a contemporary state.

The decline of feudalism, of which Hegel was fully aware, has been essentially completed. However, monarchs still exist in a few states such as Britain, Belgium, and Holland and command respect as symbols of the individuality of the state and its ultimate power of decision. In other states elected presidents have the same function; but some elected presidents, like Kurt Waldheim, symbolize difference rather than unity. In such cases we have to look for some other symbol of national unity, or for the effects of its absence.

Unlike monarchs, the feudal nobility has become irrelevant. The nobility, located in the House of Lords, played an important part in the mediation process for Hegel. They were essentially detached from the capitalist economy and so could play a neutral, mediating role between the conflicting industrial, banking, and commercial interests. But with the continuing decline of feudalism and increasing irrelevance of the Lords their mediation became less and less effective. Indeed, in the United Kingdom the hereditary Lords are gradually being abolished. So we have to look for other mediators, or for the consequence of inadequate mediation.

The civil servants also played an important part in the mediating process. According to Hegel, their interest was in the universal, the well-being of the whole society. Consequently they promoted a universal consciousness in discussions with legislators. Hegel himself was in this class, so he undoubtedly idealized it somewhat.[1] According to Kelly (1978, chap. 7, point 2) the class Hegel was referring to in Prussia included academics, churchmen, lawyers, and doctors, all well-educated. Because of their secure professional position and high status they, like the nobility, remained detached from particular occupational interests and problems and could develop and promote the big picture. Such a class scarcely exists today. Professors and civil servants are ideologically allied with the various economic interests and classes and are called on to represent those interests in society and government. Social researchers have to go where the money is, and a good proportion of research money since 1950 has come from military or corporate-sponsored research foundations that have rather definite research agendas (Diesing 1991, chap. 8). So there are few people left to mediate, unless they come from somewhere else.

Next, class structure has changed. In the early 1800s there was no separate and distinct working class, according to MacGregor (1992, 160). Craftsmen, small merchants, and machine tenders were fairly similar in outlook and experience, and people or their children moved from one occupation to another. But before long, with the rise of mass production, a distinct class of workers developed, with its own residential areas and unions. The rapid rise of unions in the mid-nineteenth century added a new participating class to the political scene, whose potentialities were emphasized by Marx.

Then mass production continued to develop and became more complex. As a result, corporations had to get larger and larger to maintain economies of scale and scope, as with automobile production (Chapter 6 above; Chandler 1990; McDermott 1991). Vertical mergers combined the various raw material producers, parts manufacturers, and final assembly plants into a single corporation spread over several states and countries. Horizontal mergers, for instance Studebaker-Packard and American Motors, improved both economies of scale and market power in oligopolistic markets. The increase in size and complexity made production planning a much more complex task, involving several layers of management and planning specialists. Banking representatives became prominent on corporate boards because banks were a crucial source of capital, financial services, and information about the economy.

One effect of the increasing complexity and interlocking of corporations was the establishment and expansion of an extremely powerful corporate executive class, including hordes of low and middle managers aspiring to top positions. This class has several subdivisions, including finance, insurance, real estate, and industrial executives. It has scarcely any resemblance to Hegel's bourgeois class of craftsmen and small merchants; indeed, it more resembles the feudal nobility in power.

Another effect was the production of many new types of labor, including various management levels. The simple labor-capital distinction of the mid-nineteenth century was gradually replaced by a rich variety of occupations (Wright 1978, chap. 2). Consequently the class consciousness on which Hegel (and Marx) depended became a more complex affair. Various segments of labor—temporaries, farm workers, white collar, blue collar, foremen, line balancers, data processors, software developers—could develop opposed interests and varying degrees of sympathy for management (V. Smith 1992). In addition, as Hegel observed, advertising and conspicuous consumption has increasingly produced a consumer consciousness that interferes with class consciousness. Also ethnic consciousness, which Hegel apparently thought would gradually vanish with the development of capitalism (¶209R) has survived and even intensified. David Harvey (1985) discusses the various kinds of consciousness that are produced in cities. Consequently, Hegel's goal of a collective consciousness has become much more complex, with variations in different countries.

Next, the increasing speed of transport and electronic transmission of money and information enabled corporations to expand worldwide and become transnational. This gave them decisive market power over both labor and government. The threat of moving production elsewhere could be used to extract subsidies from government and concessions from labor. Actual transfer to another state or country would dump out workers and their union completely. As a result the power of labor, and of local government, declined dramatically, with variations in different countries. There have been moves to internationalize labor cooperation, but they have a long way to go.

The continuing globalization of capitalism has weakened another source of community consciousness that Hegel emphasized, the family. Remember, for Hegel the family and the corporations were the two roots of the state as a community. Families used to live in one neighborhood or city for several generations, forming a large network of friendships, and still do in some countries; but now children, and parents, move all over with job opportunities, corporate transfers, poverty and desperation ... Similarly, neighborhoods—which T. H. Green, Bernard Bosanquet, and other Hegelians emphasized—have declined or disappeared as stable communities. People, and increasingly young children, are on their own, as families and neighborhoods disappear.

In summary, the community–individuality balance has shifted decisively: Individualism now dominates. The estates of nobility and middle class that represented community have essentially become irrelevant; the main class conflict has shifted from nobility–business to corporations–labor; and various other conflicts have emerged, including ethnic, religious, and gender conflicts. Consequently any remnants of community might be found in the corporations, or in some new location.

The Search for a Rational Political State

To review: We are looking for promoters of community, that is, institutions that produce a collective consciousness in the members of government, a shared interest or concern for the well-being of the whole society, and a shared understanding of the conflicting occupational interests. Second, we need communication channels that bring local information about locally experienced problems to the attention of government members. Such information allows the deputies to construct a larger picture of how the economy and other institutions are functioning, what problems are occurring and how they are related, and what might be done to remedy those problems. Presumably the information channels also bring feedback on the effects of previous government policies. They should also run in the other direction to bring information about the policymaking process back to the citizens. Third, we need people and agencies that mediate between the enormously diverse interpretations, demands, and wails of anguish that are transmitted to government. Fourth, we need policymaking and implementation structures to manage the economy and related institutions, like law, police, education, foreign relations.

In short, we need, first, consciousness-raising institutions; second, information channels; third, an enormous amount of mediation; and fourth, policymaking and implementation structures. For Hegel the corporations performed the first function in part. So we should look for voluntary associations that probably have some base in the economy and some regular connection to government. This would not include strictly local organizations like Kiwanis and Elks that have mainly sociability and charity functions. Veterans' and retired persons' associations are more difficult to categorize; they do represent a kind of occupational consciousness with a definite interest in the political process.

The second function, channeling information between citizens and government, is also performed by the occupational associations. And remember, for Hegel "it is of the utmost importance" that the masses—the workers, the poor and unemployed—should be organized and represented, though they were not in his day (¶290A). So we should look for some sort of such association too, probably labor unions.

As for the third function, mediation, we will have to look for new possibilities in the data. The mediators whom Hegel described have mostly disappeared.

A Trial Run: The U.S. Political State

Let us begin by practicing on an almost hopeless target, the U.S. political state since about 1940. Remember, Hegel thought that the United States was not even a state; but it must have developed into one since his day. First we look at the appearance; then with Hegel's help we move from appearance to essence. Essence and appearance correspond to what Creel Froman (1984) calls "the two American political systems."

American politics officially appears to be centered in the three branches of government. Congress makes domestic policy and appropriates money for policy implementation; the executive makes foreign policy and administers both foreign and domestic policy; the Supreme Court invalidates unconstitutional acts of the other two branches. In making policy, Congress consults experts and holds public hearings; and the executive department also consults experts and interested parties. Also the two branches normally work closely together, consulting constantly in committee hearings and informal contacts. If they disagree, each can check the other, with the veto power and the budgetary power, and these powers should encourage them to discuss, bargain, compromise, and reach agreement. But the ultimate power is held by the American people, the voters. If the voters do not like the performance of one or both branches, they can turn them out and elect someone else.

Toward the Essence

In 1996 the Census Bureau reported that 44 percent of Americans of voting age were not registered to vote. Of the remaining 56 percent, about half vote in a presidential election, and about 33 percent vote in off-year congressional elections. 25 percent voted in the most recent local elections here. Why? Remember Hegel's observation that when voters are an unorganized, individualistic mass, one's vote is practically irrelevant to the outcome, so there is no incentive to vote (¶311R).

How do people decide whether and how to vote? Election campaigns. Incumbents are constantly presenting themselves to targeted groups of voters as promoters of the people's interests: providing jobs, protecting health insurance, balancing the budget, lowering taxes, insuring an adequate national defense, and so on. Challengers present a different picture of the incumbents: handing out pork to special interests, raising taxes, producing budget deficits, promoting unemployment, and so on. Campaign consultants, public relations experts, and opinion pollsters advise on what to say and how to act, to present a proper (ganda) image to voters (Newman 1993). For example, they will gather a "focus group" of voters, present various campaign statements to them, and study their reactions. The statements eliciting the most positive reactions are transmitted to the speech writers for inclusion in the candidate's speech. Recently such consultants have noticed expressions of disapproval of the dishonesty of campaigns; so they include statements about the opponent's dishonesty and immoral character in the campaign speeches.

Who pays for campaigns? Mostly corporate executives, individually or organized in political action committees (PACs). Froman (1984, 118) reports that in 1982 there were 3,149 PACs, of which 2,155 were business related; labor had 350 PACs, and 644 were miscellaneous. (Jerome Himmelstein 1990, 141, reports 1,682 corporate PACs and 394 labor PACs as of 1984.) For example, private health insurance companies have contributed over $25 million over ten years to the two parties. In 1994 the health care industry, including hospitals and doctors, contributed over $2 million to Florida state legislative candidates. As more campaign money has come in, campaigns have gotten longer and longer, until campaigning is intense and almost continuous.

How do the corporate PACs decide whom to support? First, they support those incumbents who have pushed through their desired policies. The PACs find out who is supporting them from their Washington lobbyists, who discuss proposed legislation with legislators. The division of labor is clear: Congressional staffs write up legislation, assisted by trade association representatives (lobbyists), and members of Congress present a public front for reelection. When one sees a ten-second bite of a congressional speech in the House, one notices less than a dozen other congressmen sitting there, probably waiting to give their speech. Members of Congress probably do not know the details of all the complex bills their staffs draw up; for example, Michael BeVier's sponsor in the California legislature once said in a committee hearing, "Hell, if you want to know about the bill, ask them. They're the ones who wrote it," pointing to BeVier and his partner (1979, 234–235). BeVier adds, "But such candor is rare among California legislators."

However, once the staff has worked out a bill, the senator or the representative has to maneuver it through Congress by bargaining and "logrolling": I'll vote for your bill in committee if you vote for mine; I'll vote for it if you add this amendment; I'll follow the party leadership if they include my bill, and so on.

Second, business PACs also support challengers somewhat, especially challengers who make speeches in support of their desired policies, in order to establish a good working relationship. However, since challengers, even if they win, won't get in for another year or so, the payoff for supporting incumbents is more immediate.

In the case of presidential candidates the matter is more complex. Thomas Ferguson and Joel Rogers (1981, chap. 1) studied the 1980 presidential campaign in detail. "Any presidential race can be usefully thought of as consisting of two campaigns. One is public, and unfolds through the primaries and party conventions, speeches and debates, and final polls and voting results. The other is more obscure, and features the complex process by which pivotal interest groups like oil companies, international banks, weapons producers, labor unions, and even foreign companies coalesce behind particular candidates to advance their own ends" (6). In other words, the second campaign is a contest for campaign financing, which a candidate needs to stay in the first race. In 1980 each of the Republican candidates started with strong business backing. Connally had long-standing corporate interlocks with Texas corporations and banks and attracted protectionist backers, such as the National Association of Manufacturers, with early anti-Japan speeches. Then Connally got "mousetrapped" when Henry Kissinger asked him to write and deliver a controversial speech on the Middle East, which Connally thought would bring in the support of the Kissinger-Rockefeller–Council on Foreign Relations–Trilateral Commission multinationals and the oil industry. But when Rockefeller didn't show up at a fund-raiser, the free-trade interests got suspicious and avoided Connally, and the protectionists, angered by the free-trade speech, also stopped contributing. Connally ran out of money and dropped out.

Ronald Reagan had started with California business and religious right supporters; then after Connally's disappearance, he courted the multinationals, starting with California's Bechtel Corp's George Shultz and Caspar Weinberger. The latter two also represented the CFR and the Trilateral Commission. Reagan managed to keep the multinationals on his side by promising cabinet appointments (including appointments for Shultz and Weinberger), forming policy councils, and negotiating over who would be vice president. (The multinationals had been moving to George Bush.) And so on. Finally, we can ask, who benefits from all the legislation written by corporate lobbyists and congressional staffs, including all the riders and the bills that are quietly rushed through Congress in the last hours before adjournment? Also, who benefits from the work of the executive branch advisory committees? The answers to all the above questions should lead us from the appearance to the essence of the political process.

For example, the $2 million that the health care industry contributed to Florida state legislative candidates in 1994 paid off:

> A House committee unanimously approved a bill rewriting regulations for health maintenance organizations that treat Medicaid recipients. . . . The measure was loaded with dozens of special-interest amendments—many sponsored by committee members who either had received substantial campaign contributions from the medical industry or have personal financial stakes in how the bill turned out. . . . Lobbyists . . . persuaded lawmakers to add provisions to the bill that would benefit various elements of the medical industry, often while increasing costs to taxpayers and consumers. . . . Half an hour before the meeting started, all 166 seats in the Capitol's Morris Hall were taken. . . . Few of the people were casual spectators. Most were lobbyists—and they were there to make sure their clients' interests were pro-

tected. For the most part, they were successful. (*Sarasota Herald-Tribune*, March 24, 1996)

Second example: The 1995 Job Creation and Wage Enhancement Act appeared to be intended to benefit workers; but "it turned out to be a laundry list of regulatory reforms that would gut environmental protection" (*NRDC Bulletin*, February 1996).

The Essence

Main sources: Weidenbaum 1977; Destler 1980; Schwartz 1977; Domhoff 1979, 1983, 1990; Sklar 1980.

The campaign contributions and lobbying scenes direct our attention mainly to the large corporations, including banks and insurance companies. But to study corporations we will have to change terminology. A "corporation" in American English is a business enterprise. So, to avoid confusion, we shall call Hegel's "corporation" a "trade association," following Weidenbaum (1977, chap. 16), or a "policy organization."

"Most large corporations maintain one or more full-time representative in the nation's capital" (Weidenbaum 1977, 243). The Washington, D.C. corporate offices, ranging from small to large, 1) provide headquarters with information on current government policies and proposed policies; 2) lobby legislators to communicate the company's views and suggestions on pending legislation and executive actions; 3) supply corporate headquarters with analyses of current and proposed executive programs, plus advice on how the company could respond most effectively. The analyses are based in a few cases on in-house think tanks but mostly on consultation with public policy organizations such as American Enterprise Institute, Heritage, Cato, and Brookings, funded mainly by corporate foundations.

Many corporations also have representatives on advisory councils in the executive branch (Weidenbaum 1977, 252ff). Each executive department or agency has its own advisory council, staffed in part by representatives of the relevant corporations. Thus the Industry Advisory Council of the Department of Defense had twenty-six representatives of major defense contractors as members in 1972, and the Treasury Department consults committees of the American Bankers' Association and the Security Industry Association in the financing of the public debt.

Trade associations, such as the American Bankers' Association, perform the same functions as do the agencies of individual corporations. They inform members of congressional and administrative developments, testify before Congress or state legislators, make recommendations and provide data on proposed legislation, draft or help draft legislation, and lobby individual members of Congress (Weidenbaum 1977, 263). Each branch of industry has its own trade association, such as Aerospace Industries Association, Iron and Steel Institute, American Medical Association, Pharmaceutical Manufacturers' Association, American Petroleum Institute, and Timber Operators' Council.

Many corporate executives also have joined broader policy-oriented organizations, such as the Chamber of Commerce, the National Association of Manufacturers (NAM), the Business Council, and the Committee for Economic Development (CED). These organizations do not simply advise and lobby Congress; they make policy. The Council on Foreign Relations (CFR), whose membership overlapped that of the CED, planned the postwar economy—including the IMF, the World Bank, and the UN—in meetings held between 1939 and 1942 in close collaboration with the State Department and continuing in State Department committees to 1945 (Domhoff 1979, 101–109; 1990, chap. 5–6; Shoup and Minter, in Sklar 1980, 135–156). The Marshall Plan also grew out of these plans and was administered by a CED leader. In the late 1950s the CFR emphasized the importance of defending South Vietnam against the Communists, and in the early 1960s the council pushed for an accommodation with China to counter the Soviet threat (Domhoff 1983, 85ff). However, in 1968 President Johnson's fourteen Wise Men, of whom twelve were from the CFR, told Johnson to give up on Vietnam, which he did (Domhoff 1990, 136).

In the early 1970s David Rockefeller, assisted by Zbigniew Brzezinski and top Brookings Institution and CFR leaders, created the Trilateral Commission to coordinate economic planning among the United States, Japan, and western Europe (and to maintain U.S. supremacy; Sklar 1980, 76ff). Brzezinski was the first commission director, and membership included thirty-six CFR members in 1976 (Sklar 1980, 204). President Carter's foreign policy was developed by the Trilateral Commission and implemented by commission members, including his national security adviser, Brzezinski (Schwartz 1987, 107). Carter himself was a member of the Trilateral Commission, along with George Bush, and pushed Trilateral domestic policies as well. Ronald Reagan also was supported by Trilateral members, who influenced his foreign policy through Shultz and Weinberger, among others. Weinberger also pushed through the CFR-recommended (not Trilateral-recommended) big military buildup (Domhoff 1983, 88; Stockman 1986, 114–119, 300–323). Then Bill Clinton took in the CFR-Trilateral group by pushing successfully for NAFTA.

Prominent members of these policy organizations are also appointed to top and middle positions in the executive branch and to presidential policy commissions (Domhoff 1983, 136ff). Reagan appointed at least forty-three CFR-Trilateral members (Domhoff 1983, 140–141). He also appointed some fifty Hoover Institute, thirty-six Heritage Foundation, and thirty-four American Enterprise Institute members (Himmelstein 1990, 150). These are business-funded think tanks. Earlier, CFR director Henry L. Stimson served as Secretary of State or Secretary of War in three administrations, and CFR president Norman H. Davis met frequently with top executive officials (Domhoff 1990, 115ff).

All presidential appointments must be approved by the Senate, and approval can be a lengthy process. The 2,500 or so higher level nominations are submitted to the relevant Senate committee or subcommittee, which consults the relevant trade association for its approval or preferences (Riley 1987, 87–90). Thus Department of Agriculture nominations go to the Senate agriculture committee, which consults agribusiness. Since presidents know that Senate approval is necessary, they often consult informally with the relevant subcommittee beforehand about possible nominations. "It is primarily through this informal process that the Senate manages to guarantee that clientele interests will be well represented in the upper echelons of the federal bureaucracy" (Riley 1987, 90).

In addition to trade and policy associations, there are also "special interest" associations, such as AARP and labor unions, which lobby Congress and executive agencies. There are also critics, especially environmental and "public interest" groups. "Most of these critics are critics by choice. They are interested in a subject and dissatisfied with the way in which the government is handling that subject. Many have also developed the personal style of the critic, never satisfied, always questioning" (Riley 1987, 118). The agencies and subcommittees do listen to critics and special interests, especially in the public hearings that are required by law. However, they have no legal obligation to take public testimony seriously (Riley 1987, 127). Public hearings, plus occasional compliance with the demands of the critics, show that the agencies do listen to the public and do try to serve the public interest (Riley 1987, 119, 128). We have moved from essence back to appearance.

For example, I once attended a public hearing of the Nuclear Regulatory Commission, whose clientele are the utilities with nuclear power plants. Well over one hundred people had signed up to testify against some NRC waste-disposal arrangement, and the auditorium was fairly full. I noticed three well-dressed older gentlemen sitting together up near the back row; they were whispering together, pointing derisively at the speakers, and laughing quietly. I got their attention and said "Shh!" whereupon they all immediately froze in an upright position and sat quiet, solemn, and staring forward.

Back to the essence. So far we have seen the second function, information channeling in both directions, and the fourth function of policymaking, in part. However, the trade associations and policy organizations also perform the first function of consciousness raising. The trade associations presumably promote an occupational consciousness by describing the congressional or executive policy situation from an occupational perspective, and their lobbying and policymaking on executive and congressional committees promotes the general industry interest.

The policy organizations promote a more general class consciousness. This process begins with the selection of leaders for, say, the Business Council. The leaders come from specific corporations but are supposed to speak for business in general. Specific executives are recommended for leadership positions, and government advisory positions, when they have demonstrated a broader vision. "When executives were asked to identify the criteria they applied in evaluating such candidates, . . . they generally alluded to the capacity to transcend the immediate imperatives of one's own company and express a broader vision" (Useem 1987, 151).

According to Michael Useem (1987, 145ff) corporate executives develop a broader vision when they serve as outside directors on a variety of corporate boards. "Said another American executive: 'You're damn right it's helpful to be on several boards. . . . You get a more cosmopolitan view—on economic matters, regional differences, international questions, these days'" (Useem 1987, 146). So, promising executives get recommended for other corporate boards, then to government advisory boards, and eventually to positions in a policy organization.

Policy organization leaders can still experience a conflict between the need "to advance the interests of their particular business and attend to the needs of the corporate community as a whole. . . . [They] tend ultimately to rise above their particular interests to form a class which (episodically) acts in a unified and cohesive way" (Schwartz 1987, 139).

The class consciousness of such leaders is strengthened by organizational retreats to discuss the state of the economy. For example, the Business Council held a four-day conference in Hot Springs, Virginia, in May 1972, including speeches by government officials, panel discussions, and staff reports. Government participants included the chairman of the Federal Reserve, secretary of the army, secretary of state, CIA director, secretary of commerce, chairman of the Economic Advisors, and a special presidential assistant (Domhoff 1979, 73–74). The Bohemian Club in San Francisco held similar retreats attended by top government officials (Domhoff 1974). Metropolitan business clubs such as the Links Club and the Century Association in New York City and the Algonquin Club in Boston bring together corporate leaders from various associations and thus strengthen collective consciousness.

A shared class consciousness does not eliminate all differences of opinion among policy groups. Domhoff (1979) notes a persistent policy dif-

Rational Political States Today

ference between the internationally oriented CED–Business Council–CFR–Trilateral Commission group and the more national, conservative, antilabor National Association of Manufacturers and Chamber of Commerce. The NAM represents mostly smaller domestic manufacturers hurt by foreign imports, so it favors higher tariffs and nontariff barriers, lower taxes, less regulation, less welfare, less government spending. The CED-CFR group represents mostly large multinationals and banks. Jeff Frieden comments, "The Trilateral Commission is the executive advisory committee to transnational finance capital" (Sklar 1980, 69). In the 1950s and 1960s this group favored low tariffs, foreign aid, larger military spending, and more active anticommunist and pro–free market foreign policies. We have already discussed these two groups in their role as campaign contributors in the 1980 election.

So there is still room for mediation. Mediation presumably occurs during those conferences and four-day retreats and metropolitan club meetings; the leaders, or those wishing to establish a reputation for having a broader vision, would do the mediating.

Mediation may also occur on the executive agency or department advisory boards. Weidenbaum comments that "another function of advisory committees is to provide a mechanism for the exchange of views by various private interest groups" (1977, 255). However, such mediation would be limited to a specific occupational group. Each executive agency is advised by its own occupational group (Destler 1980, chap. 9). The Defense Department gets advice from military contractors; the Agriculture Department listens to agribusiness, in Destler's cases, and so on. "It is [the farm community], in the main, who continues to write farm bills" (Destler 1980, 120).

But who would do the mediating on those executive department boards? The civil servants would not, quite unlike Hegel's civil servants. Michael BeVier (1979, 33ff) reports his experience with Housing and Urban Development in an attempt he and others made to develop a subsidized housing project for the poor:

> HUD reminded me of a deaf, half-witted great aunt who is tolerated only because she had money. Actually, doing business with that agency's numerous divisions was like dealing with a dozen such biddies at once, each of whom had to be satisfied in turn, and none of whom cared what the others wanted. One division talked only about architecture, another about operating costs, another about affirmative action programs, another about rent levels, and so on. The architecture division would insist on changes which substantially increased costs, without any apparent concern for the fact that another division was demanding that costs must be decreased to allow more money for operations. . . . I remember months of frustration, frantically

rushing from one division to the next. . . . We had to get each of them to compromise enough to end up with a single development package that could in fact be built.

In this case the civil servants had to be mediated, the opposite of Hegel's cases. Possibly professors on department boards might mediate; in 1972 they constituted 58 percent of various advisory boards, compared with 31.5 percent from business and 6 percent from labor (Weidenbaum 1977, 252–257). According to Joel Bleifuss, many of these professors have their research sponsored by the corporations who are regulated by the agency. For example the EPA scientific advisory panel that reviewed the pesticide Alar had eight members, of whom seven were consultants to the chemical pesticide industry (*In These Times*, October 30, 1995). Consequently, their mediation efforts probably would be acceptable to chemical company representatives on EPA boards.

It is doubtful that mediation occurs in broader advisory committees. For example, the 1974 President's Committee on Food included representatives of Agriculture, State, Treasury, and Budget (Destler 1980, 108–120). There was frequent conflict, bargaining, and coalition-forming among the departments and their business advisors. I. M. Destler sums up the problem:

> For in the management of food policy the U.S. government faces a dilemma common to other policy areas as well. The department with most of the information and day-to-day action tends to emphasize one set of policy concerns to the neglect of others. Yet to transfer authority from it to a White House–based coordinating body would (insure that) . . . the biases of departments and agencies . . . merely become replicated in the organizational and jurisdictional divisions with the Executive Office of the President. (1980, 128)

Similarly, the 1993 Magaziner–Rodham Clinton committee on Medicare included representatives of the American Medical Association, insurance companies, large corporations who were already paying insurance, and small businesses who were not and didn't want to. Mediation and compromise were unsuccessful, and the committee failed.

However, some mediation occurs at the state and local level. Allen Whitt (1982) reports on five mass-transit referendums in California between 1962 and 1974. In general, the automobile and oil industry opposed mass transit, and central-city capitalists such as banks, insurance companies, and corporations with downtown headquarters favored mass transit. But the corporate boards of the two groups were tightly interlocked (Whitt 1982, 152, 158, 160ff). Also the corporations on the two sides did business with each other and wanted to maintain good relations (116). One politician termed the process, "interlocking corporate good will" (117). As a result, when one side strongly financed a particular campaign, the other side remained silent, and vice versa (34). "None of the campaigns was allowed openly to divide the business community into contending segments. Behind-the-scenes efforts to promote consensus and cohesion apparently succeeded rather well" (205).

Marc Mizruchi (1992, chap. 10) similarly asserts that interlocking corporate networks are the main mediating influence on corporations with differing interests, producing political cooperation. Mizruchi's assertion is based on a study of fifty-seven large corporations.

The limited scope of mediation suggests that occupation-specific legislation such as farm subsidies, the military budget, steel import controls, Medicare, or bank deregulation will be pushed by a specific trade association. If no other association objects strongly it will pass; otherwise conflict will occur.

For example:

> Out of the spotlight of Medicare debate, the nation's private health plans have obtained a series of technical changes in the overhaul approved by Congress—changes that stand to reap them billions of dollars. ... The change was one of several—dizzyingly technical and built on what many would consider minutiae—that the industry vigorously pushed for. ... In pressing for increases in the money that private plans could collect for treating Medicare patients, representatives of four trade organizations decided that the Group Health Association would take the lead, industry sources say. Association officials ... argued their case before House Speaker Gingrich ... and House and Senate Committee heads and staff. (*New York Times*, December 10, 1995)

Sometimes, rarely, a top policy organization will intervene and try to work out a compromise. Useem (1984, chap. 4) provides some examples.

But the policy organizations seem mainly to have emphasized the setting of broad policy frameworks. One example, the construction of the postwar economic order in 1939–1945 by the CFR–CED–State Department, and its management during the Cold War period, has been mentioned. Domhoff (1990, chaps. 5–8) has described this process well, based on many other studies. First, the CFR asked how large a world economic area the United States would need to maintain a healthy, growing economy. The United States needed raw materials and export markets (Hegel, ¶245–248); an adequate area for both would be East Asia, Latin America, and the U.K. colonies. Western Europe was later added to the area. The United Kingdom could be persuaded to open its colonies to the United

States through judicial use of lend-lease and other military and financial aid. Japan must be prevented from dominating East Asia in its "co-prosperity sphere." Within this area, trade in raw materials and U.S. manufactures could be promoted by: persistent lowering of tariffs and trade barriers via GATT negotiations; an export-import bank for short-term loans; a world bank to promote Third World investment (in U.S. capital goods); and a monetary fund (IMF) to help countries with temporary balance of payments deficits. The Keynesian national planners at the Treasury Department objected to the State Department–CED "business internationalists"; the State Department won (Block 1977, Ch. 3).

There was also some opposition to the detailed tariff and banking proposals from high-tariff NAM members, New York banks, and the United Kingdom, among others. CED members and CFR economists mediated and negotiated compromises on these policies. Also from 1955 to 1962 the newly developing southern textile industry wanted tariff protection, so the free-trade southern Democrats in Congress turned protectionist. CED members again negotiated a compromise, including loopholes for higher tariffs and import quotas to protect threatened industries. Such compromises continued in the late 1970s in steel and other import-threatened industries.

This 1940s–1960s policy framework included, domestically, acceptance of unions, labor-management wage bargaining, pensions, and occupational safety and health measures. The CFR-CED leadership came from large banks and export-oriented corporations, so they did not see labor as an enemy. Their focus of interest was rapid international expansion, and labor troubles would hinder that. Besides, by 1950 wage bargaining was firmly established in export industries like autos and steel. So labor leaders were welcomed to board seats on the CFR; later the Trilateral Commission included four top AFL-CIO officials.

A rightward shift in the policy framework occurred in the early 1970s. The causes of this shift are hypothesized differently by different writers, such as Schwartz (1987, chap. 13), Vogel (1989), Himmelstein (1990, chap. 5), and Domhoff (1990, chap. 10). The declining profits and worsening position of U.S. businesses in the world economy, including the first postwar trade deficits, must have contributed to this shift; also the full employment and large wage increases of the late 1960s; perhaps also the disruption by the radical New Left and the rabid environmentalists, resulting in many new government regulations.

At any rate, the CED and the Brookings Institution moved right about 1975, getting close to the NAM (Domhoff 1990, chap. 10). Don Regan and Martin Feldstein were conservative CED members who worked for Reagan. In 1972 or 1973 the Business Council set up the Business Roundtable, consisting of CEOs, to lobby Congress. The "right turn" involved lots of money for many old or new conservative foundations and think tanks like the Heritage Foundation, Cato, Hoover, American Enterprise Institute, Manhattan Institute, Olin, Bechtel, Coors, Pew, and Scaife (Vogel 1989, chap. 8)—also Hudson Institute, Foreign Policy Research Institute, Bradley, Educational Affairs, Institute for Contemporary Studies, Georgetown CIS . . . These foundations mostly (except Bechtel, for instance) expressed the ideology of the smaller national corporations represented by NAM. For example, twelve of the sixteen current directors of the Cato Institute are top executives of small corporations. Because of the huge increase in funding, these conservative institutions replaced the more liberal internationalist Ford, Carnegie, and Rockefeller Foundations as the dominant source of research money, and U.S. social science moved rightward (Diesing 1991, chap. 8).

The conservative foundations also sponsored policy studies, news analyses, syndicated articles, propaganda films, radio programs, and a talent bank of conservatives available for government appointment (Peschek 1987, chap. 1). The change also involved larger campaign contributions, advertising, and much lobbying. The new policy was antilabor, and unions were mostly shut out of government after 1980. The change also continued the previous emphasis on lower taxes, less regulation, less welfare, much more military spending, and import controls.

The Trilateral Commission, from about 1975, disagreed somewhat with this right turn. The commission agreed that labor should be disciplined, for instance by Carter's wage controls, to help make U.S. industry more competitive. But members of the commission preferred to do it cooperatively, by consultation and compromise (Tabb, in Sklar 1980, 212ff., 308ff.). They also emphasized modernizing aging U.S. manufacturing plants, relocating to the nonunion South or to low-wage countries, and promoting trade and détente with the resource-rich Soviet Union. Détente involved reducing military spending, and there Trilateral policy clashed sharply with the military-industrial complex, including both domestic business and government agencies (Wolfe, in Sklar 1980, 533ff.). The conflict raged during the Trilateralist Carter administration, and the military-industrial complex won (Wolfe 1980, 287–288).

Indeed, the conflict continues. The conservative national corporations want more military spending, which benefits U.S. armament corporations, but no U.S. military involvement in foreign conflicts like Bosnia and Zaire. They have also opposed funding for OPIC, which supports multinational investments.

The above account suggests that the United States has indeed become a state with a rational government since Hegel's time. The citizens are the corporate executives and their allies, consisting of pro-business civil servants and politicians, and think-tank and university researchers and propagandists. There is no feudal nobility. The poor, the workers, small farmers, the unemployed do not participate in government, but they didn't in Hegel's time either. Trade unions make considerable campaign contributions, so they do get hearings from a few favored members of Congress; but the overall influence of unions has declined since the corporate policy shift of the 1970s.

The business class is organized in trade associations that promote an occupational consciousness and whose leaders are appointed to government positions. They represent the individualistic side of politics. Class consciousness, the community side, is expressed and weakly promoted by the top policy organizations, who also establish the basic policy framework for each period of several decades. The policy objective of the top groups is to manage the U.S. and the world economy so as to maximize the competitiveness, profitability, and power of U.S. corporations.

The economists and other think-tank researchers and theorists provide the empirical data and predictions, ideas, and policy proposals that would fit this corporate policy objective. The executives of the large international corporations knew in general what they wanted in the 1940s: markets for their capital goods in developing countries safe from Communist influence, plus readily available finance capital for those countries. Later, the executives of smaller corporations and those threatened by international competition knew in general what they wanted: protection against unfair competition, lower taxes, less regulation, less union power . . . But the executives depended on the economists and researchers to work out the economic context, the policy details, and the public justification for the resulting policy agenda. The agenda itself would be worked out jointly in the top policy organizations and trade associations.

For example, in the 1950s and early 1960s there was much corporate-supported research on the stages of economic growth, the Third World modernizing elite, and the need for export industry rather than import substitution for rapid growth. The corporate basis for the research was the desire of the large corporations to export to developing countries, and later to move or expand their own operations there. In 1976 the Smith-Richardson foundation started supporting supply-side economic theory, which became central in the Reagan budgetary process, which supported the domestic agenda of national corporations (Himmelstein 1990, 149).

The politicians serve as coordinators and administrators of the policy-making and implementation process. If the policies work as predicted, the campaign money comes in and they get reelected. If they don't work, campaign money goes to the opponents. The politicians also serve as public fronts for the policy organizations: They take the blame and retire or are retired from office, for, say, an unpopular war to defend (military) democracy and free trade in Vietnam, promoted by the CFR-CED (Prewitt and Stone 1973, 235–236).

That's freedom to become what one wants to be, isn't it?—for a few, anyway. And besides, for the others, it's better than Stalinist or military tyranny (Prewitt and Stone 1973).

The foregoing account omits the complex intercorporate business planning, including banks and insurance companies, that is described in Munkirs (1985), Ciscel (1989), and Mintz and Schwartz (1985). Such planning occurs within the policy framework maintained by the policy organizations through government. For example, in 1941 corporate executives used their planning skills and communication networks to organize war production for the military, and this military-industrial collaboration has continued since then (Waddell 1994).

Notice that there is quite a large gap between the appearance and the essence in this case. The essence is a government by the top policy organizations and the specific trade associations; the appearance is a government by representatives of the voters. This gap creates a problem: What keeps the voters convinced that they are running the show?

One part of the answer is the steady stream of news analyses, syndicated articles, radio and television programs and talk shows provided by the business-supported conservative think tanks. Another part is the politicians' carefully crafted presentations of their policy proposals and diagnoses. Specifically, much of Carter's 1976 campaign strategy and speeches were worked out by Trilateral Commission members such as Samuel Huntington and Zbigniew Brzezinski, plus the usual opinion pollers and tacticians (Sklar 1980, 203–207). All the above sources provide the facts, values, and ideas for the public to think about politics. Also all the above sources, and especially the news media, focus on elections as the key political event. So of course voters believe they are central; they make the crucial decisions. And if politicians don't carry out their campaign promises, they can be replaced at the next election. Of course other factors are also relevant.

Now we can ask, Is the U.S. government actual? Does it work? If we look at the results, we would have to say that it did work very well in the 1950s and 1960s, the "Golden Age of Capitalism." The postwar international institutions provided the regulatory framework that enabled the large corporations to export and expand, and produced rising profit levels until 1965. Foreign aid, beginning with the Marshall Plan and continuing with World Bank loans, Eximbank loans, and so on, provided the money that developing or recovering countries needed to buy U.S. products. The U.S. military and CIA kept watch on any "socialist" politics that threatened to nationalize the foreign properties of U.S. corporations, such as United Fruit in Guatemala in 1954, and established military governments that would protect corporate property in those states. U.S. labor was rewarded by a corporate-sponsored "social structure of accumulation" that provided regular wage increases and other benefits in return for labor quiescence and collaboration. The dollar became the world's reserve currency, thus facilitating U.S. corporate investments abroad and preventing balance of payment problems and inflation pressures.

In the early 1970s the Owl of Minerva appeared, and top executives came to recognize the central contradiction of this political regime: The successful U.S. corporations, with their industrial exports, had produced their own competitors, in Germany, France, Italy, and so on. Also a monetary contradiction appeared: The accumulated international reserve dollars produced the Eurodollar market, unregulated, which produced monetary instability, overinvestment, and defaults. The source of monetary stability had produced instability.

These and other problems, such as the ending of the Bretton Woods regime in 1973, called for intensive dialogue and mediation between the national and internationally oriented policy organizations. Instead, top-level disagreement intensified, and politicians' ambivalence consequently increased. Disagreement was intensified by bureaucratic rigidity and Cold War hysteria. For example, the Committee on the Present Danger was set up to counter Trilateral attempts to promote détente. So the system has not worked perfectly in recent years; but Hegel's exemplars certainly didn't either.

Corporate States Today

Main sources: Katzenstein 1984, 1985; Scholten 1987; Pekkarinen 1992.

The Hegelian term "corporation" leads us to look at the corporatist literature of the 1970s and 1980s. These writings focus mainly on the small European corporate states, including Austria, Belgium, Netherlands, Denmark, Norway, Sweden, Finland, and Switzerland. According to Lehmbruch and Schmitter (1982, 16): "There are strong reasons to place Austria first on a scale of neo-corporatism, since it ranks very high on all relevant dimensions." Guger tells us that "Austria has been considered as a paradigm of corporatism in all its various classifications" (in Pekkarinen 1992, 338). So we shall look at Austria, while noting occasional contrasts and similarities with other states on the list.

We begin with a Hegelian theme, ¶324, 324R: Wartime forcefully brings the unity of the state to the consciousness of the citizens and thus promotes a collective consciousness. The Nazi terror of the late 1930s and World War II had this effect on the small European states. Indeed in Austria there was terror in the early 1930s, German occupation in 1938, and divided Allied and Soviet occupation until 1955. These terrible events forcefully showed the small states their weakness in a dangerous world and made people resolve to stick together. The rapidly expanding international economy in the 1950s and 1960s also demonstrated the vulnerability of small states to international competition: Their domestic industries and jobs could be severely weakened by competition from high-tech or low-wage production. Everybody would suffer from that, so everybody should work together to prevent it.

The Austrian corporate structure as of 1955 was built on pre-1930 institutions. A strong labor movement with many unions is united in a single peak union, the ÖGB, or *Österreichischer Gewerkschaftsbund*. Most large industry has been nationalized, including all the companies the Nazis took over in 1938 and returned in 1945, and those returned by the Soviets in 1955. Nationalized industries are united in a peak holding company, the ÖI, or *Österreichische Industrieverwaltung*. There are also many private companies, mostly smaller, united in the Federation of Austrian Industrialists, as well as foreign-owned subsidiaries such as Siemens. Some banks are private, some public. Thus business and finance are more divided and diverse than labor. Consequently business and labor are approximately equal in power, depending on how one defines power.

The above interest groups are represented politically in government-licensed economic chambers, with compulsory membership. The Chamber of Labor speaks for wage and salary earners and consumers; the Economic Chamber represents private business, commerce, and industry; ÖI represents public industry; the agriculture chamber represents farmers. Here we have Hegel's corporations. The private peak associations such as the ÖGB cooperate closely with their respective corporations. The corporations provide information, advice, and policy analysis to the private groups and receive policy proposals from them.

Corporations in turn provide members for fifty-six or more executive advisory committees (Katzenstein, 1984, 76ff). Business, labor, and other relevant interest groups are equally represented on each committee and work out policy details on, for example, taxation or distribution of investment capital or retraining of labor. Civil servants and economic experts also sit on these committees and play a neutral, mediating role between business, labor, and agriculture (Katzenstein 1984, 64; Pekkarinen 1992, 349). Business, labor, and agriculture also work out general economic policy on the Joint Commission (or Parity Commission), which is the top policymaking organization. Decisions are unanimous, not by majority vote.

Of the two major parties, the Socialist Party mainly represents labor and the People's Party mainly represents business. However, the two parties governed in coalition from 1955–1966, and again since 1986, and share similar policy views.

Mediation occurs at all levels of policymaking. The ÖGB mediates between different unions—those representing nationalized industry, foreign-owned industry, and smaller producers such as textiles (Pekkarinen 1992, 224ff). It also mediates between different union policy groups—Socialist, Communist, and Catholic—to work out agreed industrial policy proposals. The Economic Chamber engages in the more difficult mediation between different segments of business such as large exporters and import-threatened small business. Cross-mediation also occurs; for example the Catholic faction in the labor movement supports the People's Party and thus mediates between the parties. Labor owns stock in the national bank and sits on its investment and monetary policymaking board. Civil servants mediate the policy proposals brought by labor and industry to the Joint Commission and the other advisory committees. Finally the presidents of the labor, agriculture, and economic chambers meet prior to the convening of the Joint Commission to work out an agreement if necessary.

The generally agreed policy framework is to increase productivity, maintain full employment and wage increases, control inflation, maintain or increase exports, and protect or restructure or compensate small import-threatened industry such as textiles. There have been shifts of emphasis with changes in the economic climate; for example, increasing budget deficits in the late 1970s made a balanced budget more important and full employment less important in the 1980s (Pekkarinen 1992, chap. 11). Also financial support shifted from the high-employment, nationalized industries to small business (Pekkarinen 1992, 255–257).

Mediation in policy implementation is also important but difficult. The problem is that implementation is usually monitored, and adjusted, by the interest group most closely involved; but this group would tend to adjust implementation in its favor. For example, the chemical industry would be intensely aware of a new chemical regulation, but workers and nearby homeowners might be marginally aware of it. Consequently the union and the industry association would both have to monitor implementation and report to their members.

The results: An unemployment rate of about 1.5 percent in the 1970s and about 3.5 percent since 1980 (Pekkarinen 1992, 343) was maintained by countercyclical monetary and fiscal and wage policy, bank lending to ailing firms to maintain their workforce, public works construction in recession times, shorter work weeks and longer unpaid vacation times in the public and nationalized sectors, a shift of employees from declining to expanding product lines, vocational retraining, and early retirement. A low inflation rate was maintained by countercyclical fiscal policy in the early 1970s, including budget surpluses and repayment of government debt, and control of prices by the Joint Commission. Export growth and 3.5 percent GDP growth was achieved by policies of attracting foreign investment, wage restraint by unions, government promotion of private saving and investment focused on selected high-tech export niches, and, later, expanding capital exports and production abroad.

Most of the foreign capital imports and Austrian product exports were from and to Germany, supported by the policy of tying the Austrian schilling to the Deutschmark in 1973.[2] In other words, Austria opened itself first to the most convenient and promising part of the threatening world economy. The increasing Austrian foreign investments since 1988 were focused on eastern Europe; current plans are to shift up to one third of domestic production to eastern Europe, especially Slovakia. By 1990 Austrian capital exports were triple the amount of imports (OECD, 1993). Domestically, weak companies were supported by national bank loans and temporary subsidies for new machinery; some survived, others failed.

Policymaking was flexible, with fairly rapid adjustments of errors. For example, when wage increases in the early 1970s put pressure on business, the unions exercised more restraint after 1975. When Austrian steel began sustaining large losses in the 1970s due to world overproduction, the losses were at first covered by oil industry profits to maintain full employment; then workers agreed to ten unpaid vacation days per year and earlier retirement; then government subsidized and modernized older plants; then companies shifted from unprocessed steel to manufactured goods and specialty engineering products and, in 1981, to electronics (Katzenstein 1984, 207–215). In general, policy adjusted to short-term world market pressures, provided a cushion and retraining for market losers, and as a result maintained roughly the same national division of income.

Note that there is no planning–market reversal in this sort of policy process. Neither dominates the other, and each influences the other. Policymaking adjusts continually, incrementally, and locally to change in world markets and adjusts the national market, but of course it cannot control the national or world market the way oligopolist planning did in the Chapter 6 cases. Katzenstein comments, "The Austrian model is based on ... a parallelism of plan and market" (1984, 60). Contrast, for example, the many changes in Austrian steel policy in the 1970s and earlier with the rigidity of U.S. steel, which was followed by sudden collapse and multiple plant closings in 1979–1983.

The Austrian experience suggests the possibility that a rough, approximate planning–market balance can be temporarily maintained if the planning itself is dialectical. That is, Joint Commission planning consists of a dialogue among opposites—business, labor, agriculture—in which differing interpretations of prospective economic problems are presented and discussed. Such a process provides triangulation, that is, multiple sensitivities to, and interpretations of, emergent local and international developments. In contrast, planning in a successful U.S. oligopoly focuses only on the short-term interest of the corporation, with the two goals of maximizing profits and market share dominating the planning. Sometimes there is room for slightly different perspectives on the board; more often the CEO, such as Roger Smith of GM, decides autocratically.

The OECD survey (1993, 45) summarizes the Austrian economic performance:

> As a small open economy . . . Austria has followed a trade-oriented growth strategy and progressively liberated its import and capital flow regimes. The pressures of international competition have favored a rapid shift of resources into high-productivity lines of production, resulting in a pace of technological progress above the OECD average. The access to foreign markets has allowed economies of scale, degrees of specialization, and choices for consumers and investors which otherwise would have been impossible to realize in the small domestic market. . . . Austria has experienced an historically unprecedented period of strong growth in living standards. . . . Productivity, which had initially been one of the lowest in the OECD, is now one of the highest in the open industrial sectors.

The OECD adds that despite a small 1992 downturn in which Austria did better than the OECD Europe average, future prospects are good because of full EC membership and increasing investment in eastern Europe.

In addition, Austrian air pollution was the lowest of any highly industrialized country in 1985 (Kornai 1992, 179).

Now we look briefly at a contrasting corporate state, Switzerland. Swiss unions are weak and small, representing from 30 to 38 percent of the work force in the 1970s, about half of Austria's percentage (Katzenstein 1984, 101). They are also politically divided and conflicting, including moderate metalworkers and watchmakers, militant public employees, and some radical unions. Most unions also disagree strongly with Socialist Party programs. The big multinational corporations and banks are closely related through interlocking corporate boards, the Swiss Federation of Commerce and Industry, and other peak associations. There is also a Swiss Association of Small Business and a Swiss Farmers' Union.

Farmers, small business, big business, and labor are all represented in the policymaking process, and each has veto power. Big business is obviously the most economically powerful of the four by far; but big business supports full employment and investment in agriculture and small business. Agriculture enjoys tariff protection and five-year plans for expansion in certain areas and has expanded production greatly. Labor favors high rates of R&D in big business, knowing that it will bring them higher wages and more job security, which they are not guaranteed by business-dominated Switzerland (Scholten 1987, 87).

The Swiss example brings out one aspect of democratic corporatism, fairly equal participation in policymaking. Big business and especially the banks could control the state; indeed, Blaas (in Pekkarinen 1992, 369) calls Switzerland a case of paternalistic liberal capitalism, not corporatism (he doesn't ask, What induced the paternalism?). But business consults on equal terms with other interest groups, including labor. In interviews with members of the Swiss inner business circle, Kriesi found that the Swiss labor federation was named the largest number of times as having a decisive voice. The employers' federation was second (Lehmbruch and Schmitter 1982, 143). In the 1970s, government was run by a four-party coalition including the weak socialists. Conversely, in Austria the Socialist Party, supported by most labor, took power in 1970 and kept it; but in 1976 it strengthened the representation of the People's Party and their small-business supporters in a new Industry Planning Commission. Socialist Austria has developed policies that produced stronger export industries and GDP growth; for example, in the 1960s the ÖGB union decided that since industrial productivity was low on a world scale, investment was more important than wage increases. Full employment was next on the list, to be achieved by higher exports; wages could come later, and did come in the 1970s. Later Austria decided that balance of payments was of immediate importance, and downplayed wage growth again (Pekkarinen 1992, 350ff). Conversely, multinational capitalist Switzerland produced agricultural prosperity, high wages, and only 1 percent annual GDP growth in the 1970s. Of course other factors also influenced these results.

In Austria and Switzerland, the outward appearance of policymaking is fairly close to the essence and can be described briefly. Austrian election campaigns last a few weeks and are quiet and uneventful. Seven of the nine provinces have long been governed by a Socialist-People's coalition. The national parliament routinely approves the proposals of the Joint Commission and the advisory boards. The Swiss parliament meets for twelve weeks a year. Swiss political parties are financially weak (Scholten 1987, chap. 3) and so can't campaign much. Any organized group has the right to demand a referendum on a proposed policy; in practice the threat of calling a referendum is a bargaining chip that each corporate group can use in the advisory committee bill-drafting process. A referendum would delay the already slow bargaining process further (Papadopoulos 1995, 427–429). But the main appearance is the sequence of policy outcomes in both countries, which benefit all major occupational groups and preserve a broad range of career opportunities for all.

Of the other corporate democracies discussed by Katzenstein, the Low Countries have institutions similar to Switzerland, and the Scandinavian countries are similar to Austria. Charles Sabel (1982, chap. 5; 1989; Piore and Sabel 1984), Daniela Gobetti (1996), and others have discussed a similar political organization in the small regional *economica diffusa* of northern Italy, such as Emilia-Romagna. Here production and finance are coordinated within a region by collaborative labor-management planning in association with regional banks. Both management and labor are organized in regional associations, and local politicians mediate between them (Gobetti 1996, 67–69).

Pekkarinen (1992, chap. 1) distinguishes Austria from the Scandinavian countries on a different dimension. He describes Austria as consensual; that is, labor, industry, and agriculture came together out of national solidarity, like a family. Katzenstein puts it this way: Labor participates in government "not as a pressure group attempting to extract economic benefits for its members but as a participant shaping its decisions" (1984, 37). The Nordic countries came together through conflict and bargaining; labor and business learned that they had to collaborate because neither could dominate the other but each could make great trouble for the other. So they came together to avoid destructive class conflict. Thus relative power equality is more important in this sort of corporatism than in the Austrian-Swiss-Dutch consensual version, and community consciousness is less important than in the consensual states.

When we compare the Austrian model with Hegel's 1821 model, we see the effects of changes in the world economy since Hegel's time, plus some details unique to Austria.

First, in both cases war was a factor promoting national unity; but for little Austria war was a terrible shock, with three great armies rolling over it and occupying it for seventeen years. Hegel's Napoleonic wars weren't that bad. The drastic change to "total" war since 1914 has made Hegel's moderate remarks about war, ¶338–339, obsolete: "States recognize each other as states"; "agreements about taking prisoners"; "war be not waged against the peace of family and private life." The result is a much stronger basis for collective consciousness than in Hegel's time. War has replaced the nobility as a source of community.

Since 1960 or so the rapidly opening world economy has presented a longer-term threat to the small states, especially to their local industry. Industry had to become and remain world-competitive, or it would be bankrupted or bought out by the rising multinationals, and that would impoverish the whole country and shift control of the national economy abroad. "Industrial peace is crucial for the Swiss economy, which, because of its relatively open nature, requires a high degree of international competitiveness" (Scholten 1987, 87). "Germany's partition after 1945 made the country smaller and enhanced its perception of vulnerability and dependence on world markets. A consensual style of politics came to prevail" (Katzenstein 1989, 347).

An example of what could happen to the small states is provided by the Emilia-Romagna economy of northern Italy. This formerly independent cooperative community, eulogized by Charles Sabel and others, gradually came under the control of large multinational corporations in the 1980s (Harrison 1997, 81–89). In 1977 the multinational conglomerate Olivetti bought Sasib, one of the largest companies in the district, as part of a large food processing machinery empire. Sasib then bought various smaller local firms using Olivetti capital, beginning in 1984, plus eight larger firms spread through Italy, and then set up operations in five foreign countries as well. Other multinationals, including Nestle, Kraft, and Unilever, then bought most of the remaining local firms. Presumably technological collaboration continues on a local level, but production has become more standardized for multinational markets, and the goal is maximum profit for the MNC owners. The flexible specialization lauded by Sabel and others is disappearing.

The recognition of this threat has provided the main source of community consciousness for the small states.

The Austrian corporations operate like Hegel's corporations, with one big difference: Labor and small farmers have their own corporate representatives on the Joint Commission. Hegel would have been very pleased with that. As a result, Hegel's insoluble problem of unemployment and poverty has been solved, temporarily. Labor and farmers have an equal voice, so they can sensitize and remind business and banking representatives of farmer and labor problems and worries: job security, wages, Hungarian agricultural imports, and so on. Consequently, full employment and wage increases have been among the basic policy goals since the 1960s. They certainly were not policy goals in Hegel's England during 1800–1821. All representatives on the Joint Commission could collaborate in analyzing and dealing with these problems and could share the costs: unpaid vacations, public works spending during recessions, risky bank loans to ailing firms, job retraining paid for by highly progressive taxes, rent control, employer-paid unemployment compensation, more efficient export industries . . . Business marketing experts could advise farmers on new processing techniques to compete with the superior quality Hungarian chicken imports; small urban and suburban wine growers could be subsidized as scenic tourist and weekend attractions.

Interestingly, the English 1820 solution to unemployment and poverty has been reversed in Austria and Switzerland. As Hegel observed, the surplus workers could be exported to the colonies to start a new life (and import surplus British goods). Now, in Austria and Switzerland guest workers are imported from poor countries to fill the vacancies in boom times and are sent home in slack times. Thus continuing full employment has been achieved at the expense of the guest workers. However, surplus capital goods are still exported to the developing eastern European countries, as in Hegel's time.

The mediation process is different from the process in Hegel's time, as we expected it to be. Mediation between different branches of labor and among different industries still occurs within the peak associations, and the civil servants on the Joint Commission still mediate between labor, industry, and agriculture. But there is also mediation through cross-cutting corporate membership. Thus labor representatives on the National Bank board can bring labor's point of view into discussions about investment decisions and, conversely, can educate union leaders about the world of finance and its problems. Similarly, Catholic workers in the People's Party can maintain that party's sympathy and partial understanding of labor and thus keep the two major parties in a more amicable relationship.

Such cross-cutting mediation prevents the corporations from becoming entirely separate entities, each with its own class consciousness, united only at the top. This latter phenomenon is called "pillarization" and has occurred in the Netherlands (Lehmbruch and Schmitter 1982, 24, chap. 2; Scholten 1987, 126, 137). Hegel warned of the danger of pillarization in ¶255A. The corporate leaders promoted pillarization through rhetoric and symbolic politics, to maintain power over their own "baronies" and to prevent drifting of followers away to some other or some new corporation. As a result the larger economic picture is not transmitted down the pillars, so the rank and file maintain their narrower class or occupational consciousness. Another result is to rigidify the process of bargaining and consensus formation at the top, since the leaders are as interested in maintaining their own control as they are in protecting the whole country. Ziya Önis (1995, 111) notes that such rigidity has also occurred in Sweden.

But if the followers continue to press for advantages for their own occupation or class, then the leaders have to provide some direct benefits in order to maintain their own position. Consequently a shared Joint Commission–type policymaking for the whole economy tends to turn into bargaining over the benefits. This easily leads to distribution of more benefits than the economy can provide (Scholten 1987, 13), and the benefits become mirages. This degenerative tendency in corporatism shows the crucial importance of mediation and consciousness raising at middle and lower levels of the corporations, as Hegel noted.

Finally, the problems that the corporate states face are more desperate than the problems Hegel discusses. Hegel's state had the task of managing its own economy: providing infrastructure, education, welfare, controlling prices, safety inspections, and crime. The problems are within the state, and the goal is to maintain a society in which people can develop themselves as they wish. In the contemporary small states the problems mainly come from outside, from the world economy, and the goal is to survive in a continually changing world. (Belgium is an exception; its internal cultural differences are a continuing problem.) Consequently, policy in the corporate states must be flexible, ready to adapt to some new technology, new political developments in eastern Europe, new multinational corporate investment shifts, emerging markets for new products, new OPEC policy, and so on. Policy changes might require retraining of workers for new occupations, family moves to different towns or to Hong Kong (where multinationals like BASF have branches), early retirement, gradual dissolution of some industry, and so on. Such shifts constrain individual self-development to take unexpected and perhaps undesired forms. Hegel may not have liked that. In addition a prolonged world economic stagnation might break up the whole collaborative arrangement, with the desperate, near-bankrupt corporations downsizing and going their own way, as Schmitter worries (Lehmbruch and Schmitter 1982, 277).

Also, short of a world economic crisis, the world economy impinges most directly on the consciousness of the multinationals like Volvo, Shell, Siemens, and Nestle. These companies are always necessarily ambivalent between a national, community consciousness and a world-market competitive consciousness. Consequently, mediation within the Commerce and Industry Federation, the peak industry association, will always be difficult. A failing company will desperately ask for help, and a successful expanding multinational will be able to go its own way, ignoring others' troubles. Labor and agriculture do not have that option (Scholten 1987, 140–142).

Recent developments in Swedish politics illustrate these world economic pressures, along with other problems (Marshall 1996). Large Swedish corporations are increasingly interested in seeking higher profits and lower wage rates by moving production abroad. Wages have increased in part because of growing rivalry between blue-collar and white-collar workers; the whites want to maintain their higher wages and the blues want to catch up. Consequently labor has essentially abandoned the policy of wage restraint in industries threatened by foreign competition and has focused on companies with higher profits as a basis for wage demands. The result is inflationary pressure and a disintegration of the centralized bargaining and policymaking process.

The problem of world finance capital is worse. Money knows no national boundaries; it moves anywhere in the world in seconds, in pursuit of expected low inflation rates and high expected profit or interest rates. No state can control the flow of finance capital any more. Consequently, the small corporate states are forced to maintain a low inflation rate and nondevaluation policy to prevent finance capital flight. Without adequate finance capital, the social democratic policies of targeted investment, full employment, strong export industry, adequate wages and hours, countercyclical fiscal policy, and so on become impossible (Notermans 1993; Moses 1994). Ton Notermans and Jonathon Moses disagree on details but agree on the above picture, including the top priority of anti-inflation policy and monetary stability.

Austria understood this problem in the early 1970s and linked the schilling to the Deutschmark as a monetary anchor. By 1980 the monetary link had taken top priority (Notermans 1993, 138). The other countries caught on later.

"When philosophy paints its grey in grey, then has a shape of life grown old." In Hegel's state, community consciousness was produced by mediation, mainly provided by the remnants of the feudal community and the civil servants. In the small corporate states the main source of community is their small size and the growing threat (and opportunity) from the world economy. Community has gotten smaller, and the economic basis of individuality has grown ever larger. The imbalance increases. The small states have joined or are joining the European Union (EU), which is moving toward a common currency by 2002 and gradually toward a common economic policy.

The development of the EU is a complex, multifaceted, indeterminate process, but at present the individualist aspects are developing faster than the community aspects (Marks et al. 1996). The individualist aspects are called "negative integration" (Marks et al. 1996, chap. 2); they consist of strengthening the European Common Market by eliminating tariffs and other trade restrictions, setting up a common currency with standard interest rates and reserve requirements set by a central bank, and establishing uniform standards for financial and insurance services. The trade restrictions that are being reduced include selective government subsidies, product quality and safety standards, transport weight and safety standards, and national employment qualifications for particular occupations. Insofar as such standards are made uniform for EU member countries, products, transport, and workers can move freely within the EU. The effect of continuing negative integration is to enable people and corporations, their money, and their products and services to move anywhere in the EU; this fosters individuality and helps business.

The community aspects, called "positive integration," are focused almost entirely on industry and agriculture. Nearly 80 percent of total EU expenditure is currently devoted to promoting the economic development of poorer regions and countries, such as southern Italy, Greece, and Spain; encouraging new industrial development in areas of declining industry such as steel; and maintaining subsidies for small farmers (Tsoukalis 1997, 202–219). So the community being developed is an industrial, and of course financial, community in which the richer areas redistribute wealth to the poorer industrial areas to make them more equal, and in which farmers are also protected. Environmental protection regulations have also been strengthened. EU funds come mainly from customs duties and 1 percent of the value-added tax (VAT); so consumers pay for industrial development (Tsoukalis 1997, 215).

Local community-support measures involving the concerns of the middle class, workers, and the poor have mostly been left to the individual member states. These measures include health and safety rules at work, health and retirement insurance, education, welfare, and public goods such as parks, public radio, and the arts. Many member-state representatives, and also Jacques Delors, have strongly urged the adoption of more community and socialist-oriented policies, such as worker participation in management, equal pay and opportunities for women, a charter of workers' rights, a minimum EU wage, and so on. In the 1980s, such policies were blocked mostly by U.K. Tory representatives and also by European business federations. Business has been much more active at the EU level than labor has (Tsoukalis 1997, 115, 121–137, 275).

Apparently the main aim of the federation of European employers is to promote industrial growth in order to maintain European competitiveness with the United States and Japan. Other concerns are present but secondary.

The preparation for joining the EU common currency created a new set of problems that put heavy stress on the Austrian policymaking process: drastic budget-cutting to reach the EU target; resulting recession and unemployment worsened by the German recession (Germany faced the same budget problems); 5,000 business failures in 1995; a "dialogue of the deaf" between business and labor over a proposed wage freeze; and even disagreements between the two coalition parties, Socialist and People's. A big issue is whether to develop a coalition of the small corporate states to counter German-French hegemony or to become subservient to German politics.

But these are temporary stresses. The EU will be a new chapter in world history, which at least has transcended the many centuries of European wars.

Notes

1. Marx pointed out this idealization of the civil servants; but Marx in turn idealized the future industrial working class. It's hard to avoid idealizing something—corporate executives, the market, some future government, our country, the Third World modernizing elite, rational individuals . . .

2. In 1973 the world fixed-currency regime established in 1944 was ended, and national currencies began to float freely. A fixed or rising currency would attract foreign investment and later promote domestic investment abroad, whereas a falling currency would temporarily promote exports but then contribute to inflation and capital flight.

8

The Useful Dialectic

Finally, we examine how dialectical thinking can help us locate persistent problems in some current institutions—family, economy, and government—and help us or someone to devise solutions; that is, we shift from structure to agency. Here we follow Hegel's example. Hegel used his dialectical understanding of political structures and processes to lecture and write about constitutional changes that were occurring or should occur in Württemberg, Prussia, and England (Bogdandy 1989, 240).

Social Problems

We begin with the family. Since only two adults are involved, the actions of each should have a strong effect on the development of the marriage. In no other social relation can one person be so efficacious, or ruinous, as in marriage. So knowing the dialectic can be quite useful here.

Marriage is an endless learning process. The most difficult thing to learn and accept is the oppositeness, not merely difference, of the beloved. The difficulty consists first in coming to recognize our own onesidedness, and after that to accept and come to understand the Other. This is perhaps more difficult for men, because as Hegel observed, men tend to focus on achievements in the external world, on getting things done, rather than on people's inner feelings. We naturally think that this is the normal way to maturity: learn some skills, get a job, learn your way around the world, accomplish something. How could that be onesided?

Learning proceeds through conflict and surprise. However, knowing about dialectic should lessen the surprise and facilitate recognition of one's own onesideness. After all, everything is onesided and needs its opposite to complete itself. This in turn implies mutual respect, partnership.

In a partnership each partner is better at certain tasks, so a division of labor is worked out accordingly. The assignment of tasks produces further conflict, and this calls for mediation, discussion, dialogue. After all, that's how dialectic proceeded in Plato, didn't it? Continuing conflict and dialogue gradually produces understanding of the other—and of oneself. Such understanding also enables one to absorb some of the outlook and skills of the partner, and perhaps to develop hidden abilities and sensitivities. Men have a sensitive but undeveloped "feminine" side, and vice versa. That's how a continuing synthesis proceeds: Each opposite absorbs some of the other, while remaining opposite.

So far we have discussed sharing and combining; but combining requires separateness. Community requires individuality and difference. So each partner needs time away from the other, to maintain separateness. Also people must accept difference, disagreement, in some areas; dialogue has its limits.

Next, knowing about dialectic (and reading the master–slave dialectic in the *Phenomenology*) can sensitize a person to the dominance–submission relationship and its instability. In Hegel's time the husband was culturally defined as dominant: He was the breadwinner, and he owned and managed the family capital. We have learned what suffering and conflict such a relationship can cause; and women have, with much effort, shifted the culturally defined relationship toward approximate equality since then, assisted by economic developments. The dialectic of the family has gradually, over two centuries, produced the changes in women that induced them to struggle for redefined family roles.

The problem is that a dominance–submission relationship is readily, painfully apparent to the submissive partner but not to the dominant one. He will feel that everything is fine, things are normal, and will be shocked by the wife's strange behavior or when she suddenly moves out. What happened to family values? Instead, he has to look at himself and ask, "Do I feel satisfied with this marriage because I'm getting my way? Am I ignoring her wishes, her feelings? Am I doing my share?" To answer these questions adequately requires a developed people-orientation rather than an exclusive task-orientation, so some men will find the questions to be puzzling. Probably the master in the *Phenomenology* didn't think of himself as a master either; he was just an ordinary hardworking farmer, with lazy slaves.

Finally, people change over time, and each partner has to accept and adapt to the other's changes. I omit discussion of all the problems of personal maturation, because Hegel doesn't discuss them.

Next we consider the planning–market dialectic of Chapter 6. An understanding of this process should be helpful to government and corporate officials involved in managing segments of the economy. The basic point, which such officials undoubtedly understand, is that neither a pure competitive market economy nor a totally planned economy is possible. Each, when it dominates the other too much, is unstable and tends to produce trouble and perhaps a reversal of domination.

A standard problem, noted in Chapter 6, is that successful planning gets routinized. Success tends to blind the planners to the changes that market processes and technology are always producing; the planning rule is, "If it works, do it again, even better." But in addition one tends to look for problems in the same location where they have appeared before, instead of being sensitive to hints of new troubles of a different kind. Conversely, unregulated markets tend to run wild until the smaller competitors are eliminated by bankruptcy or buyout and the remaining oligopolists learn to regulate the market. The problem, then, is to develop a combination of moderate, limited competition and limited, flexible planning.

The Austrian Joint Commission has succeeded fairly well at this task. To summarize the solution briefly: First, planning, like family, should be a partnership of opposites whereby each side contributes its own perspective, insights, and skills to the planning dialogue. The opposites could be business and labor, as in Austria, or domestic and multinational corporations, as in the United States, or agribusiness and small farmers' cooperatives. Next, the world economy and financial system, a complex planning–market mixture, set the limits or constraints within which corporate planning must operate. Even the United States oligopolists could not control the world market, and Austrian planners certainly do not. Within these limits, planning is focused on helping weaker competitors, up to a point, and thereby maintaining the community consciousness that sustains the political system and its planning. Workers accept wage restraints and work harder in order to temporarily subsidize or restructure declining industries or to strengthen export industries. Industries help maintain fairly full employment by shifting workers to higher demand areas, reluctantly accepting shorter work weeks and longer paid vacations, and by encouraging retraining. Planners look for new export opportunities that some troubled corporations can shift into in order to expand their production. Some price and wage level limits are negotiated and set countercyclically, but competition occurs within these limits and in the large nonregulated areas. Government subsidizes public goods like the arts, libraries, parks, education, and public transport. (For details see Katzenstein 1984; 1985.)

The main problem in developing or maintaining a temporary plan–market balance is the adaptation of planning to existing production processes and market structures. As markets and technology have become more complex, successful planning also has had to become more complex. For example, Alfred Sloan's planning process, which partly separated production planning and financial planning, was appropriate to a developing finance capitalism in which centralized financial markets coexisted with decentralized and later international production processes. Later, Japanese, Swedish, and Austrian industrial planning was appropriate to a developing global market in which industrial nations competed with one another.

Increasing globalization calls for more complex industrial-financial-social planning, for instance in the future European Union. Bennett Harrison (1997, chaps. 6, 7, 9) has described a transnational form of financial and production planning now occurring in Japan, Europe, and occasionally the United States. The planning is distributed across a network of large corporations and their subsidiaries, which are connected by cross-ownership of shares, exchange of technical specialists, long-term loans and purchase agreements, and mergers—but most basically by trust. Such networks are called *keiretsu* in Japan. Planning includes coordinating production plans, sharing the relevant technical knowledge and collaborating in further research, sharing information about market opportunities and barriers in foreign countries, and changing plans as market circumstances change. "Each partner brings to the marriage its own specialty—technology, financial power, access to government regulators or procurement officers—and its own constellation of small firm suppliers" (Harrison 1997, 138). Usually the largest firms in a network provide the finance and purchase the products of the smaller firms, whereas other firms provide technology or distribution channels or local government contacts, but the mix varies. Some networks connect several relatively equal firms plus their subsidiaries, whereas others are dominated by a lead firm (Harrison 1997, 144–145).

Such planning consists mainly of sharing information and technical knowledge, including especially information about each firm's production plans. Henry Milner (1989, 32–37) argues that such planning is market-efficient because it reduces uncertainty and thus enables a network of firms to collaborate in production. He also points to the importance of mutual trust in reducing transaction costs, citing D. C. North (1981). When firms can trust each other, based on long collaboration, they need not maintain legal staffs and emergency plans to guard against possible cheating, nonpayment, cancellation of contracts, or other trickery. Trust also can be maintained by the enforcement power of a leading firm in the network.

A possible future form of planning for a global economy is suggested by Paul Cockshott and Allin Cottrell (1997, 349–355). They propose to use computers with Lotus 1-2-3 type programs to solve up to a million simultaneous equations. Each equation would state the causal connections between several economic variables. Thus the effects of a change in one variable, such as exchange rates or oil prices, on all other variables can be calculated by the computer. Such planning, like the planning Harrison describes, would be indicative, that is, it would supply information rather than commands to local governments, manufacturers, unions, and banks on the expected future changes in supplies, prices, unemployment, and so on. These units in turn can supply feedback on their changing plans, which would be used to update the central plan.

In other words, such planning can provide information on expected changes in employment, prices, and supply levels, which would enable producers and investors to adjust their production and investment plans, and governments to adjust their short-term countercyclical policies. The result would be a close and constant interaction between planning and markets.

Such planning may seem utopian; but its predecessor, the Keynesian Klein-Goldberger economic model of the 1950s, involving twenty-two or more simultaneous equations (Hoggatt and Balderston 1963, 177–180) would have seemed equally utopian a century earlier. Mathematics has long been an increasingly important part of the forces of production; computers have destroyed Hayek's argument against the possibility of industrial planning. And since in this new kind of planning labor would be involved, as in Austria, Sweden, and other countries, planning would not be limited to the goals of maximum economic growth and ever-increasing profits. It would include goals of minimal unemployment; job security; challenging rather than routine, meaningless work; and minimal environmental destruction.

A third example of practical use, in metropolitan politics, is provided by Joel Rogers (*In These Times*, October 18, 1998). He begins by describing a dialectical process of urban decay that has occurred in various American cities. First, as urban population expands, more middle class and richer people move to the suburbs. Moving is encouraged by government construction of roads and other infrastructure out to the suburbs, under pressure from developers and auto corporations. Some of these roads can produce urban destruction; for example Robert Moses's Cross Bronx Expressway ruined a whole neighborhood (Caro 1974, chaps. 36–38).

The result of suburbanization is a lower urban tax base, which produces poorer schools, decaying infrastructure, less welfare, and attempts to raise taxes somehow. These effects encourage more moves to suburbs, including relocation of businesses, banks, and retail stores. Less welfare and less urban employment opportunities increase poverty, desperation, crime, drugs, and police, which encourage suburbanization, business closing or relocation, and protective isolation of remaining rich urban districts.

Some cities try to attract business back into town with subsidies; for example Detroit in 1983 destroyed a whole community, Poletown, to provide free empty space for a GM manufacturing plant. GM was free to shut down the plant any time, but Poletown was gone.

The dialectic here is the community–individuality contradiction. The process begins with individuality dominant: People feel free to move wherever they please, and the suburbs are made more attractive by developers and rapid transport downtown. These moves gradually weaken the urban community: Mobility weakens the sense of neighborhood community because people are moving out and in all the time; a weaker tax base causes deterioration of community institutions, including schools, the arts, welfare, maintenance and repair. A weaker community weakens individual development via worse education, fewer job opportunities, fewer informal social groups, unsafe streets, deteriorating community meeting places such as sports fields, pubs, churches . . . The resulting degeneration and desperation of the underclass frightens others into withdrawing; and so on.

Rogers proposes a policy to reverse this process. First, local, state, and national governments should spend money on public transit systems linking many parts of the city, rather than on highways linking suburbs to downtown offices. This would enable people to both live and work in the city and thus to participate more in city activities. Second, city government should encourage metro businesses to link together through trade, technical and financial collaboration, development planning, and joint marketing and worker training. Such collaboration is similar to the *keiretsu* planning described in Harrison (1997). Government would assist in technical training, financial support, subsidies to new businesses that would enrich the local network, and regional investment funds drawn from local banks and pension plans. Third, government could protect smaller businesses that have urban links to other businesses by maintaining industrial zoning; this would prevent developers from buying up factories and converting them to gentrified housing. For example, Goose Island in Chicago. Also government and local business could attract or spin off new businesses with potential links by redeveloping vacant, abandoned areas and offering other development assistance. But low-wage and polluting industries would not be encouraged to stay.

The result would be increased productivity and an increasing sense of community among local businesses and employees, which would keep them in the city and improve employment and the city's tax base. This would allow the city to improve education, parks, transport, and welfare and thus would facilitate individuality, individual and business development. Finally, a successful development process gradually would draw the suburbs into a metropolitan planning process and develop a metropolitan community.

This reversal-of-domination policy depends heavily on agency; it seems to require a wealthy, intelligent, well-organized, ideal communitarian political organization to descend from the heavens and take over a city government. However, Rogers asserts that "across the country you can already find different pieces of the project I am recommending here." He also lists cities that seem to be moving toward such a policy: Portland, Cleveland, Milwaukee, and St. Paul–Minneapolis (but not Detroit, New York, and Los Angeles). He argues that a potential alliance, waiting to be organized and activated, exists among local businessmen, labor, and other groups in such cities.

A fourth example of practical use consists of maintaining or improving the essence of one's own political system. This use is probably limited to full-time political officials; but officials act on the advice of scholars.

A political insider will probably appreciate the importance of mediation. U.S. top industrialists have long recognized the importance of mediation and accommodation between the international corporations represented by the Trilateral Commission, CED, and CFR, and the smaller protectionist-oriented firms in the NAM and the Chamber of Commerce. But mediation between industry and labor, or between health insurance companies, employers, doctors, and hospitals is more difficult and requires government officials and some source of community consciousness.

Hegel mentions a different kind of mediation in ¶295–297, mediation of civil servants who have developed an individual or department consciousness. One example is BeVier's experience with the "old biddies" in the California HUD, who were concerned only with following the rules of their own department (Chapter 7 above). Destler's account of the 1974 Committee on Food (Chapter 7) is another example; representatives of Agriculture, State, Treasury, and Budget each pushed the concerns of their own department, and nobody cared about the assigned food problem. Apparently such processes are commonplace in Washington. In the first case BeVier apparently succeeded in broadening the HUD officials' consciousness; but on the food committee and similar advisory groups the mediation would have to come from the top.

This problem is bound to be much more serious today than in Hegel's time, because of the great expansion of government activity since then. The expansion in turn was required by the ever-increasing complexity of economic and social life. Expansion requires more bureaucratic complexity, and this inevitably produces a very narrow consciousness in the ordinary civil servant. Hegel's "universal class" has essentially disappeared (if it ever existed), along with the nobility.

Pillarization is another recurring problem, which encourages conflict and pushes all mediation up to the top levels. The solution is cross-membership, which brings members of opposed interest groups together and encourages consciousness-broadening at lower levels. Another possibility is Hot Springs and Bohemian Club–type retreats that bring together members of opposed interest groups.

An experienced insider also will be sensitive to signs of deficient mediation. One example from Switzerland would be an increase in referendum petitions. Interest groups that are dissatisfied with some proposed policy can threaten to call for a referendum, as a form of filibuster. So an increase in referenda is a sign of increasing dissatisfaction and conflict. Phillippe Schmitter (Lehmbruch and Schmitter 1982, chap. 9) discusses various other kinds of trouble that a sensitive politician will have to notice and manage.

Mediation between different segments of labor is even more difficult, as the examples of Sweden, Switzerland, France, the United Kingdom, and the United States show. Labor has become so diversified that migrant or guest workers, corporate data processors, airline pilots, steelworkers, supervisors, bank clerks, and nurses have little in common. For Hegel class consciousness was a crucial step toward community consciousness; but even in the small corporate states, working-class consciousness seems to be the most difficult kind to achieve and maintain at present. Ollman examines the many barriers to working-class consciousness, apart from the growing diversity of labor (1979, chap. 1). The forces of production gradually have torn apart the growing labor solidarity of a century ago.

In the United States, occupational consciousness is perhaps the only achievable and maintainable goal at present for labor. One first step might be to organize the unorganized occupations like nurses and temporaries, and to strengthen weak unions like the Farm Workers. This will require continuing assistance from the richer and more active unions. Continuing association of very different unions also can contribute to an eventual beginning of class consciousness. This step is being taken already, as mine workers help organize janitors, utility workers, and public employees in various cities. There is also a Los Angeles Manufacturing Project, whose goal is to organize Los Angeles's entire manufacturing workforce with the help of stronger unions like the teamsters.

Next, the bureaucratized unions must be democratized, with term limits, circulation of leadership, and more membership participation. This will facilitate the upward communication of membership experiences and concerns and the downward communication of the larger political picture (including new problems), as well as reduce the constant tendency to pillarization, routinization, and insensitivity to change.

Cross-membership can be cultivated in city-wide organizations that include chapters of all unions represented in the city. Such organizations also can get involved in local politics. Another possibility is an organization that unites all union chapters whose members work for a particular multinational corporation. Naturally such an organization also can try to participate in the politics of their corporation.

Finally, union officials will have to deal with the accommodation–aggressiveness contradiction, which has weakened Swiss unions and, even more, U.S. unions since the 1920s, where it appeared as the anticommunist–communist conflict. Both extremes are unstable and tend to turn into their opposite. Revolutionary fervor in the United States always began with conflict among the self-proclaimed vanguards, and this conflict absorbed their attention until they were ousted. Either the corporations were aroused and activated, as in the 1970s, and labor was defeated; or anticommunists took over and the unions became bureaucratized and quiescent. In either case, the result was subservient, accommodating unions. In good times annual pay increases soothed the membership, and a self-perpetuating leadership managed the unions ever more comfortably without membership interference. Even occupational consciousness was scarcely promoted by such unions; all that mattered to most members were pay increases and grievance rights. But in hard times, with downsizing, no pay increases, and benefit reductions, such unions had no active membership that would permit the bureaucrats to resist their corporate bosses. Eventually the aroused members started electing a more aggressive leadership, and quiescence ended.

The solution to the accommodation–aggressiveness conflict, as you must know by now, is a partnership and dialogue between opposite kinds of unionists, the accommodators and the "revolutionaries," or the realos and the fundis. The Swiss and Austrian experience with such dialogue, including mediation by moderate unionists, can show us the extreme difficulties of such a process. But the result could be a flexible, adaptive union, based on an active membership with at least an occupational consciousness. As for class consciousness, the Owl of Minerva cannot help us here.

And Socialism?

The dialectic can help here, but not by making a prediction. Socialism must grow within capitalist development, if at all, just as capitalism slowly grew within feudalism. So we might find some early signs of a future social order developing quietly within the present.

One way to start is by looking for signs of a reversal of domination. Ake Sandberg et al. (1992) provide a detailed account of such a process underway in Sweden since the 1970s. In 1938 labor and employers reached an agreement *(Saltsjöbaden)* that they needed each other and had to work together. Labor wanted good wages and job security, but that depended on economic growth, which management would provide by organizing production and allotting work. That was standard Fordist capitalism, similar to U.S. agreements ten years later. By 1970 various Swedish union locals were complaining about boring, monotonous Taylorized work; and some managers were looking ahead for ways to increase product quality and to redesign production for more complex, high-tech products in a changing world economy. The two sides came together, via conflict of course, on agreements to jointly discuss restructuring of work. Labor wanted skilled, challenging jobs; management wanted profits in a changing economy.

At first management had to provide the ideas for work reorganization, and workers could comment on how they might work in practice. Over the years workers gradually got familiar with the technical problems of job design and production control and could contribute more to the discussion. Management came to appreciate their increased understanding. The redesigned production process also required more detailed worker control. Groups of workers would discuss a production problem, set the pace of work, and shift the flow of materials.

One result was a rich, challenging work process, intense and stressful; another was high quality products, and profits. According to Christian Berggren (1980) worker control at SAAB improved product quality 50 percent over several years. Gradually workers learned to participate in administration, maintenance, quality control, and in the planning and scheduling of tasks. Unions began to emphasize employee responsibility for production planning and sometimes looked ahead to a possible workers' collective. Management emphasized worker commitment to the company, perhaps through profit sharing; more autonomy for production units; limiting management mainly to budgetary and financial control; and shifting the remaining unskilled jobs to temporaries, part-timers, and outsourcing. No participation for them.

Is that socialism? No, of course not. One cannot extrapolate a local, short-run, temporary development into the long run. It merely shows "how a new mode of production can naturally grow inside an old one." The characteristics of the change in this case seem to be: 1) Two fairly equal opposites, each needing the other to be complete and adequate, form a partnership. 2) Their sense of community is reinforced by their weakness in the face of a threatening world economy. 3) The partners gradually, through conflict, work out a division of tasks that fits their special abilities: Management takes care of finance and budgeting and marketing, whereas labor takes care of production. 4) Through practice, and training by management, labor learns to manage its own collective work; it "finds itself in the other" and develops "a mind of its own": unalienated work. 5) To management's satisfaction, another result is higher productivity growth (Gordon 1996b, 145–149).

More recently the municipal workers' union, which is made up mostly of women, has reorganized the welfare departments to achieve both greater efficiency and richer, self-managing jobs. They did this in successful opposition to an attempt by management consultants to fragment and Taylorize and outsource welfare work (Curtin and Higgins 1998, 85–86).

Contrast this development with Soviet autocratic planning. Here management was given its quotas to fill, and labor was given its orders. Consequently there was no development of worker capacity for self-management; workers remained serfs or were forced into servitude, except for in the informal economy. Soviet planning moved *away* from socialism.

Another contrast is with planning at General Motors in the 1960s and 1970s, as described by Maryann Keller (1989, 23–28, 58, 61, 100–103). Here labor was not involved at all. Sloan's organization structure distinguished a central financial planning agency and several semi-independent departments devoted to production planning, and this resembled the Swedish bipolar organization. However, in contrast to the Swedish case, the two planning agencies were "spinning in two separate orbits." Financial planners were concerned with the numbers—production costs, percent return on investment (ROI), a standard quality index; they knew nothing about production. The production departments were concerned with getting maximum financial input; indeed they competed with each other for resources. So instead of a dialogue between opposites, there was a conflict of opposites. The only solution was autocratic rule by the CEO, which occurred in 1980.

To understand how the Swedish development occurred one must look at its larger context: Swedish society, one of the small corporatist societies discussed in Chapter 7. These societies are high in community, and this facilitates labor–management cooperation. David Gordon (1996a) observes that labor–management cooperation is highest in Sweden and lowest in the United States among the developed capitalist countries. Conversely, the United States is highest in the ratio of management-level employees to workers, and highest in the wealth–poverty spread. Poverty rates are highest in the United States and lowest in Sweden and Norway, among developed countries (Milner 1989, 201).

Milner gives a complex, detailed account of the institutions, values, practices, and history that have maintained Swedish solidarity more or less. The account shows that Sweden is fairly similar to Austria in its culture and politics.

An international level of community institutions could conceivably develop eventually in the European Union, which includes Sweden. But the dynamics described briefly in Chapter 6 would seem to make any such large-scale socialism impossible for quite some time. The increasing size and market power of the multinational corporations has moved us into a new feudalism, which is still developing. The dukes and barons are the corporations and the banks, which like their feudal predecessors engage in alliances and wars to expand or protect their domains. Tactics include alliances within a planning network, official or tacit cartels, horizontal and vertical mergers, hostile buyouts, billion-dollar lawsuits, and all sorts of government assistance, subsidies, and military support. Some of the barons, like Rupert Murdoch (known as KRM), expand worldwide; others, like Robert Maxwell, are destroyed and their baronies divided up.

IMF policy since 1982 has increased the power of the multinational banking conglomerates such as the New York Citigroup. IMF loans to desperate Third World countries such as Indonesia have included a requirement that the borrowing country remove all restrictions on the entry and exit of any foreign financial capital. And since the IMF also protects foreign investors against loan defaults, international investment has become essentially risk-free. The insurance against loan defaults is paid by the poor masses in the "developing" countries. This IMF policy will probably help the multinational banks become the global emperors, "the principal regulators" of the new world feudalism (Cox 1987, 267).

The power of the feudal lords consists of their money, plus the worldwide corporate organization and corporate interlocks and the ever-expanding hierarchy of managers that enables them to mobilize their power in battles and negotiations with other lords and with governments. Indeed, the demand for power, in the form of ever-increasing profits, is perhaps the main impetus for ever-increasing economic growth and the ever-increasing exhaustion of the earth's resources.

As with the earlier feudalism, there is still room for some small, semi-autonomous cooperative or socialist production systems to find their own niche in the world economy, but the future of these small developments is doubtful; look, for example, at the fate of Emilia-Romagna.

Conclusion

The main purpose of this book has been to show how one can do dialectical research today in order to locate the dynamic tendencies and cross-pressures of present society. Then what? The present chapter has reversed the focus; it deals with agency, praxis, problem-solving. It attempts to show how one can use dialectical research and thinking to interpret a current problem and devise an attempted solution. All the examples are of small, local problems; but it is conceivable that a larger problem could also be managed. For example, the problem of reorganizing a large, successful, smug, bureaucratized, routinized corporation, or a government, would be difficult (Mitroff et al. 1994). A still larger national or global reform would be impossible.

A large, global dialectical reversal is possible some day, and a dialectical thinker might see signs of its approach and hope to participate. But to hasten the presumed process along by staging a revolution would be disastrous. It should be clear by now that there can be no "great leap forward" to pure capitalism, or pure Muslim fundamentalism, or any other utopia. Such revolutionary attempts have produced a period of mass misery and terror, and a replacement of the old guard by a similar new guard.

New institutions grow slowly out of the old ones, and the old persist in revised form *(aufgehoben)* in the new. Changes in eastern Europe are the latest example (Bartlett 1997); the old authority structures, political practices, and social relations persist and change slowly after a transfer of power. There are many earlier examples in the "less developed countries." Hegel learned this lesson from the French Revolution, but failed to convey it persuasively enough; utopian thinking persists. Progress comes slowly, if at all.

This approach to socialism is the opposite of Lenin's (and Althusser's) absurd rhetoric about finding the "weakest link" in the world chain of capitalism; once that link is broken, the chain will fall off the whole earth. Capitalism and the emerging new feudalism isn't an external chain; it is the totality of developing institutions of modern society.

Bibliography

Agger, Ben. 1989. *Fast Capitalism*. Urbana: University of Illinois Press.
Albert, Michael, and Robin Hahnel. 1978. *Unorthodox Marxism*. Boston: South End Press.
Aronson, Ronald. 1995. *After Marxism*. New York: Guilford Press.
Avineri, Shlomo. 1972. *Hegel's Theory of the Modern State*. Cambridge: Cambridge University Press.
Bahr, Hans-Dieter. 1971. "Historischer Materialismus in Hegel's Geschichts philosophie." *Praxis International* 8, no. 1–2: 139–160.
Balasko, Yves. 1988. *Foundations of the Theory of General Equilibrium*. Boston: Academic Press.
Bales, Robert. 1953. "The Equilibrium Problem in Small Groups." In *Working Papers in the Theory of Action*, ed. T. Parsons, R. Bales, and E. Shils. New York: Free Press.
———. 1955. "Role Differentiation in Small Decision-Making Groups." In *Family, Socialization, and Interaction Process*, ed. T. Parsons and R. Bales. Glencoe: Free Press.
Ball, Terence, and James Farr. 1984. *After Marx*. London: Cambridge University Press.
Barber, Benjamin. 1988. "Spirit's Phoenix and History's Owl." *Political Theory* 16, no. 1: pp. 5–28.
Bartlett, David. 1997. "Ownership Structure and Economic Policy in Eastern Europe and Latin America." *Politics and Society* 25, no. 2: pp. 202–233.
Bates, Robert. 1981. *Markets and States in Tropical Africa*. Berkeley: University of California Press.
Bauer, Gregory, and John Carlson. 1994. *Monetary Policy and Inflation: 1993 in Perspective*. Cleveland: Federal Reserve Board.
Berggren, Christian. 1980. "Changes in the Organization of Work in the Swedish Engineering Industry." *Acta Sociologica* 22, no. 4.
Bernstein, J. M. 1984. "Left Hegelians." In *The State and Civil Society: Studies in Hegel's Political Philosophy*, ed. Z. A. Pelczynski. Cambridge University Press.
BeVier, Michael. 1979. *Politics Backstage*. Philadelphia: Temple University Press.
Block, Fred L. *The Origins of International Economic Disorder*. Berkeley: University of California Press.
Bogdandy, Armin. 1989. *Hegels Theorie des Gesetzes*. Freiburg: Karl Alber.
Borrus, Michael. 1983. "The Politics of Competitive Erosion in the U.S. Steel Industry." In *American Industry in International Competition*, ed. John Zysman and Laura Tyson. Ithaca: Cornell University Press.

Bosanquet, Bernard. 1899. *Philosophical Theory of the State*. London: Macmillan.
Bosserman, Phillip. 1968. *Dialectical Sociology*. Boston: Porter Sargent.
Branchflower, David, and Andrew Oswald. 1994. *The Wage Curve*. Cambridge: MIT Press.
Brod, Harry. 1992. *Hegel's Philosophy of Politics*. Boulder, Colo.: Westview Press.
Butow, Robert. 1961. *Tojo and the Coming of the War*. Princeton: Princeton University Press.
Card, David, and Alan Krueger. 1995. *Myth and Measurement*. Princeton: Princeton University Press.
Caro, Robert. 1974. *The Power Broker: Robert Moses and the Fall of New York*. New York: Random House.
Chandler, Alfred. 1990. *Scale and Scope*. Cambridge: Harvard University Press.
Ciscel, David. 1989. "Galbraith's Planning System As a Substitute for Market Theory." *Journal of Economic Issues* 23, no. 2: 411–418.
Cockshott, W. Paul, and Allin Cottrell. 1997. "Value, Markets, and Socialism." *Science and Society* 61, no. 3: 330–357.
Coleman, James S. 1990. *Foundations of Social Theory*. Cambridge: Harvard University Press.
Coletti, Lucio. 1973. *Marxism and Hegel*. London: New Left Books.
Cox, Robert W. 1987. *Production, Power, and World Order*. New York: Columbia University Press.
Crenson, Matthew. 1971. *The Unpolitics of Air Pollution*. Baltimore: Johns Hopkins University Press.
Cullen, Bernard. 1979. *Hegel's Social and Political Thought: An Introduction*. New York: St. Martins.
Curtin, Jennifer, and W. Higgins. 1998. "Feminism and Unionism in Sweden." *Politics and Society* 26, no. 1: pp. 69–93.
Dallmyer, Fred. 1993. *G.W.F. Hegel: Modernity and Politics*. Newbury Park: Sage.
D'Costa, Anthony. 1993. "Restructuring and Development of the Steel Industry." In *Trading Industries, Trading Regions*, ed. Helzi Noponen, Julie Graham, and Ann Markusen. New York: Guilford.
Denemark, Robert, and Kenneth Thomas. 1988. "The Brenner-Wallerstein Debate." *International Studies Quarterly* 32, no. 1: pp. 47–65.
Destler, I. M. 1980. *Making Foreign Economic Policy*. Washington, D.C.: Brookings Institution.
Dewey, John. 1934. *Experience and Nature*. Chicago: Open Court.
D'Hondt, Jacques. 1988. *Hegel in His Time*. Peterborough, Ontario: Broadview Press.
Diesing, Paul. 1962. *Reason in Society*. Urbana: University of Illinois Press.
———. 1982. *Science and Ideology in the Policy Sciences*. New York: Aldine.
———. 1991. *How Does Social Science Work?* Pittsburgh: University of Pittsburgh Press.
Domhoff, G. William. 1974. *The Bohemian Grove*. New York: Harper.
———. 1979. *The Powers That Be*. New York: Random House.
———. 1983. *Who Rules America Now?* New York: Simon and Schuster.
———. 1990. *The Power Elite and the State: How Policy Is Made*. New York: Aldine.

Downs, Anthony. 1957. *An Economic Theory of Democracy*. New York: Harper.
Edelman, Murray. 1964. *The Symbolic Uses of Politics*. Urbana: University of Illinois Press.
Epstein, Ralph. 1928. *The Automobile Industry*. Chicago: Shaw.
Feenberg, Andrew. 1991. *Critical Theory of Technology*. New York: Oxford University Press.
Ferguson, Thomas, and Joel Rogers, eds. 1981. *The Hidden Election: Politics and Economics in the 1980 Presidential Campaign*. New York: Random House.
Findlay, J. N. 1958. *Hegel: A Re-Examination*. New York: Collier.
Fligstein, Neil. 1990. *The Transformation of Corporate Control*. Cambridge: Harvard University Press.
Friedrich, Carl. 1953. *The Philosophy of Hegel*. New York: Modern Library.
Froman, Creel. 1984. *The Two American Political Systems*. Englewood Cliffs, N.J.: Prentice-Hall.
Gadamer, H. G. 1976. *Hegel's Dialectic*. New Haven: Yale University Press.
Galambos, Louis, and Joseph Pratt. 1988. *The Rise of the Corporate Commonwealth*. New York: Dial Press.
Gelderman, Carol. 1981. *Henry Ford*. New York: Dial Press.
Georgakis, Dan, and Marvin Surkin. 1975. *Detroit: I Do Mind Dying*. New York: St. Martins.
George, Alexander. 1993. *Bridging the Gap*. Washington, D.C.: U.S. Peace Institute Press.
Giddens, Anthony. 1984. *The Constitution of Society*. Cambridge: Polity Press.
Gilligan, Carol. 1982. *In a Different Voice*. Cambridge: Harvard University Press.
Gobetti, Daniela. 1996. "Regularities and Innovation in Italian Politics." *Politics and Society* 24, no. 1: pp. 57–82.
Gondolf, Edward et al., eds. 1986. *The Global Economy*. Boulder, Colo.: Westview Press.
Gordon, David M. 1996a. "Conflict and Cooperation." *Politics and Society* 24, no. 4: pp. 433–456.
_____. 1996b. *Fat and Mean*. New York: Free Press.
Gottlieb, Roger. 1987. *History and Subjectivity*. Philadelphia: Temple University Press.
Greer, Ed. 1968. *Big Steel*. New York: Monthly Review Press.
Gunder Frank, Andre. 1967. *Capitalism and Underdevelopment in Latin America*. New York: Monthly Review Press.
Hardimon, Michael. 1994. *Hegel's Social Philosophy: The Project of Reconciliation*. Cambridge: Cambridge University Press.
Harris, H. S. 1995. *Hegel. Phenomenology and System*. Indianapolis: Hackett.
Harrison, Bennett. 1997. *Lean and Mean: Why Large Corporations Will Continue to Dominate the Global Economy*. New York: Guilford.
Harvey, David. 1985. *Consciousness and the Urban Experience*. Baltimore: Johns Hopkins University Press.
Harvey, John T. 1996. "Long-Term Exchange Rate Movements." *Journal of Economic Issues* 30, no. 2: pp. 509–516.

Hasnat, Baban. 1998. "Integrated International Production and Non-Market Activity." *Journal of Economic Issues* 32, no. 2: pp. 333–340.
Hegel, G.W.F. [1807] 1967. *Phenomenology of Mind*. Trans. J. B. Baillie. New York: Harper.
———. [1821] 1942. *Philosophy of Right*. Trans. T. M. Knox. Oxford: Clarendon.
———. 1956. *Philosophy of History*. Trans. J. Sibree. New York: Dover.
Heilbroner, Robert. 1980. *Marxism: For and Against*. New York: Norton.
Himmelstein, Jerome. 1990. *To the Right*. Berkeley: University of California Press.
Hirschhorn, Larry, and Carole Barnett, eds. 1993. *The Psychodynamics of Organization*. Philadelphia: Temple University Press.
Hoggatt, Austin, and Fred Balderston, eds. 1963. *Symposium on Simulation Models*. Cincinnati: Southwestern Publishing.
Hudson, Ray, and David Sadler. 1989. *The International Steel Industry*. London: Routledge.
Hyppolite, Jean. 1969. *Studies on Marx and Hegel*. Trans. John O'Neill. New York: Harper.
Ingrao, Bruno, and G. Israel. 1990. *The Invisible Hand*. Cambridge: MIT Press.
Jamme, Christof, and Elisabeth Weisser-Lohmann, eds. 1995. *Politik und Geschichte. Zu den Intentionen von Hegels Reformbill-Schrift*. Bonn: Bouvier.
Katzenstein, Peter J. 1984. *Corporatism and Change: Austria, Switzerland, and the Politics of Industry*. London: Cornell University Press.
———. 1985. *Small States in World Markets*. London: Cornell University Press.
———. 1989. *Industry and Politics in West Germany*. Ithaca: Cornell University Press.
Kaufmann, Walter. 1965a. *Hegel: A Reinterpretation*. Garden City: Doubleday.
———. 1965b. *Hegel: Texts and Commentary*. Garden City: Doubleday.
Keller, Maryann. 1989. *Rude Awakening: The Rise, Fall, and Struggle for Recovery of General Motors*. New York: Morrow.
Kelly, George A. 1978. *Hegel's Retreat from Eleusis: Studies in Political Thought*. Princeton: Princeton University Press.
Kojève, Alexandre. 1969. *Introduction to the Reading of Hegel*. New York: Basic Books.
Kornai, Janos. 1992. *The Socialist System*. Princeton: Princeton University Press.
Kovel, Joel. 1997. "Negating Bookchin." *Capitalism, Nature, Socialism* 8, no. 1: pp. 3–35.
Lamoreaux, Naomi. 1985. *The Great Merger Movement in American Business, 1895–1904*. Cambridge: Cambridge University Press.
Lawson, Tony. 1997. *Economics and Reality*. London: Routledge.
Lehmbruch, Gerhard, and Phillippe Schmitter, eds. 1982. *Patterns of Corporatist Policymaking*. London: Sage.
Liebeschütz, H. 1967. *Das Judentum in Deutschen Geschichtsbild von Hegel bis Max Weber*. Tübingen: Mohr.
Linklater, Andrew. 1990. *Beyond Realism and Marxism*. London: Macmillan.
Lukacs, Georg. 1923. *Geschichte und Klassenbewusstsein*. Berlin: Malik. 1967. Reprint, Amsterdam: de Munter.
Lynn, Leonard. 1982. *How Japan Innovates: A Comparison with the U.S. in the Case of Oxygen Steelmaking*. Boulder, Colo.: Westview.

MacGregor, David. 1992. *Hegel, Marx, and the English State.* Boulder, Colo.: Westview Press.
MacIver, Robert. 1947. *The Web of Government.* New York: Macmillan.
MacIntyre, Alasdair, ed. 1972. *Hegel.* Notre Dame: University of Notre Dame Press.
Magaziner, Ira, and Robert Reich. 1982. *Minding America's Business.* New York: Random House.
Maker, William, ed. 1987. *Hegel on Economics and Freedom.* Macon, Ga.: Mercer University Press.
Mandel, Ernest. 1975. *Late Capitalism.* London: New Left Books.
Mannheim, Karl. [1929] 1936. *Ideology and Utopia.* Trans. Louis Wirth and E. Shils. New York: Harcourt, Brace.
Marcuse, Herbert. 1941. *Reason and Revolution.* Boston. Beacon.
Marks, Gary et al. 1996. *Governance in the European Union.* London: Sage.
Marshall, Mike. 1996. "The Changing Face of Swedish Corporatism: the Disintegration of Consensus." *Journal of Economic Issues* 30, no. 3: pp. 843–858.
Marx, Karl. [1844] 1970. *Critique of Hegel's Philosophy of Right.* Trans. Joseph O'Malley. Cambridge: Cambridge University Press.
McDermott, John. 1991. *Corporate Society.* Boulder, Colo.: Westview Press.
Meikle, Scott. 1979. "Dialectical Contradiction and Necessity." In *Issues in Marxist Philosophy,* ed. John Mepham and D. Rubin. Atlantic Highlands, N.J.: Humanities Press.
Meyer, John, and Clinton Oster. 1987. *Deregulation and the Future of Intercity Passenger Travel.* Cambridge: MIT Press.
Milner, Henry. 1989. *Sweden: Social Democracy in Practice.* New York: Oxford University Press.
Mintz, Beth, and M. Schwartz. 1985. *The Power Structure of American Business.* Chicago: University of Chicago Press.
Mitroff, Ian, and Warren Bennis. 1989. *The Unreality Industry.* New York: Birch Lane Press.
Mitroff, Ian, Richard Mason, and Christine Pearson. 1994. *Frame Break: The Radical Redesign of American Business.* San Francisco: Jossey-Bass.
Mizruchi, Marc. 1992. *The Structure of Corporate Political Action.* Cambridge: Harvard University Press.
Morishima, Michio. 1992. *Capital and Credit.* Cambridge: MIT Press.
Moses, Jonathon. 1994. "Abdication from National Policy Autonomy: What's Left to Leave?" *Politics and Society* 22, no. 2:125–148.
Munkirs, John. 1985. *The Transformation of American Capitalism.* Armonk, N.Y.: M. E. Sharpe.
Newman, Bruce. 1993. *The Marketing of the President.* Thousand Oaks, Calif.: Sage.
Norman, Richard. 1976. "On Dialectic." *Radical Philosophy,* no. 14.
Norman, Richard, and Sean Sayers. 1979. *Hegel, Marx, and Dialectic.* Atlantic Highlands, N.J.: Humanities Press.
North, Douglass C. 1981. *Structure and Change in Economic History.* New York: Norton.
Notermans, Ton. 1993. "The Abdication from National Policy Autonomy." *Politics and Society* 21, no. 2: pp. 133–168.

OECD. 1993. *OECD Economic Surveys: Austria*.
Ollman, Bertell. 1971. *Alienation*. London: Cambridge University Press.
———. 1979. *The Social and Sexual Revolution*. Boston: South End Press.
———. 1993. *Dialectical Investigations*. New York: Routledge.
———. ed. 1998. *Market Socialism: The Debate Among Socialists*. New York: Routledge.
Önis, Ziya. 1995. "The Limits of Neoliberalism." *Journal of Economic Issues* 29, no. 1: pp. 97–120.
Ottman, Henning. 1977. *Individuum und Gemeinschaft bei Hegel. Hegel im Spiegel der Interpretationen*. Berlin: de Gruyter.
Papadopoulos, Yannis. 1995. "Analysis of Functions and Dysfunctions of Direct Democracy." *Politics and Society* 23, no. 4: pp. 421–448.
Parsons, Talcott, and R. F. Bales, eds. 1955. *Family, Socialization, and Interaction Process*. Glencoe: Free Press.
Pekkarinen, Jukka et al., eds. 1992. *Social Corporatism: A Superior Economic System?* Oxford: Clarendon Press.
Pelczynski, Z. A., ed. 1971. *Hegel's Political Philosophy: Problems and Perspectives*. Cambridge: Cambridge University Press.
———, ed. 1984. *The State and Civil Society: Studies in Hegel's Political Philosophy*. Cambridge: Cambridge University Press.
Peschek, Joseph. 1987. *Policy-Planning Organizations, Elite Agendas, and America's Rightward Turn*. Philadelphia: Temple University Press.
Pinkard, Terry. 1988. *Hegel's Dialectic: The Explanation of Possibility*. Philadelphia: Temple University Press.
Piore, Michael, and Charles Sabel. 1984. *The Second Industrial Divide*. New York: Basic Books.
Piven, Francis Fox, and R. Cloward. 1971. *Regulating the Poor: The Functions of Public Welfare*. New York: Random House.
Piven, Francis, and R. Cloward. 1985. *The New Class War*. New York: Pantheon Books.
Plant, Raymond. 1973. *Hegel*. Bloomington: Indiana University Press.
———. 1980. "Economic and Social Integration in Hegel's Political Philosophy." In *Hegel's Social and Political Thought*, ed. Donald P. Verene. Atlantic Highlands, N.J.: Humanities Press.
Prasch, Robert E. 1995. "Toward a 'General Theory' of Exchange." *Journal of Economic Issues* 29, no. 3: pp. 807–828.
Prewitt, Kenneth, and Alan Stone. 1973. *The Ruling Elites*. New York: Harper.
Pugh, Emerson W. 1995. *Building IBM*. Cambridge: MIT Press.
Rayack, Elton. 1987. *Not So Free to Choose*. New York: Praeger.
Reck, Andrew. 1960. "Substance, Subject, and Dialectic." In *Studies in Hegel*, ed. Andrew Reck. New Orleans: Tulane University Press.
Riley, Dennis D. 1987. *Controlling the Federal Bureaucracy*. Philadelphia: Temple University Press.
Ritter, Joachim. 1969. *Metaphysik und Politik*. Frankfurt: Suhrkamp.
Rosdolsky, Roman. 1968. *Zur Entstehungsgeschichte des Marxschen Kapital*. Frankfurt: Europäische Verlagsanstalt.

Rostow, W. W. 1960. *The Stages of Economic Growth*. Cambridge: Cambridge University Press.
Sabel, Charles. 1982. *Work and Politics*. Cambridge: Cambridge University Press.
_____. 1989. "Flexible Specialization and the Re-Emergence of Regional Economies." In *Reversing Industrial Decline*, ed. Paul Hirst and J. Zeitlin. New York: St. Martins.
Sandberg, Åke, Gunnar Broms, Arne Grip, Lars Sundström, Jesper Steen, and Peter Ullmark. 1992. *Technology, Change, and Co-determination in Sweden*. Philadelphia: Temple University Press.
Sayers, Sean. 1985. *Reality and Reason: Dialectic and the Theory of Knowledge*. Oxford: Blackwell.
Schacht, Richard. 1972. "Hegel on Freedom." In *Hegel*, ed. Alasdair MacIntyre. Notre Dame: University of Notre Dame Press.
Scheit, Herbert. 1973. *Geist und Gemeinde. Zur Verhältnis Religion und Politik bei Hegel*. Munich: Anton Pastet.
Scherrer, Cristoph. 1991. "Governance of the Automobile Industry." In *Governance of the American Economy*, John Campbell, et al., eds. Cambridge: Cambridge University Press.
Scholten, Ilja, ed. 1987. *Political Stability and Neocorporatism*. London: Sage.
Schwartz, Michael, ed. 1987. *The Structure of Power in America*. New York: Holmes and Meier.
Sherman, Howard. 1976. "Dialectics As a Method." *Insurgent Sociologist*. Summer.
_____. 1991. *The Business Cycle*. Princeton: Princeton University Press.
_____. 1995. *Reinventing Marxism*. Baltimore: Johns Hopkins University Press.
Simon, Herbert. 1955. "A Behavioral Model of Rational Choice." *Quarterly Journal of Economics* 69: 99–118.
_____. 1982. *Models of Bounded Rationality*. Vol. 1–2. Cambridge: MIT Press.
Sklar, Holly, ed. 1980. *Trilateralism*. Boston: South End Press.
Smith, Steven. 1989. *Hegel's Critique of Liberalism*. Chicago: University of Chicago Press.
Smith, Tony. 1993. *Dialectical Social Theory and Its Critics*. Albany, N.Y.: SUNY Press.
Smith, Vicki. 1992. *Managing in the Corporate Interest: Control and Resistance in an American Bank*. Berkeley: University of California Press.
Spruyt, Hendrik. 1994. *The Sovereign State and Its Competitors*. Princeton: Princeton University Press.
Stace, W. T. 1924. *The Philosophy of Hegel*. London: Macmillan.
Steinberger, Peter J. 1988. *Logic and Politics: Hegel's Philosophy of Right*. New Haven: Yale University Press.
Stepelvich, Lawrence, and David Lamb, eds. 1983. *Hegel's Philosophy of Action*. Atlantic Highlands, N.J.: Humanities Press.
Stillman, Peter, ed. 1987. *Hegel's Philosophy of Spirit*. Albany, N.Y.: SUNY Press.
Stockman, David. 1986. *The Triumph of Politics*. New York: Avon.
Strohmeyer, John. 1986. *Crisis in Bethlehem*. Bethesda, Md.: Adler and Adler.
Tawney, R. H. 1926. *Religion and the Rise of Capitalism*. New York: Penguin.
Taylor, Charles. 1975. *Hegel*. Cambridge: Cambridge University Press.

———. 1979. *Hegel and Modern Society*. Cambridge: Cambridge University Press.
Tiffany, Paul. 1988. *The Decline of American Steel*. New York: Oxford University Press.
Tsoukalis, Loukas. 1997. *The New European Economy Revisited*. London: Oxford University Press.
Tversky, Amos. 1972. "Elimination by Aspects: A Theory of Choice." *Psychological Review* 79, no. 4, 281–299.
Useem, Michael. 1984. *The Inner Circle*. New York: Oxford University Press.
———. 1987. "The Inner Circle and the Political Voice of Business." In *The Structure of Power in America*, ed. Michael Schwartz. New York: Holmes and Meier.
———. 1993. *Executive Defense: Shareholder Power and Corporate Reorganization*. Cambridge: Harvard University Press.
Vercelli, Allesandro. 1991. *Methodological Foundation of Macroeconomics: Keynes and Lucas*. Cambridge: Cambridge University Press.
Vogel, David. 1989. *Fluctuating Fortunes*. New York: Basic Books.
Waddell, Brian. 1994. "Economic Mobilization for World War II and the Transformation of the U.S. State." *Politics and Society* 22, no. 2: pp. 165–194.
Walton, A. S. 1984. "Economy, Utility, and Community in Hegel's Civil Society." In *The State and Civil Society: Studies in Hegel's Political Philosophy*, ed. Z. A. Pelczynski. Cambridge: Cambridge University Press.
Weidenbaum, Murray. 1977. *Business, Government, and the Public*. Englewood Cliffs, N.J.: Prentice-Hall.
Weiss, Frederick, ed. 1974. *Hegel: The Essential Writings*. New York: Harper.
Whitt, J. Allen. 1982. *Urban Elites and Mass Transportation*. Princeton: Princeton University Press.
Wright, Erik Olin. 1978. *Class, Crisis, and the State*. London: Verso.
Yaghmaian, Behzad. 1998. "Globalization and the State." *Science and Society* 62, no. 2: pp. 241–265.

Subject Index

Actual 21, 23, 37, 38, 39, 44, 47, 49, 55, 61
Airlines 115–117
Alienation 43, 53
Antitrust policy 110, 114, 123–124
Appearance 19–21, 30–32, 38, 52, 133–137, 139, 153
Apple Computer 114, 115, 118, 120
Arbitration 56
Aufgehoben 27–29, 65, 87, 129, 173
Austrian politics 148–152
Auto industry 106–110

Bretton Woods 123, 148
Bureaucratic conflict 114
Business Council 138, 140, 144
Business cycle 88, 102

Capital
  economic 79–80, 90–94, 118–119
  family 49
  universal (social) 53, 58
Capitalism, stages of 78–79
  dialectic of 88–94
Cartels 111, 123, 124
Children 50, 57, 82–83, 86
Cities 14, 17, 62
Civil Aeronautics Board (CAB) 115
Civil service 58, 64, 65–66, 149–150
  idealized 130
  routinized 66, 141–142
Class conflict 109, 170–171
Class consciousness. *See* Consciousness, class
Classes 54
  bourgeois 54, 62, 146
  civil service; *See* Civil service
  executive 131
  labor 90, 131

nobility; *See* Nobles
Colonies 57
Committee for Economic Development (CED) 138, 141, 143–144
Committee on the Present Danger 148
Commons 64
Communication channels 133, 137–138
Community 44, 47, 53, 58, 154, 171
Computers 113–115
Concept 37
Conscience 46
Consciousness
  class 54, 58, 97, 131, 140, 146, 168
  collective 132, 148
  community 67, 87, 130, 132, 155, 158
  corporation 67
  occupational 59, 64, 65, 97, 140, 146, 168
  raising 58, 64, 140
Conspicuous consumption 52, 53
Constitution 61, 63–66
  United States 68–69
  United Kingdom 64
Content 37, 38, 40, 41
Contract 44
Contradiction 26, 27, 30, 48, 77, 124, 169
  self-contradiction 56, 57
Corporation 59, 62, 64, 65, 66, 70
  industrial 122
  policymaking; *See* Planning
  political 149
Corporatism 148
Council on Foreign Relations (CFR) 136, 138–139, 141, 143–144
Crime 56
Crown 63, 64, 65, 67
Culture 10

183

ideal 10
material 10

Dialectic 25–36
    accommodation-aggressiveness 169
    dependent-interdependent 50–53
    domination-submission 83–85, 162
    idealism-materialism 89
    individuality-community 74–75,
        96–98, 132, 146, 158–159, 162, 166
    internal-external 29
    Kantian 4
    laws 27
    love-furniture 49
    masculine-feminine 82–85
    negate the negation 44
    objective 30–35, 38, 56
    plan-market 104–127, 151, 162–165
    reduction of dominance 85
    reversal of dominance 81, 86, 105, 124, 126
    structure-agency 26
    subjective 30–35, 38: empirical aspect 31; method 31–35, Chapter 6; presentation aspect 33–35
    subjectivity-objectivity 40, 41, 42, 55
    synthesis 26, 40, 42, 50, 74, 82–85, 86, 89
    thesis–antithesis–synthesis 25, 26, 40, 73
    universal and particular 31, 32, 34, 39–40, 43, 47, 52, 55–56, 73, 94–96
    use-value 43, 49, 51, 77–82
    whole-part 5, 33
Dialogue 26, 64, 97
Distinction
    fact-value 2
    is-ought 2, 3, 38
    government-society 2, 3
    past-present 18, 22
    philosophy-social science 2, 23, 38
    universal-particular 18
Divergent cognitive style 22
Duty 46, 47

Emilia-Romagna 154, 155, 172
English Reform Bill 6, 31, 62, 67
Environmental Protection Agency (EPA) 95–96

Equilibrium 79
    ceteris paribus (limited) 105, 128
    Walrasian (general) 127, 128
Essence 19–21, 23, 30–33, 37, 38, 48, 58, 61, 74, 105, 137–146
Estates 37, 63
Ethical Life 46
Executive 65–66
Exploitation 91, 93
Export-Import Bank 144
Exports 57, 88–91, 93
Externalities 56
Extravagance-want 51
Euro 79
European Union 158–159

Family 47–50, 82–85, 161–162
    dialectic 82–85
    problems 83, 161–162
    recent changes 84–85, 132
Federalist Papers 63, 68–70
Federal Trade Commission (FTC) 95, 123–124
Feudalism
    declining 13–14, 16–18, 43, 87, 129–130
    emerging 172
Finance capital 127, 158
Forces of production 89, 125, 168
Fordism 106–107, 124, 170
Ford Motor Co. 106, 115, 126
Form 37, 38, 40, 41
Freedom, definition of 2, 41
French Revolution 16, 17, 28
Functional interdependence 27

Geist 9–11
    absolute 10–11: art 10–11; philosophy 11; religion 10–11, 28–29; social science 11
    objective 9–10, 19, 22, 25, 46, 89
    subjective 9, 22, 45; *See also* Subjectivity
    Volksgeist 10
    Weltgeist 10
    Zeitgeist 10
General Motors 106–109, 119, 166
Good 46
Government 63–66, 129–160
Great leap forward 173

Index

Guestworkers 156
Gunpowder 14

Hegel
  intellectual development 28–29
  interpretations of 1–7
  Logic 34
  Phenomenology 9, 34
  Philosophy of History 11–16: Greek world 12–13; Oriental world 11–12; modern time 13–16: Protestant Reformation 14–15; music 15–16
Historicism 4
Holism 5
Holy Ghost 9, 15, 28, 66
House of Lords 64, 130

Idea 37, 38, 40, 46, 49
Idealism-materialism. *See* Dialectic, idealism-materialism
Implementation 95, 123–124, 133, 150
Individualism-community. *See* Dialectic, individualism-community
Intel 114–115
Interdependence 50
Interlocking corporate networks 127
IBM 113–115, 119, 122
International Monetary Fund (IMF) 92, 138, 144, 172

Jesus 13, 28
Jews, emancipation of 17
Joint Commission 149–150, 155, 156
Judge 44, 55
Jury 55

Klein-Goldberger model 165

Labor 78, 80–81
  household 93–94
  power 78
  theory of value 53, 77, 80–81
Law 6, 37, 54–56, 94–96
Lawyers 55–56, 96
Leader, game of 107
Learning curve 121
Legislature 63–65
Logic
  deductive 2, 3, 18

deontic 3
dialectic 4
  syllogistic 25, 26
  symbolic 25
Love 47, 48–49
Lucky Goldstar 90

Market 4, 50–53, 103–124
  power 19, 131, 132
Marriage. *See* Family
Marshall Plan 138, 147
Marxist theory 7–8, 22, 147
Masculine-feminine. *See* Dialectic, masculine-feminine
Masculine perspective 47, 161
Material base
  family 49
  state 58, 59, 62, 65
Mechanization 53
Mediation 50–52, 64, 65, 73, 130, 133, 141–143, 150, 156, 167, 168
  cross-mediation 150, 156
  of civil servants 66
Mergers 95, 103, 109, 116, 120, 123–124, 126, 131, 167
Microsoft 114–115, 118
Ministry of International Trade and Industry (MITI)
Money 43, 78, 79, 81, 123, 158
Monarch 64–65, 67, 70, 129–130
Monopoly 113–115
Morality-non-morality 44
Mutual funds 79–81

National Association of Manufacturers (NAM) 136, 138, 141, 144, 145
New Left 144
Nobles 16, 17, 43, 54, 58, 62, 64, 70, 126, 129–130, 172
Nuclear Regulatory Commission (NRC) 139

Occupational associations 137–138
Occupational Safety and Health Administration (OSHA) 95
Oligopoly 103–104
Opposites
  ambivalent 32
  interdependent 32

polarized 32
Organization of Petroleum Exporting
    Countries (OPEC) 91, 104, 114, 119, 120, 122, 125
Overproduction 57, 90–93

Patriarchy 48
Pergau Dam 92
Pillarization 156, 168
Planning
    corporate 121–124
    dialectical 151–152, 163
    General Motors 107, 171
    indicative 165
    industrial 104, 106
    industrial-financial-social 107, 127
    intercorporate 147, 164
    oligopolistic 103–104, 107, 110, 112, 119–124
    routinized 109, 119–120, 121–122, 163
    Soviet 122, 125–126, 171
Plea bargaining 96
Poletown 166
Policy organization 137–146
Political action committees (PAC) 134
Political parties 66
Ports 57, 70, 89, 90, 91, 92
Poverty 57–58, 62, 93, 97–98
Power 90, 98, 108, 112, 146, 149, 172
Price leadership 110
Price wars 110, 116, 120
Prisoner's Dilemma game 110
Profit 78–80, 91, 93, 97, 107–115, 126
Property 42, 69, 97
Protestant Reformation. *See* Hegel,
    Philosophy of History
Prussian censorship 6, 17, 61, 64
Public
    authority 56–58
    goods 56
    opinion 63, 64–65

Reason 4, 18, 31
Reconciliation 28–29
Reduction of domination. *See* Dialectic
Referendums 142, 153, 168
Reform Bill. *See* English Reform Bill
Relations of production 89
Retreats 140, 168
Reversal of domination. *See* Dialectic

Right-wrong 37, 39, 42, 44, 46

Seaports. *See* Ports
Selfcontradiction. *See* Contradiction
Self-determination 60, 61
Self-related negativity 45
Serfs, serfdom 16, 54, 62, 70, 78, 87, 125
Sherman antitrust law 95, 123
Slavery 42, 43, 70
Socialism 169–170, 172
Social structure of accumulation 107, 148
Sonata form 75
Soviet Union. *See also* Planning, Soviet
Speenhamland 57
Spiral, planning-market 126–127
Stage of difference 50–53
    of similarity 53–55
State 59–68
Steel industry 110–113
    Austrian 151
Subject 35–36
Subjectivity 40, 41, 42, 46
Swedish politics 156, 157
Swiss politics 152–153
Synthesis. *See* Dialectic

Tariffs 110, 119, 144, 158
Taylorism 57, 80, 170, 171
Technology 14, 89, 106, 113–114, 125
Thought 37
Trade association 137
Translation problems 37–38
Trigger Price Mechanism 112
Trilateral Commission 136, 138, 141, 144, 145
Triplicity 25, 53, 54, 73

Understanding 18, 26, 41, 52, 63, 68
United Auto Workers (UAW) 107
Use-value. *See* Dialectic

Vanguard 91, 169
Vietnam War 138

Wartime 67, 148, 154
Wild competition 116, 117, 121, 125
Work 25, 36, 42, 53, 57, 78, 82
World Bank 91, 92, 93, 123, 138, 144, 147
World finance capital 158
Wrong. *See* Right

Author Index

Agger, Ben 94
Albert, Michael 27, 94
Althusser, Louis 173
Aristotle 26
Aronson, Ronald 8
Avineri, Shlomo 6, 25, 39, 61, 66

Bahr, Hans-Dieter 89
Balasko, Yves 128
Bales, Robert 19–21, 23, 26 ,31, 32, 48, 84
Ball, Terence 10
Barber, Benjamin 22
Barnett, Carole 122
Bartlett, David 173
Bates, Robert 92
Bauer, Gregory 121
Bennis, Warren 67
Berezovsky, Boris 126
Berggren, Christian 170
Bernstein, J. M. 89
BeVier, Michael 135, 141, 167
Bhaskar, Roy 10, 19
Blaas, W. 153
Bleifuss, Joel 142
Block, Fred 144
Bogdandy, Armin 6, 7, 16, 54, 161
Borrus, Michael 110
Bosanquet, Bernard 7, 59, 66, 132
Bosserman, Phillip 23, 30, 36
Branchflower, David 19
Brod, Harry 6, 16, 30, 68
Brzezinski, Zbigniew 138, 147
Bush, George 136, 138
Butow, Robert 65

Calhoun, John 69

Card, David 19
Carlson, John 121
Caro, Robert 165
Carter, Jimmy 138, 145, 147
Chandler, Alfred 131
Ciscel, David 147
Chodorov, Nancy 85
Clinton, Bill 138
Cloward, Richard 57
Cockshott, Paul 164
Coleman, James 40
Coletti, Lucio 89
Connally, John 136
Cottrell, Allin 164
Cox, Robert 172
Crenson, Matthew 112
Cullen, Bernard 53
Curtin, Jennifer 171

Dallmyer, Fred 53
Davis, Norman 139
D'Costa, Anthony 112, 113
Denemark, Robert 88
Descartes, Rene 18, 26
Destler, I. M. 137, 167
Dewey, John 7, 15
D'Hondt, Jacques 1, 61
Diesing, Paul 11, 84, 94, 131, 145
Domhoff, G. William 137
Downs, Anthony 68

Edelman, Murray 67
Engels, Friedrich 77
Epstein, Ralph 106

Farr, James 10
Feenberg, Andrew 125

Ferguson, Thomas 135
Fichte 25
Findlay, J. N. 26, 30
Fligstein, Neil 95, 123–124
Ford, Edsel 120
Ford, Henry 106, 120, 121
Frieden, Jeff 141
Friedrich, Carl 21
Froman, Creel 133, 134

Gadamer, H. G. 1, 30
Galambos, Louis 109
Gelderman, Carol 106, 120
Georgakis, Dan 107
George, Alex 120, 122
Giddens, Anthony 10
Gilligan, Carol 82, 84, 85
Gobetti, Daniela 154
Gondolf, Edward 110
Gordon, David M. 27, 171
Gottlieb, Roger 10, 83
Green, T. H. 7, 132
Greer, Ed 112
Gunder Frank, Andre 90
Gurvitch, George 36

Hahnel, Robin 27, 94
Hardimon, Michael 4, 29
Harris, H. S. 10, 53
Harrison, Bennett 155, 164
Harvey, David 132
Harvey, John T. 121
Hasnat, Baban 105
Hayek, Friedrich 128, 165
Heilbroner, Robert 25, 33, 89
Higgins, W. 171
Himmelstein, Jerome 135, 139, 144, 146
Hirohito, Emperor 65
Hirschhorn, Larry 122
Hobbes 18
Hume, David 18
Huntington, Samuel 147
Hyppolite, Jean 75

Ingrao, Bruno 128
Israel, G. 128

Kant, Immanuel 2, 7, 19, 25, 46, 73, 84

Katzenstein, Peter 148, 163
Kaufman, Walter 22, 26, 30
Keller, Maryann 106, 119, 121, 171
Kelly, George A. 129, 130
Kennedy, John F. 111
Keynes, J. M. 88, 102
Kissinger, Henry 136
Kojeve, Alexandre 25, 26, 28, 30, 36
Kornai, Janos 126, 152
Kovel, Joel 27
Kriesi, Hans 153
Krueger, Alan 19

Lamoreaux, Naomi 120
Lawson, Tony 19
Lehmbruch, Gerhard 148, 156
Leibniz, 18, 26
Lenin, 173
Liebeschutz, H. 1
Linklater, Andrew 7
Locke, John 2, 18, 51, 68, 70
Lorenzo, Frank 116
Lukacs, Georg 22
Lynn, Leonard 110

MacGregor, David 6, 21, 31, 54, 66, 82, 131
MacIver, Robert 7
Magaziner, Ira 113, 125, 142
Mandel, Ernest 33
Mannheim, Karl 11
Marcuse, Herbert 25
Marks, Gary 158
Marshall, Mike 157
Marx, Karl 4, 6, 34, 39, 89, 90, 129, 131, 160
Mauss, Marcel 87
Maxwell, Robert 172
McDermott, John 70, 131
Meikle, Scott 30
Meyer, John 115
Milner, Henry 164, 171
Minsky, Hyman 79, 128
Minter, William 138
Mintz, Beth 147
Mitchell, Wesley 88
Mitroff, Ian 67, 173
Mizruchi, Marc 143

Index

Montesquieu 70
Morishima, Michio 128
Moses, Honathon 158
Moses, Robert 108, 165
Mozart, Wolfgang 15–16, 22, 48
Munkirs, John 147
Murdoch, Rupert 172

Newman, Bruce 134
Norman, Richard 89
North, Douglass C. 164
Notermans, Ton 158

OECD 151, 152
Ollman, Bertell 7, 25, 31, 33, 36, 127, 168
Onis, Ziya 156
Oster, Clinton 115
Oswald, Andrew 19
Ottman, Henning 5, 7

Papadopoulos, Yannis 153
Parsons, Talcott 19–21, 23
Pekkarinen, Jukka 148
Pelczynski, Z. A. 12
Peschek, Joseph 145
Petry, Michael 62
Pinkard, Terry 3, 26
Piore, Michael 154
Piven, Francis Fox 57
Plant, Raymond 6, 11, 17, 28,
Plato 13, 26
Popper, Karl 4
Prasch, Robert E. 105
Pratt, Joseph 109
Prewitt, Kenneth 147
Pugh, Emerson 113

Rayack, Elton 40
Reagan, Ronald 136, 138, 144, 146
Reck, Andrew 1
Reich, Robert 113, 125
Ricardo, David 12, 52
Riley, Dennis D. 139
Ritter, Joachim 16, 17, 61
Rockefeller, David 136, 138
Rogers, Joel 135, 165–167
Rosdolsky, Roman 31

Rostow, Walt Whitman 91
Rousseau, J.J. 51

Sabel, Charles 154
Sandberg, Ake 169–170
Say, J. 17, 52
Sayers, Sean 25, 27, 30
Schacht, Richard 2
Scheit, Herbert 11, 12, 28, 30
Schmitter, Phillipe 148, 156, 157, 168
Scholten, Ilja 148
Schumpeter, Joseph 120
Schwartz, Michael 137, 147
Sherman, Howard 30, 88, 102, 103
Shoup, Laurence 138
Shultz, George 136, 138
Simon, Herbert 121
Sklar, Holly 137
Sloan, Alfred 107, 124, 163, 171
Smith, Adam 7, 17, 52, 53, 57, 78
Smith, Roger 119, 152
Smith, Steven 22, 62
Smith, Tony 25
Smith, Vicki 132
Spruyt, Hendrik 14
Stace, W. T. 10
Steinberger, Peter J. 75
Steuart, James 17, 28
Stillman, Peter 9
Stimson, Henry 139
Stockman, David 138
Stone, Alan 147
Strohmeyer, John 110, 118, 120
Surkin, Marvin 107

Tabb, William K. 145
Tawney, Richard H. 14
Taylor, Charles 61, 87
Tiffany, Paul 110
Tsoukalis, Loukas 7, 159
Tversky, Amos 121

Useem, Michael 95, 140, 143

Veblen, Thorstein, 128
Vercelli, Allesandro 128

Vogel, David 144, 145

Waddell, Brian 147
Waldheim, Kurt 130
Walsh 61
Walton, A. S. 88
Weidenbaum, Murray 137

Weinberger, Caspar 136, 138
Whitehead, Alfred North 4
Whitt, J. Allen 142
Wolfe, Alan 145
Wright, Erik Olin 131

Yaghmaian, Behzad 105